Edwin Morgan

For
Alexandra Griffiths
'Sandra'

Edwin Morgan

Inventions of modernity

COLIN NICHOLSON

Manchester University Press

Manchester and New York

distributed exclusively in the USA by Palgrave

Copyright © Colin Nicholson 2002, 2009

The right of Colin Nicholson to be identified as the author of this work has been asserted by him in accordance with the Copyright, Designs and Patents Act 1988.

Published by Manchester University Press
Oxford Road, Manchester M13 9NR, UK
and Room 400, 175 Fifth Avenue, New York, NY 10010, USA
www.manchesteruniversitypress.co.uk

Distributed exclusively in the USA by
Palgrave, 175 Fifth Avenue, New York NY 10010, USA

Distributed exclusively in Canada by
UBC Press, University of British Columbia, 2029 West Mall,
Vancouver, BC, Canada V6T 1Z2

British Library Cataloguing-in-Publication Data
A catalogue record for this book is available from the British Library

Library of Congress Cataloging-in-Publication Data
A catalog record for this book is available from the Library of Congress

Front Cover: 'Bees' Nest by Edwin Morgan, used with the permission of
Carcanet Press

ISBN 13: 978 0 7190 6361 9

First published 2002 by Manchester University Press

First paperback edition 2009

Printed by Lightning Source

Contents

Acknowledgements   *page* vi

Abbreviations   viii

Introduction   1

1 Apocalypse and after   14

2 A self-fashioning Scot   31

3 From Glasgow to Mayakovsky   59

4 A cognitive mapping   82

5 Out, in space   104

6 Reconfiguring subjectivity   137

7 Not fade away   169

   Edwin Morgan: 'Pieces of Me'   195

   Bibliography   202

   Index   212

Acknowledgements

Although he is in no way responsible for the use I make of information he supplied, or for me reading him wrong to the light, I thank Edwin Morgan for conversations about his writing, for permission to quote from his work and to include 'Pieces of Me', and for answering with grace and patience all my subsequent queries. He gave me much but I needed more, and colleagues regularly fed me information, as Roger Savage well knows. I am indebted to a host of others in different ways, including generations of Edinburgh students whose enthusiasms for Morgan's writing provided a range of insights and ways of reading. Cairns Craig first suggested this book; John Kirk helped it on its way; and Olga Taxidou, Sarah Carpenter, Penny Fielding, Lee Spinks, Charles Jones, Ian Campbell, Allan Hood and Ian Brown gave useful advice. Arkadi Tcherkassov showed me the pulse of Soviet dissidence, and Olga Shapyrina, Vera Shamina and Maria Kosyreva explained Russian references. Bókay Antal generously shared his knowledge of Hungarian poetry, and Ferencz Gyözö suggested how Morgan's translations might find a Hungarian response. Szamosi Gertrud and Komaromy Szolt offered other guidance. Tom Bee gave me ideas about visual text and its electronic transmission; Theo Broekmans and Josefien Braam chased references across the Internet. The Scottish Poetry Library is as ever an invaluable resource, now attractively housed in its premises off Edinburgh's High Street; and for the sabbatical leave without which *Inventions of Modernity* would not have been written, I thank Roger Savage, Cairns Craig and the Dean of the Arts Faculty at Edinburgh University. Colleagues at Edinburgh's University Library were uniformly helpful; as was the Department of Special Collections at Glasgow University Library, whose dated catalogue of Morgan's manuscripts helped to organise my reading. Hamish Whyte's interim bibliography proved a godsend, and he showed me the Morgan papers in Glasgow's Mitchell Library. The British Council in Budapest jointly with the Hungarian Grants Committee sponsored a research and curriculum development programme between the universities of Edinburgh and of Pécs in southern Hungary, which gave me space to re-write. The hospitality and generosity of the Baltezarevic family in the Serbian city of Niš allowed me to finish the process. Together with her colleagues in Edinburgh University Computer Users Support Group, Crystal Webster showed endless patience. On a longer time scale and a broader spectrum, so did Liz.

I owe a particular debt of gratitude to Carcanet Press for making an extensive range of copyright material available to me on generous terms, including permission to quote from Morgan's *Collected Poems, Collected Translations, Sweeping out the Dark* and *Virtual and Other Realities.* Grateful acknowledgement is also made to Mariscat Press for permission to quote from *Hold Hands Among The Atoms* and *Demon,* and to Polygon for permission to quote from *Edwin Morgan: Nothing Not Giving Messages, reflections on his work and life.*

Parts of chapter 5 appeared in *The Yearbook of English Studies,* 30, 2000, pp. 221–33.

Abbreviations

B   *Beowulf: A Verse Translation into Modern English*, University of California Press, Berkeley, 1952.

CP   *Collected Poems*, Carcanet, Manchester, 1990.

CT   *Collected Translations*, Carcanet, Manchester, 1996.

D   *Demon*, Mariscat, Glasgow, 1999.

Essays   *Essays*, Carcanet New Press, Cheadle Hulme, 1974.

HH   *Hold Hands Among the Atoms*, Mariscat, Glasgow, 1991.

IP   *Instamatic Poems*, Ian McKelvie, London, 1972.

NNGM   *Nothing Not Giving Messages: Reflections on his Work and Life*, Hamish Whyte, Edinburgh, 1990.

SD   *Sweeping Out The Dark*, Carcanet, Manchester, 1994.

VR   *Virtual and Other Realities*, Carcanet, Manchester, 1997.

WHV   *Wi The Haill Voice, 25 Poems by Vladimir Mayakovsky*, Carcanet, Oxford, 1972.

Introduction

To understand another person's utterance means to orient oneself
with respect to it, to find the proper place for it in the corresponding
context. ... Meaning belongs to a word in its position between
speakers; that is, meaning is ... the effect of interaction between
speaker and listener produced via the material of a particular sound
complex. (Mikhail Bakhtin)[1]

I don't feel British. I don't feel, certainly, English. I don't feel anything but Scottish. ... So, yes, I would like a Scottish Republic really.
That's what it comes down to. (Edwin Morgan)[2]

At two o'clock on the afternoon of 7 October 2000, while spot beams
swept Glasgow's Tramway Theatre and probed its audience, a computer
desktop visually projected onto space above the stage simulated a down-
loading operation, and for the rest of the day Edwin Morgan's trilogy on
the life of Jesus presented a real-time figure using the idioms of experience
at the turn of the twenty-first century. Conflict in Roman-occupied
Palestine produced a politicised if enigmatic Nazarene confronting a web
of institutional and social manipulations generated by imperial collusion
among Pharisees, Sadducees, scribes, priests and officials. In unpromising
context Morgan's protagonist developed a celebration of love inclusive
enough to acknowledge his own fathering of a child and embrace the
homosexuality of his disciple John the Beloved, who speaks what could
serve as the trilogy's epigraph: 'there is in love / a great strength; by it,
indeed, we live. / And love is love whatever flesh it inhabits'.[3] Earlier,
during his first temptation of Jesus, Lucifer is pleased that their encounter
'is beginning to be a conversation', and his satanic verses resonate a structured intention to bring the unthought into dialogic relationship.[4]
Morgan habitually thinks of voice in relation to drama, and as late as 1992
was describing himself as 'a kind of non-dramatist dramatist' with a strong
interest in 'presenting characters ... to make them as distinctive and real as
I can in short space, to give them all the life I can'.[5] Ten years before he
made this remark he had prepared acting versions of two medieval plays,

one Dutch and one French – an experience he has identified as the beginning of his interest in the stage.[6] In 1992 he published his verse translation into Glaswegian dialect of Rostand's *Cyrano de Bergerac*, in 1999 his version of Marlowe's *Doctor Faustus* was published; and in his eightieth year (2000), when *A.D.* was acted, his translation into Scots of Racine's last secular tragedy, *Phaedre*, was also played and published.[7] The formal stage may have come relatively late into Morgan's career, and original drama later again, but the man of theatre who stepped into the spotlight at the curtain call for *A.D.* had a long-established track record as performing poet and dramatiser of speech.

In 1998 with the Scottish National Jazz Orchestra behind him, Tommy Smith asked an Edinburgh audience to welcome 'the legendary Edwin Morgan'. 'Planet Wave', a poem sequence set to music by Smith and commissioned by the Cheltenham Jazz Festival for its first airing a year earlier, then played sound effects and rhythmic combinations unlike anything the audience had heard before. In a timely reminder that legend derives from what is read, *PN Review* printed the poem just before its performance in Edinburgh's Queen's Hall; and listening to Morgan in that energetic context it was difficult not to hear a self-guying and celebratory 'outing' as he picked up his story and a personalised creation history got under way:

> Don't ask me and don't tell me. I was there.
> It was a bang and it was big. I don't know
> what went before, I came out with it.
> Think about that if you want my credentials.
> ....
> out through what was now space, out
> into the pulse of time, out, my masters,
> out, my friends, so, like a darting shoal,
> like a lion's roar, like greyhounds released,
> like blown dandelions, like Pandora's box,
> like a shaken cornucopia, like an ejaculation.[8]

Given the Morgan treatment, the Big Bang theory of universal origin articulates an appropriate myth for the times, and Pandora, fashioned by Vulcan as first mortal woman, associates relevant text. In one version of the tale, Jupiter's gift to Pandora contained all the world's ills, let loose when it was opened; evidence of male codes determining female behaviour then blaming her across time as an old tale and a coat of many colours. But somewhere along its transmission lines this story changed: the box contained only good, lost when it was opened – except for hope, left hiding in a corner. Either way, Pandora activates permissive scoring for Morgan's Promethean subjectivity at large and enjoying itself in 'Planet Wave', striding oceans and aeons in the shaping of its account: 'Is this the lucky planet? / Can you down a pint of lava, make love / to the Grand Canyon, tuck a thunderbolt / in its cradle? Yes and no, folks, yes and no. / You must have patience with the story'. While syncopation tested possibility, Morgan's time-travelling voice told of cave-dwellers' uses of fire and craft; showed people building their ark of survival against 'The Great Flood', and surrendering to music at the completion of an Egyptian pyramid; and recalled vivid detail from a tenth-century Viking funeral on the Volga.

Over a long and productive life Morgan has entertained a large and varied audience, moving people from laughter to concentration in many countries. His 1952 translation of *Beowulf* entered curricula in Australia and in the USA, where it enjoyed an extraordinarily long print life. As well as several Scottish Arts Council awards he was given the 1972 Hungarian P.E.N. Memorial Medal; and an OBE in 1982 when *Poems of Thirty Years* was published. Three years later he spent the prize-money for his versions of Attila József on a Concorde day-trip to the North Pole. For a globetrotter who always came home, Morgan's unusual civic status was confirmed when Glasgow named an international writing festival (part of its 1990 European City of Culture franchise) after his 1973 collection *From Glasgow to Saturn*. In 1999 he was appointed City Laureate, and published his redaction of Marlowe's *Faustus*, a year later he received the Queen's Gold Medal for poetry and published his Scots version of *Phaedre* (which won the Wiedenfeld Prize for translation), as well as his Jesus trilogy, a sequence of poems called *Demon*, and a revised and expanded *New Selected Poems*. Not a retiring way to welcome the new century: but this public and productive citizen is also a private and reclusive figure, who in Tom Leonard's affectionate description of him as 'Cultural attaché to the legendary city of Morganiana' is 'said to exist behind a door marked "Morgan" in an unobtrusive block of flats off the Great Western Road'. From here 'translations and original poems go out daily to magazines all over the world, while the city director converses by golden telephone with the spirits of some dead but perky Russian Futurists'.[9]

For Kenneth White, reading *Poems of Thirty Years* in 1982 felt like a 'gradual process of getting spaced out': 'for this virtuoso has a finger in every pie, from the meat pies you get in the local greasy spoon to the cherry pies they make in Nebraska'.[10] Morgan certainly covers a lot of territory. The 1985 *Selected Poems* (which was to sell in excess of 20,000 copies) persuaded Denis Donoghue that 'the force of Morgan's imagination is its variousness';[11] and one of Morgan's Italian translators is not

alone in finding this variousness 'disorienting and enriching at the same
time'.[12] Reading *Themes on a Variation* in 1989, Iain Crichton Smith
helped to explain why by noting a characteristically extensive range:

> Morgan's poetry has always been large, vigorous and imaginative.
> It has been energetic and various ... composed of straight narrative,
> concrete poetry, sci-fi, satire. It has been life enhancing, technol-
> ogy-welcoming, adventurous, protean. More than the work of
> most poets it welcomes the 20th century, with its gadgets, its para-
> doxes, graffiti, new languages, torn advertisements, unconscious
> jokes, voyages. It writes of heroes and heroines, its Marilyn
> Monroes, Edith Piafs, etc, those who have lived their lives fully to
> the point of extinction, those whom we consider to be its paradigms
> and its victims.... Its range of languages is gargantuan, using Latin,
> French, demotic Glasgow, grave Academe, the language of the
> computer and of geology.[13]

A voracious appetite for language has led Morgan to translate into
English and Scots from Italian, Russian, German, Spanish, French,
Portuguese, Anglo-Saxon, ancient Greek, Dutch, Khmer, Armenian and
Hungarian – 'working with cribs on the last three, although he now gets
by in Hungarian'.[14]

Morgan's imagination routinely ranges from a poetry of local place
and ethical space through high formal rhetoric to clowning, constantly
experimenting and as constantly sensitive to the primacy of responsibil-
ity towards the Other. Plato would certainly have censored Morgan's
sometimes-stellar negotiations of and with alterity, though they share a
passion for ambitious projection. Evidently, the Glaswegian takes pleasure in variegating the play of voice in Athenian dialogue in ways sympathetic to Hannah Arendt's suggestion that the role of the philosopher
is 'not to rule the city but to be its "gadfly", not to tell philosophical
truths but to make citizens more truthful', though truths abound in
Morgan's work.[15] As we shall see, Morgan is pointed about Plato; yet
'I'm not a political animal really,' he said in 1972, 'except I have now
and again very strong feelings about things, but they're more feelings
than thought-out intellectual positions.' He added that he would 'rather
use the word radical than socialist' (NNGM p. 49), and it has long been
evident that the only acceptable discipline would be his own, exercised
as technical experiment, formal variety, meticulous phrasing and the
emotional impact of structured feelings. Within an older, broader notion
of politics as the space where individuals realise their nature as rational,
sentient beings, Morgan's literary criticism assumes socially active

reference and his poetry articulates a kaleidoscope of perceptions to speak a living here and now both publicly and privately inflected. Fascinated by the zany, the arcane, the absurd, the possible futures anciently set and possible pasts figured futuristically, his interest in social, personal, linguistic and cultural othernesses comes to us in a poetics of communicative rationality which operates through often mind-bending syntax. Repeatedly scouting semantic frontiers where centripetal pressure separates and centrifugal energy draws together, Morgan's song book reconfigures the personal and the political partly because space conventionally reserved for the personal – 'all that is present and moving, all that escapes or seems to escape from the fixed and the explicit and the known … this, here, now, alive, active, "subjective"' – has been significantly co-opted into a public domain.[16] The personal and private is now routinely projected as public and social;[17] and Morgan's writing repeatedly navigates these intersections as boundary-crossing self-disclosure, such that a late poem can refer to 'peeling layer on layer like a flaying', and end:

> No tide
> will ever wash away the ash you hide
> of pain, or love, or pain or love denied.[18]

Alan Bold detected 'very little tender human contact between people' in Morgan's work;[19] but looking for love and loss in the poetry, Iain Crichton Smith found 'strange movements of solitude, random messages of love', and quoted lines from 'The Divide':

> I keep thinking of your eyes, your hands.
> There is no reason for it, none at all.
> You would say I can't be what I'm not,
> yet I can't not be what I am.[20]

Smith identified 'the real Morgan that is the poet' in lines from a sequence of 'Unfinished Poems':

> Pain to know,
>   pain not knowing.
> Pain to love,
>   pain not loving.
> Pain on the rack
>   and in the rocking-chair.
> Wrong to meet,
>   wrong not to.
> Wrong to be barren
>   wrong to bear. (CP p. 377)

Morgan's sexual orientation took some years to clarify in writing, as the obliqueness and compression of the early verse testifies. But over the years of its difficult emergence personal candour came to authenticate a public poetry's integrity, and *Inventions of modernity* has no argument with Smith's reading of Morgan as wearer of many masks across an extensive range of meaning-making practices, including a private poet at times 'naked and desolate'.[21]

There is no doubt about the city Morgan identifies as home, yet Morgan territory typically undermines cognitively privileged habits of observation, preferred value systems and dominant cultural assumptions. His experimentalism habitually activates meaning strategically at odds with current or fashionable epistemologies and attitudes, as when a verse-letter addressed to 'An Iraqi Student' at the time of the Gulf War mobilises concern about loss of epistemic anchoring:

> One thin line of thought in words, not shifting
> as sands are – well, not quite so shifting, language
> shifts with anchors dragging – must manage
> like a camel train to make its measured progress
> through missile banks, camouflage fatigues, gas-masks
> clustered like decapitated insects –
> future ruins already dusted
> by the desert wind.[22]

As it invents, translates, historicises, ventriloquises and records speaking sensibilities, insofar as Morgan's work reconstructs cultural history and memory, it defines him as a major poet in our time. His different take on early twentieth-century groundings for the modernism that now encodes his own succession includes Hugh MacDiarmid, for many years largely absent from accounts of new writing immediately before and after the First World War. Partly as a consequence of this difficult relationship, Morgan's lines of enquiry and networks of association are differently disposed. Robin Fulton reminds us that MacDiarmid was something of a predator:

> With the enthusiasm and frequent inaccuracy of a voracious auto-didact he has rifled world literature, history and science for material which can be absorbed into his own prevailing concerns. The movement is inwards, and fidelity to the sources is not highly regarded. With Morgan, the movement is outwards, and in his translation and criticism fidelity towards and respect for the sources is paramount.[23]

Fulton remembers as characteristic an exercise Morgan published in 1969: 'a study of three poems about Brooklyn Bridge, by Hart Crane, Mayakovsky and Lorca ... followed by translations of Mayakovsky's Russian into Scots and of Lorca's Spanish into English'.[24] Forming as it does part of the alternative social and personal infrastructures Morgan imagines for a native country historically subordinated within discursive economies centred elsewhere, the exercise brings into sharp relief his differences from the Eliot–Pound axis still influential at mid-twentieth century. It also fundamentally complicates, as does much of Morgan's output, culturally privileged senses of predominantly Anglo-American post-war reinventions of modernism.[25] Wary of conceptual apparatuses governing perception and cognition, Morgan's treatment of narratives grand or otherwise marks him out as transformer of a cultural inheritance that includes a 'Modernism' that was achieving currency as critical discrimination in the 1960s, when Morgan was securing his own national and international reputation. The genealogies through which he references his present inscribe a tradition for his individual talent that constitutes nothing less than a reconstructed modernism which both challenges its English valences as established by Leavisite protocols and proprieties, and subverts its United States incarnation by landscaping cultural and political effects for the carefully engineered historical blindnesses and strategic neutralities of an autotelic New Criticism. The ideology of modernism Fredric Jameson set out to demystify in 1975 had already been radically reconfigured in Morgan's creative interventions, where binaries conventionally assembled to differentiate modernist from postmodernist practice already articulate as topic, theme and interaction.[26] Morgan's poetry prophetically if incidentally transcends a postmodernism more recently if prematurely declared 'dead as a theoretical concept and, more important, as a way of developing cultural frameworks influencing how we shape theoretical concepts'.[27] Exhaustion and silence are not part of his project, but neither is God the Father (or any other deity) except, recurrently, as figure of invention. Typically construing divinity as an effect in language, Morgan's secular aesthetic incorporates that effect as a transforming agency for human subjects. Suspicious of social or spiritual hierarchies, hostile to the discursive and political practices they generate and validate, and usually preferring demons to angels, he locates grand narrative in small story and reverses the procedure as occasion requires, dispersing centred subjectivity to imagine fuller becomings.

Teaching in the English Literature department of a Scottish university, Morgan could hardly have been unaware that curricula and canons are narratives of a kind, narratives that determine criteria of competence and/or illustrate how they may be applied.[28] In Morgan's scheme of things narrativised criteria must stretch or give way to accommodate alternative need, and what has been said about Jean-François Lyotard's account of subjectivity addresses an effect of Morgan's poetry: 'to force our lips open, so that we speak where before there was only a silence imposed by a seemingly inexorable logic'. To stimulate this reactivation the sublime will be brought back into time as 'the politics of a world which will explode into all kinds of voice, and which will frown upon the traditional silence of exit and loyalty'.[29] Morgan ended a British Academy lecture in 1977 with the suggestion that the sublime was 'being reborn in science fiction, and the last refuge of the sublime is in the stars', where he also locates voice.[30] If that extends a cosmic dimension for exercises in interiority cast as vividly realised *mises en scènes*, and Morgan is an expert scene-setter who habitually projects aspects of himself into other existences, he renders the local in vital idiom. Living in Glasgow, he has said, 'your ear is attuned to the broadest kind of Glasgow speech as well as what you're using yourself': 'I enjoyed different kinds of speech, and I think I was probably thinking about that fairly early. I'm not quite sure how early; perhaps I was collecting different accents and making some-thing of it' (NNGM p. 120). Heterology is what he is about, and trans-individual differentiation has long been a tactic in poetry that sustains conceptions of a future for which an 'Ariel Freed' from Prospero's con-trol still reaches: 'only to have no shore, no landfall, / no runway, no eyrie, no goal and no fall!'[31] It will then seem, but is not, perverse to sug-gest that a paradigm shift from modernism's groundless, transcendent subjectivity towards new forms of subjectivity based on the notion that everyone is conditioned by the idea of limit, sketches a future already the-matised and breached in Morgan's rhythms:

> Limit-subjectivity will come to be understood as grounded in history, politics, culture and intersubjectivity, and will come to be defined in terms of its reflexive appreciation of those grounds, and of their consequences for the exercise of the subject's agency.... It will focus in on what we intuitively grasp but cannot quite express.[32]

Insisting on expressibility and recognising a grounded, limited subjec-tivity as all that is on offer in socially structured practice, Morgan works at and against frontiers of the possible:

> Imagine anything the world could, it might
> do; anything not to do, it would.
> A plume of act flies as it spins by. (CP p. 348)

Transgression of limit is integral to his forms of attention:

> Not seeking order, or the measured disorder
> of chaos theory, but pressing every border,
>
> scouring, tracing, probing and extending
> whatever tries to tell him it's an ending,
> breaking whatever tells him it's unbending.[33]

Perceptions of the real inform these travelling perspectives. A late poem called 'Day's End' sees public business and private pleasure continuing as usual, while: 'The homeless in their doorways clutch the cold, / Still real, still waiting for the tale to be told'.[34] Telling that tale is a theme Morgan constantly varies, and his commitment to story is firm:

> I like that element of poetry and I don't want to give it up. Even if you have a difficult poem like 'Waking on a Dark Morning' [CP pp. 513–15], there's a story there too: if it's looked at closely it is actually about waking on a dark morning in a bedroom with curtains, furniture and so on; the clues are there. It's obviously difficult in many ways but it's meant not to be nonsense; it's meant to show the gradual coming to consciousness of somebody who is waking up. I love story telling; I love novels and films too, where there's still a strong emphasis on story. Anyway, I don't give up story.[35]

Morgan's speakers tell many a tale in assembled (and dispersed) legions of alterity that together constitute a post-war metanarrative of cultural maturation. As part of the practice of difference he customarily centres the marginalised and re-positions the socially excluded. For example, in 'The Heart of Midlothian', he rewrites the fate of 'a born imp of Satan' to rescue him from Walter Scott's treatment of Jeanie Deans' illegitimate son, called The Whistler, who unwittingly kills his father and is sold into American plantation slavery: 'The young man had headed a conspiracy in which his inhuman master was put to death, and had then fled to the next tribe of wild Indians. He was never more heard of; and it may therefore be presumed that he lived and died after the manner of that savage people, with whom his previous habits had well fitted him to associate':[36]

> He's in a tepee now, his logs are sawn.
> He mimics the wild beaks and wings of dawn,
> an undrawn life worth more than all the drawn.[37]

Outsiders find space in this poetry. As, from early work onwards, do earth-bound travellers and planetary explorers: 'Planet Wave' includes hymns in praise of Magellan and to Copernicus for his 'wave of thought that got the earth to move'.[38]

As a way of marking out manageable space, and to find a way through, I adopt wherever possible a writing and publication chronology. But within poem sequences and sometimes across collections I take Morgan's lead and jump back and forth to find relationship. I have freely plundered the interviews and statements in *Nothing Not Giving Messages* and thank Hamish Whyte for bringing them together. Since Morgan is large and contains multitudes, others will read him in their own way: nothing else would do for a poetry recurrently involving freedom from coercion and restraint, and where only the structure of perception and argument at hand is operative. His verse raises questions about the status and function of thought and feeling in a literate democracy: I identify some of these as they arise in and across particular poems and sequences. Because Morgan's writing spans over half a century, *Inventions of modernity* includes a seriatim account of the aesthetic practices and associated ideologies he uses and refuses.

My first chapter describes contexts in which he began work, when the priority for Scots usage in verse was a public argument. Of relevance at that time was a now largely forgotten Scottish prominence in the New Apocalypse movement that flourished briefly in the 1940s. Together with a precursor surrealism, which was always an attempt to rediscover a political role for art in the world, apocalyptic poetics suggested openings, and Morgan seems never to have abandoned its commitment to experimental renewal.

Using these contexts to bring out personal repressions and political implications in the early verse, chapter 2 looks at libertarian comedy in 'The Vision of Cathkin Braes' and at the modernising impact of his *Beowulf* translation. It also charts developing disagreements with Hugh MacDiarmid, which constitute a significant motif in twentieth-century Scottish culture; and then reads the 'Whittrick' sequence as early evidence of Morgan's dialogic imagination.

Admiration for Vladimir Mayakovsky's technological dynamism carries into a range of Morgan's writing, which updates Futurism's hi-tech city to include computer poems, cyberspace and space travel. Chapter 3 reads political technique and Scottish focus in the sound world invented for his Mayakovsky translations, and connects them with a sequence of 'Glasgow Sonnets' published in the same year as *Wi the Haill Voice* and the Glasgow shipyard working occupation of 1972.

Chapter 4 reads translations of Eugenio Montale as a tactic of self-discovery, and the texts translated into English for *Sovpoems* (1961) as part of a singular modernist reconstruction. Slight in size but not in scale, and little read at the time, *Sovpoems* issued a plea for sanity when nuclear annihilation was a clear and present cold-war danger. This fourth chapter then traces Morgan's gay poetry as it developed during the 1960s, and describes his concrete and related work. Against the background of a recurrent surrealism the chapter considers a seemingly contrary but in effect complementary attraction to a poetry of documentary realism in *Instamatic Poems* (1972), designed to present verbal snapshots of events reported in the daily press.

Chapter 5 picks up a more expressive development of gay poetry and considers surreal adaptations in *From Glasgow to Saturn* (1973); then turns to a newly mobile sequencing in *The New Divan* (1977), to science-fiction poetry including 'Memories of Earth', and an imaginary republic closer to Bakhtin's than Plato's. One of this republic's constituencies is the radically gendered classical pantheon of an 'Alphabet of Goddesses'.

Chapter 6 treats *Sonnets From Scotland* (1984) as reconstructive political testament arising from the failure of the 1979 referendum on devolution, and considers issues related to cinematic and televised representations of subjectivity raised by *From the Video Box* (1983); it also includes the reflective post-Communist-era formulations of *Hold Hands Among The Atoms* (1991). Translations included in *Sweeping out the Dark* (1994) encode different attitudes to the vanishing narrative of Communist promise partly through the work of Attila József, whom Morgan considers 'one of the major poets of the [twentieth] century'.[39]

Chapter 7 approaches gender issues raised by 'A Voyage', examines image-making practices in the environment of digital simulation scripted by *Virtual and Other Realities* (1997), and looks at cultural priorities inscribed in a 1999 sequence called *Demon*. The book ends with an autobiographical sequence of poems by Morgan here published for the first time.

Notes

1 V. N. Vološinov, *Marxism and the Philosophy of Language* [1929], cited in Pam Morris (ed.), *The Bakhtin Reader*, London, 1994, p. 35.

2 Edwin Morgan, 'Nothing Is Not Giving Messages', interview in *Edwin Morgan: Nothing Not Giving Messages: Reflections on his Work and Life*, ed. Hamish Whyte, Edinburgh, 1990, p. 142. Hereafter NNGM.

3 Edwin Morgan, *A. D. A Trilogy of Plays on the Life of Jesus*, Manchester, 2000, p. 148.
4 *Ibid.*, p. 70.
5 Interview in Colin Nicholson, *Poem, Purpose and Place: Shaping Identity in Contemporary Scottish Verse*, Edinburgh, 1992, p. 74.
6 Edwin Morgan, *The Apple-Tree: A Medieval Dutch Play*, Glasgow, 1982; *Master Peter Pathelin*, Glasgow, 1983. See Bill Findlay, *Motivation and Method in Scots Translations, Versions and Adaptations of Plays from the Historical Repertoire of Continental European Drama*, unpub. doct. diss. (Edinburgh: Queen Margaret University College), 2000, vol. 1, p. 242.
7 Edwin Morgan, *Christopher Marlowe's Doctor Faustus*, Edinburgh, 1999; *Phaedre: A Tragedy*, Manchester, 2000.
8 Edwin Morgan, 'Planet Wave', *PN Review*, 24:3, January–February 1998, p. 18.
9 Tom Leonard, 'Poster for POETSOUND '84', Third Eye Centre, Glasgow, 1984, cited in Kevin McCarra, 'Edwin Morgan: Lives and Work', in Robert Crawford and Hamish Whyte (eds), *About Edwin Morgan*, Edinburgh, 1990, pp. 7–8.
10 Kenneth White, 'Morgan's Range', *Cencrastus*, 12, 1983, p. 32.
11 Denis Donoghue, 'Ten Poets', *London Review of Books*, 7:19, 7 November 1985, p. 21.
12 Marco Fazzini, 'From Glasgow to Outer Space: Edwin Morgan's (Un)Realities', in *Crossings: Essays on Contemporary Scottish Poetry and Hybridity*, Venezia Lido, 2000, p. 84.
13 Iain Crichton Smith, 'Vintage Morgan', *Cencrastus*, 32, 1989, p. 13.
14 Peter McCarey, 'Edwin Morgan the Translator', in Crawford and Whyte (eds), *About Edwin Morgan*, p. 90.
15 Hannah Arendt, 'Philosophy and Politics', *Social Research*, 57:1, 1990, p. 81.
16 Raymond Williams, *Marxism and Literature*, Oxford, 1977, p. 128.
17 Geoffrey Hawthorn and Camilla Lund, 'Private and Public in "Late-Modern" Democracy', in J. Good and I. Velody (eds), *The Politics of Postmodernity*, Cambridge, 1998, pp. 41–2.
18 Edwin Morgan, 'To the Librarians, H. W. and H. H.', in *Virtual and Other Realities*, Manchester, 1997, p. 71.
19 Alan Bold, *Modern Scottish Literature*, London, 1983, p. 79.
20 Edwin Morgan, *Collected Poems*, Manchester, 1990, p. 369. Hereafter CP.
21 Iain Crichton Smith, 'The Public and Private Morgan', in Crawford and Whyte (eds), *About Edwin Morgan*, pp. 39–53.
22 Edwin Morgan, *Hold Hands Among The Atoms*, Glasgow, 1991, p. 76.
23 Robin Fulton, *Contemporary Scottish Poetry: Individuals and Contexts*, Loanhead, 1994, p. 13.
24 *Ibid.*, p. 15.
25 Alan Sinfield, *Literature, Politics and Culture in Postwar Britain* [1989], London, 1997, pp. 182–202; Ihab Hassan, *The Postmodern Turn: Essays in Postmodern Theory and Culture*, Ohio, 1987, pp. 91–2.
26 Fredric Jameson, 'Beyond the Cave: Demystifying the Ideology of Modernism', in *The Ideologies of Theory: Essays 1971–86*, vol. 2: *The Syntax of History*, London, 1989, pp. 115–32, reprinted in Francis Mulhern (ed.), *Contemporary Marxist Literary Criticism*, London, 1992, pp. 168–87.

27 Charles Altieri, 'What is Living and What is Dead in American Postmodernism: Establishing the Contemporaneity of Some American Poetry', *Critical Enquiry*, 22:4, 1996, p. 764.
28 Jean-François Lyotard, *The Postmodern Condition: A Report on Knowledge*, Manchester, 1979, p. 23.
29 Roy Boyne, 'Postmodernism, the Sublime and Ethics', in Good and Velody (eds), *The Politics of Postmodernity*, pp. 212, 217.
30 Edwin Morgan: 'Provenance and Problematics of "Sublime and Alarming Images" in Poetry', *Proceeding of the British Academy*, LXIII, 1978, p. 313.
31 Morgan, *Virtual and Other Realities*, p. 101.
32 Boyne, 'Postmodernism, the Sublime and Ethics', p. 211.
33 Morgan, *Virtual and Other Realities*, p. 63.
34 *Ibid.*, p. 98.
35 Interview with Morgan, 17 August 1998.
36 Walter Scott, *The Heart of Midlothian*, ed. Clare Lamont, Oxford, 1982, p. 506.
37 Morgan, *Virtual and Other Realities*, p. 53.
38 Morgan, 'Planet Wave', p. 21.
39 Edwin Morgan, 'Attila Jószef', *The Dark Horse*, 11, 2001, p. 36.

1 Apocalypse and after

Critical understanding of self takes place ... through a struggle of
opposing 'hegemonies' and of opposing directions, first in the ethical field and then in that of politics proper, in order to arrive at the
working out of a higher level of one's own concept of reality.
(Antonio Gramsci)[1]

Born in 1920 in Glasgow's West End to socially conservative, churchgoing Presbyterian parents, Edwin Morgan grew up an only child first in
Pollockshields then Rutherglen. Quiet and introspective, he was
unhappy as a schoolboy at Rutherglen Academy, toyed with the idea of
leaving early to become a carpenter, but took bursary examinations to
complete his schooling with three years at Glasgow High, where he
became aware of his homosexuality and where he first started writing;
winning prizes in his last year for English composition, for French, and
for prose and verse contributions to the school magazine. He intended
going to art school, but changed his mind at the last minute and enrolled
at Glasgow University in 1937. 'Nocturne: Ruins and Music' was the first
of several pieces that appeared in the *Glasgow University Magazine* over
the next two years, during which time undergraduate encounters with
French and Russian writing had significant impact. Both symbolist practice and Mayakovsky's Bolshevik Futurism offered possible strategies that
would subsequently clarify. 'I didn't put myself to school with
MacDiarmid or with any of the earlier Scottish poetry', Morgan recalled
in later years: 'it was there and I enjoyed it, but it wasn't what compelled.
Even during my last years at school and at university I was feeling my way
gradually into other ways of looking at things'.[2]

Conscripted in 1940, Morgan came under pressure for registering
as a Conscientious Objector, and adapted his pacifism to the requirements of the time by enlisting in the Royal Army Medical Corps, spend-
ing the war as a Quartermaster's clerk sometimes called on as
stretcher-bearer with the 42nd General Hospital in Egypt, the Lebanon
and Palestine. Not until *The New Divan* appeared in 1977 would he work
through some of these wartime experiences. Demobilised in 1946, he

picked up his university studies and after a curriculum that included Political Economy, French, History and Russian, graduated in 1947 with a First in English Language and Literature. At the age of twenty-seven he was offered a teaching post in Glasgow University's English Department, where he took early retirement from his professorship in 1980; by which time he had produced a prodigious body of poetry and numerous critical essays.[3]

While serving in the Middle East Morgan read whatever he could lay his hands on, relying on friends in Scotland to keep him supplied with books. But notwithstanding school and undergraduate promise he experienced considerable difficulty getting started again after the war, and later drew attention to some of the potentially disabling contexts in which he and others found themselves:

> Although Englishmen do not have to worry about their relation and attitude to Scotland, the Scots have, and have long had, to worry about their relation and attitude to England, or to the English-speaking world. No country, which has once been independent, and is then overshadowed in union with a more powerful partner, can develop naturally and happily. Its political history is officially closed, but emotionally it remains unfinished. Its cultural traditions soon begin to show a lack of integration, and though this does not preclude fine work in a variety of styles it does mean that the steady maturing and enriching of traditions which is characteristic of the greatest cultures is constantly frustrated, either by a sentimental native conservatism or by desperate attempts to imitate the modes of the dominating neighbour culture.[4]

Finding a language of self-constitution was for Morgan further and radically problematised by a socially imperative concealment of sexual orientation: his 1950 essay 'Women and Poetry' raised proto-feminist colours in an uncongenial climate.

With choice of poetic medium in 1940s Scotland in continuing dispute, Morgan pursued his talent by developing a perception of Scots and English as sister languages in what he later called the 'ur-historical sense that the Scots tongue developed originally out of the Northumbrian dialect of Anglo-Saxon'.[5] These different sound-worlds never felt alien, and his resolution of an argument about the preferred use of Scots relates to culturally colonised circumstance in distinctive ways. The world was then a different place, with approved forms of spoken and literary English still both a globally and domestically effective power – thanks partly to the international prestige enjoyed by a rigorously class-based

BBC – and Scotland a country where political independence from London's dispensing centre was for many of its citizens neither a credible nor a desirable prospect. A movement in favour of Home Rule would later develop irreversible momentum, but the late 1940s were not the late 1970s; and if a devolution referendum at the later time did not achieve what many hoped for, the question could at least be put and command a majority of votes cast. Thirty years earlier disagreement about what constituted fit speech and idiom for a self-governing country was raising considerable heat and dust among rival practitioners. Morgan came back to this after a time overseas that had been an eye-opening experience of self-exploration, and a shock of cultural difference that included what he called the revelation of his first encounter with medieval Scottish poetry (NNGM pp. 122–3). It is difficult to overestimate the continuing impact of the discovery while abroad of a native literary history that helped form useable perspectives which would significantly reconfigure master narratives both locally developed and imported. Back in Glasgow, with a movement to establish vernacular Scots as a contemporary medium influencing a domestic cultural agenda, and a landslide Labour government in Westminster (decisively supported by Scotland's industrial electorate) putting in place structures of social practice to improve life opportunities for millions of people north and south of the border, literary choices could and did problematise both cultural identity and political self-definition.

Morgan first appeared in print following demobilisation in the *Glasgow Herald*'s correspondence columns, where in 1946 a sometimes acrimonious dispute about the name, nature and cultural viability of Scots followed a BBC broadcast in which James Fergusson had dubbed such writing 'Plastic Scots'. An episode that opens a window on to the lack of integration to which Morgan refers was stimulated when the *Herald*'s 'Editorial Diary' cited the authority of the state broadcasting system ('the BBC ... has this week rechristened synthetic Scots, that fantastic, original language which has become the raw material of some of our poets') in a belittling sally against a developing vernacular. 'The BBC prefers to call it *plastic Scots*, on the theory that it can be compounded of any gobbets of language which, once thrown together, can then be punched into any shape the poet likes. It is not (quoting from memory) *like any tongue ever spoken or written between Shetland and the Solway*'.[6] On the following day, under the sub-heading 'Short Course in Plastic Scots', the *Herald*'s diarist advised any would-be scribblers that writing at least one ode to Hugh MacDiarmid was *de rigueur*. 'After all, he invented synthetic Scots, from which the plastic form is derived'. The first reply was duly signed by C. M. Grieve pointing out that linguistic experimentation was a feature common to modern writing, that problems of intelligibility were accordingly not confined to writing in Scots, that all languages were synthetic, and (perhaps unsettlingly for Morgan in his mid-twenties), that English anthologists 'eschew almost all contemporary Scottish poetry not written in it'.[7] In a subsequent letter MacDiarmid claimed that 'the entire Scottish contribution to English poetry could be excised without noticeable detriment to the latter': 'all recent English critics and literary historians have testified to the fact that wherever modern Scottish poets have written both in English and in Scots their best work has been done in the latter'.[8] The exchange continued for several weeks, with MacDiarmid returning to the fray and Maurice Lindsay calling both radio programme and *Herald* attack 'mean-spirited, pointless and foolish'; with Douglas Young, Lallans poet, academic Classicist and combative leader of the Scottish National Party weighing in, and with Fergusson declaring his belief that 'these writers are not so much positively concerned with reviving, re-creating, or inventing a Scots language, as negatively obsessed, from political and not poetical motives, with getting away from English'.[9] During the course of this 'negative obsession' Morgan wrote two letters to which we shall return. Some of the cultural politics in contention were laid out in three anthologies also appearing in 1946: James Fergusson's *The Green Garden: A New Collection of Scottish Poetry*, Maurice Lindsay's *Modern Scottish Poetry: An Anthology of the Scottish Renaissance 1920–1945*, and MacDiarmid's larger *Golden Treasury of Scottish Poetry* first published in 1940 but now re-issued in a second edition.

With a recognisable blend of pseudo-scientific polemic, pronounced anti-English sentiment and sharp writing delivering astute observation, MacDiarmid's *Golden Treasury* introduction welcomed the fact that since the 1920s a revival of literary Scots had gone hand in hand with political developments on Scotland's nationalist wing. He described Scotland as a Gaelic country, emphasising what he called the 'essential Irish Gaelic sources of our national beginnings', and voicing a desire to transcend 'largely false' divisions between Highland and Lowland, between Scots and Scottish Gaelic: 'If the new Scottish literary movement which began just after the Great War were to produce major literature it could only do so by resuming and renewing the traditions of our ancient Gaelic heritage'.[10] With an Irish revival of native language in view, led by the Gaelic League that in the 1890s generated impetus for political independence, MacDiarmid was looking to extend the impact of his revolutionary interventions of the 1920s. Rather than English, he maintained, the growing end of Scottish poetry was in Scots: 'an ever-increasing number of our younger poets are reverting to that medium, and writing in a Scots which is a synthesis of all the dialects into which Scots has degenerated and of elements of Scots vocabulary drawn from all periods of our history' (p. xxiv). Lindsay's anthology, planned during the war years to publicise self-definitions that had been 'started as a deliberate search after national culture [in] parallel to the political Scottish Nationalist movement', nailed its colours to the mast by using as epigraph the same MacDiarmid stanza – 'The Little White Rose' – with which its author had prefaced his own selection.[11] Conversely, not only does Fergusson's *The Green Garden* make no mention of *The Golden Treasury*, his selection excludes Gaelic writing on the grounds that it 'does not belong to the main stream of western European culture', and describes as legitimate but unsuccessful recent experiments with 'two new variants ... a medley of old and modern words, labelled by its critics "synthetic Scots"':

> and a phonetic form of debased modern Scots, of somewhat Balkan appearance on the printed page, styled by some of its practitioners 'Lallans'. ... I cannot but suspect that the motive in each case has been political rather than literary: a desire to find a new medium of expression, which should not be English.[12]

Since its selection ends with Burns because the traditions that interest its editor cannot subsequently be traced (p. xix), readers of *The Green Garden* would not be troubled by this Balkanisation. Editorial politics were further disclosed in the terms used to present a controlling perception Fergusson thought of as typically Scottish: 'English poets have generally been pioneers and experimenters; they are always bursting their chains and breaking out into fresh adventures of form and rhythm. The Scots ... hugged their chains and wreathed them with flowers ... . This passion for creating intricate beauty within strict self-imposed limits is something innate in the Scottish aesthetic character' (p. xvi). That 'self-imposed' is at least disingenuous; and hugging one's chains defines a paradigmatic cultural cringe in the face of discursive dominance. What MacDiarmid called the surviving values of a 'pro-English "courtier school"' here generates property's proprieties to give Fergusson his title: 'While I think of English poetry as a spacious landscape ... Scottish poetry appears to me rather as ... the Green Garden which haunted the imagination of Scottish poets for three hundred years' (pp. xxiv–xxv).[13]

Cultural gardens can be planted as compensatory nostalgia, and by describing Fergusson as led to this 'courtly' image by a Scottish adherence to tradition, a reviewer in the *Times Literary Supplement* half-recognised the tactic and the strategy.[14] When the union of the crowns took the Scottish court south, enshrining English practice as ruling and appropriate discourse for essentially rural and agrarian traditions of writing, its terms and priorities buttressed and reinforced security of tenure for a Scottish land-owning class. Scotland more generally moved into England's orbit and subsequently threw native energies into Britain's empire building.[15] Fergusson's father and grandfather had been Governors-General of New Zealand, an office his brother Bernard was to assume from 1962 to 1967 before being created Lord Ballantrae of Aucherne and the Bay of Islands in 1972, the year in which he took up the chairmanship of the British Council. Bernard was also a rhymer who drew from MacDiarmid in 1948 the accusation that he was a liar and a coward (albeit at the time commander of the 1st Battalion, the Black Watch, in Germany) for taking part in a separate denigration of writers in Scots, this time solicited by the editor of the Scottish *Daily Record*. That editor had, Fergusson remembers, 'induced a few Scottish writers to flyte each other, and invited me to participate. This was when the writers of the so-called Scottish Renaissance were in full spate, pouring out verse in what they called "Lallans" or Lowland Scots, which my brother James happily dubbed "Plastic Scots"'.[16] Meanwhile, brother James's book had been reviewed in a leading English journal and its compiler given broadcasting time to air views then identified by a Scottish newspaper as the BBC's; tracing a complicit periphery's cultural incorporation into valorising power located elsewhere, and complicating the opposing hegemonies Gramsci thought functional to advancing self-awareness.

Although Douglas Young considered the aristocratic strain in Fergusson's anthology complementary to the proletarian elements promoted by MacDiarmid, the latter habitually saw language divisions as largely class-based in the sense that he recognised Scots in the speech of a native working class.[17] As the argument unfolded, promoters of literary Scots emphasised its speech-patterns as part of the sound world of lived experience: but as R. Crombie Saunders (a contributor to Lindsay's anthology) pointed out, while a majority of Scottish people 'still speak some Scots dialect of more or less impurity … they write in an English which has surprisingly little relationship to it'.[18] Young had already allowed that most users of Scots for verse 'nowadays speak English in daily intercourse, and read and write it'; and MacDiarmid well understood that Scots was used in print for few contemporary purposes save poetry.[19] But MacDiarmid was arguing for the advancement of self-determination through commitment to what he called a *Kulturkampf* against invasive English practice; a struggle that entailed making 'the political sympathies of our literature identical with our national interests'.[20] Not an easy battle in a dramatically unequal contest for the survival of a native lexis and its timbre. Apart from control of the airwaves, London's governing systems exercised effective control over the setting of standards for basic learning programmes across Scotland's schools. In what became perhaps the most influential early twentieth-century text book on the production and reproduction of a preferred English sound world, Daniel Jones was open about his sources for best practice:

> 'The pronunciation represented [in the Everyman *English Pronouncing Dictionary*] is that which I believe to be very usually heard in everyday speech in the families of Southern English people who have been educated at the public schools.... It is probably accurate to say that a majority of Londoners who have had a university education, use either this pronunciation or a pronunciation not differing greatly from it'.[21]

To raise questions about an imported cultural policing of Scottish custom and practice, including the promotion and development of speech patterns set by standardising educational norms in English, MacDiarmid used a 1934 report by a research committee of Glasgow's local association of the Educational Institute of Scotland. At issue is not whether the subaltern can speak but rather the rules of engagement laid down for its speaking:

> Too often censure was founded on the assumption that 'Proper English' is the language spoken by Englishmen, whereas the 'bairn from Falkirk' and the 'Glesca keelie', on finding themselves in the same pen at Wembley with a Cockney, a Tyke, a Lancashire lad, a Stafford potter, and a Durham miner, might wonder if they had not been misdirected to the Tower of Babel ... . In most cases Glasgow pupils enter the schools with one language only, the Central Scottish Dialect, and they proceed to learn to write Standard English. As the result of education the vernacular is gradually eliminated from written work, but it persists in colloquial use [and] is the medium of expression naturally employed by the Glasgow child, who may interrogate the teacher during a Dictation lesson with such a question as 'Whit cums efter "after"?' In the playground children who try to speak Standard English are generally laughed at, whilst in the classroom a lapse into the mother tongue is greeted with hilarity.[22]

Morgan pushed his boat into these politicised cross-currents of a post-war contest over proper speech and acceptable script, navigating on the one hand Edwin Muir's advice to his countrymen to cast aside Scots as a 'trash of nonsense' and on the other MacDiarmid's assertion that no Scottish poet using the medium of English has managed to write first-class work.[23] His first letter in the 'plastic Scots' controversy suggested that most attempts at vernacular verse do not ring true because they do not have 'the sense of a period of language standing solidly behind them' and therefore involve too self-conscious an attempt at recreating 'the linguistic effects of a tradition now broken'. In the absence of a living tradition such interventions find themselves working against 'a force too strong now to oppose – that of Standard English'.[24] 'I write Scots as I know it', Douglas Young wrote a few days later and picking up Morgan's phrase, 'a living tradition'. A culture living in speech acts and sound world is not the same as historical continuity in textual practice, and on the same day as Young's retort Morgan's second letter suggested that attention to their preferred audience requires poets to follow their own inclinations, writing in 'a Scots mixture' if they find themselves thinking and feeling in the medium. If, on the other hand, they speak and hear 'a northern variant of the standard language', they should feel free to concentrate their energies on enriching and rejuvenating it.[25]

A permissive approach did not win favour with either MacDiarmid or Young. At a public meeting in Glasgow in December 1946, with the former in the chair, the latter spoke against deviation from Lallans. The lecture quickly became a pamphlet and *'Plastic Scots' and the Scottish Literary Tradition* traces the emergence of native speech and script from early times to present usage, on the way describing as Reformation quislings such anglicising propagandists as John Knox:

> The effect of English predominating in the pulpit was that English predominated also in the Parliament, which was largely taken up with ecclesiastical disputes. Moreover the General Assembly of the Kirk, transacting in English, was as important as Parliament. Lallans continued to be used in the family, for common business, for poetry, and in the law-courts, but a large-scale Lallans prose failed to develop. A dichotomy was accentuated in the Scots mentality by this bilingualism.[26]

MacDiarmid hauled Muir over the coals for his change of heart about the scripted viability of Scots, and Maurice Lindsay had subsequently suggested that because Scottish poets had a choice of two and sometimes three languages, 'unless he can use them all with equal skill, his Scottish

psyche must feel, in some degree, frustrated'. Lindsay advertised his
anthology as 'a representative culling of the best fruits of the first twenty-
five years of the Scottish Renaissance'; and looking back at the movement
in 1954 Morgan's 'Modern Makars' essay puts Gaelic writing at a distance to consider aspects of Muir's, MacDiarmid's and Sydney Goodsir
Smith's writing:

> The choice between Lallans and English involves a great deal of
> heart-searching and probably a great deal of experimentation, and
> deciding to use only the one and to drop the other is almost as
> hazardous a solution as deciding to keep on using both: since
> each has a reality for the Scottish writer – however hard put to
> it the poet may be in defending his 'esoteric' or 'synthetic' *jur-
> mummlan whummlan*, and however nest-fyling the defender of
> English may appear ... . If a poet is to develop naturally and com-
> pletely he wants to have a basic linguistic medium that he can
> take for granted, and he wants to know what this medium is at
> an early point in his career, so that he can devote all his energies
> to exploring and advancing it.[27]

We can hear personal pressures in this – by 1954 Morgan was discovering the flexible instrumentality of Scots, having done Anglo-Saxon
as well as Mayakovsky's Russian experiments into the medium.[28] He was
also writing in and translating into English. Since the early 1930s
MacDiarmid had been writing mostly in English while continuing to
argue in favour of Scots; becoming, as Morgan now put it, 'what he most
abhors, an Anglo-Scot: he is that quite inescapably: he speaks English,
and he writes English prose. Why therefore should he not write English
verse?' But Morgan is sensitive to the pressures involved in MacDiarmid's
language shift: 'That he had to do this, against his own expressed conviction about the adaptability of Scots, is a measure of the blocking and
paradoxical circumstances of modern literary Scotland'. Morgan separates himself from Gaelic but ends his essay with the conviction that even
in their English translations Sorley MacLean's poems were evidently not
dying: 'we are in the troika, for better or worse, and as we rush forward
we try to imagine what harmony might reconcile the various tongues
that call to us'. Morgan recognises this diversity as both problem and
opportunity for 'the steady growth and maturing of character and of
style': 'On the debit side [a Scottish writer] has dissipation of energy,
along two or perhaps three linguistic and psychological tracks; on the
credit side he has the vigour and the dialectical impetus that come from
this difficult and challenging situation'.[29] While the full-throated name

he gave to his Mayakovsky translations speaks in the voice he adopted to engage revolutionary experimentalism, a personal resolution of independence at this earlier time can't have been easy. In 'Modern Makars' Morgan quotes to refuse something he had heard several times in 1946, whether in MacDiarmid's *Golden Treasury*, in the argument over 'plastic Scots', or in Douglas Young's pamphlet: 'We have often been told that "no Scots writer ever wrote first-rate poetry in English"'. Meanwhile, some of the finest poems to come out of the British armed forces during the Second World War were written in Gaelic by Sorley MacLean; Hamish Henderson's *Elegies for the Dead in Cyrenaica* won the 1948 Somerset Maugham Award; W. S. Graham had published his first volume; and from Morgan, it seemed, nothing. But if the years after 1946 were for him a period of 'restless readjustment and unsatisfactory achievement', they were not without activity. Other contexts then in play were to exercise continuing effect.[30]

When Dylan Thomas's poetry was making Morgan's pulse race towards the end of the 1930s, surrealism was a more broadly based excitement. Morgan was in tune with the movement and remembers 'a great deal of discussion of a poetry that enjoyed calling up irrational elements' (NNGM p. 54). Morgan was seventeen when he met (William) Sydney Graham: 'my first poet, and only a year and a half older than myself, so the bond between us was close'.[31] Writing to Morgan from Greenock in 1938, Graham reported 'reading over some of your poems the other night, aloud. The room was singing and dreaming with the sound of them. Three of the dream poems fused into me and made me cry – they must be good'.[32] Graham may have been reading Morgan's responses to Verlaine, 'When the Blind Dream' and 'Twilight'; and perhaps 'Maya: Dream-Reality/Reality-Dream', which do, at any rate, connect with verse Morgan himself was reading at the time.[33] Dylan Thomas's first collection *18 Poems* (1934) includes a dream/twilight element, and the sonnet sequence 'Altarwise by owl-light' in his second, *Twenty-Five Poems* (1936), evidently fertilised Morgan's attention: he would learn to develop formally structured dream and fantasy into spectacular effect.[34] In 1940 a Scottish current in the European ferment of left-wing ideas and literary intentions came on stream with an anthology of criticism, poems and stories called *the new apocalypse*. The Glaswegian poet J. F. Hendry's introduction conscripted the biblical resonance of *Revelation*'s visionary iconoclasm (and the interactive universe of poems such as Thomas's 'The force that through the green fuse') into a radical concern with 'the collapse of social forms and the emergence of new and more organic ones'. In the last year of peace the intensities of the time called for an intensity of response: in order to attain 'optimum living fusion between man and total environment', Hendry claimed, apocalyptic writing 'occurs where expression breaks through the structure of language to become more organic'. Perhaps with a corrective eye to *Revelation*'s hallucinated and image-fusing shifts, Hendry added 'without thereby impairing language as means of communication'.[35] A year later, in 1941, Hendry co-edited a companion volume, *the white horseman: prose and verse of the new apocalypse*, that took its epigraph from D. H. Lawrence:

> The rider on the white horse! Who is he then? ... He is the royal me, he is my very self and his horse is the whole MANA [force, vitality, power] of a man. He is my very me, my sacred ego, called into a new cycle of action by the Lamb and riding forth to conquest, the conquest of the old self for the birth of a new self. It is he, truly, who shall conquer all the other 'powers' of the self. And he rides forth, like the sun, with arrows, to conquest, but not with the sword, for the sword implies also judgement, and this is my *dynamic* or potent self. And his bow is the bended bow of the body, like the crescent moon.[36]

Royal is not a term of respect in Morgan's lexicon, and neither sacred nor male ego-mystique robed in conquest denote values he would readily espouse. He was abroad when *the white horseman* appeared and did not get back to writing for another five years, so when he became aware of the book is moot. He described as 'apocalyptic' post-atomic poems he wrote soon after his return to Scotland, where attempts to find space in (radically adjusted) biblical rhythms proved unsustaining, and he moved in different directions. But Morgan's post-war repertoire would develop forms that push syntax beyond breaking point, and although it soon became evident how difficult he would find it to sympathise with aspects of a poetic mission to present a rhetoric from which 'the guiding and controlling presence of a speaking subject ... has been excluded', by the same token he knew selfhood as 'a site in which experience is to be acted out as conflict'.[37] Morgan would go on to thematise the birth of a new self, would continue putting adventurers in motion against large, sometimes interplanetary backgrounds, and could find elements in the movement politically congenial. The notion of a public activism stimulated by recycling myth as personal experience lies behind what G. S. Fraser called his 'general theory' of apocalypse in poetry, which records a resolve 'to realise some of the dimensions and characteristics of man's submerged being'. Fraser also acknowledged the relationship with surrealism – 'one might even call [apocalyptics] a dialectical development of [surrealism]: the next stage forward'.[38] In the same anthology Hendry's essay on 'myth and social integration' identified Freud's discovery of the influence of the sub-conscious on everyday life as his main contribution to political thought, and saw apocalyptic writing as an activist extension of psychoanalysis to society. Whereas Freud 'sought to adapt the individual, as often as not, to the desires of society', apocalypse writers would work the other way: 'Apocalypticism represents ... the restoration of order to myth, a pattern of myth, individual and social', which in the urgent priorities of the time should correspond to a socialist arrangement of society.[39] A sense of shared purpose had made sufficient headway by 1943 for Maurice Lindsay in *Poetry Scotland*'s first issue to identify 'two main camps' of Scottish writing in English: 'the older poets with Edwin Muir as their leader, and the Scottish writers of the New Apocalypse'; the latter lightly represented in this collection because they were 'nearly all in the forces and serving overseas'.[40] Some years before the American Beat movement got under way, and riding the wave of optimism that gave electoral victory to a reforming Labour Party, Hendry's 1945 statement of the movement's practice and purpose, 'The Apocalyptic Element in Modern Poetry' in *Poetry Scotland*'s second issue called for sexual oppression to be resolved into 'a unity and equality of love in the same way as the social struggle for power must be resolved into real economic and political equality'. In terms of artistic production, he wrote, surrealists are 'among the more intelligent of our romantics' and 'we must push on to the social solution, which Romanticism in the past failed to find'.[41]

Though he couldn't know it, Hendry was tapping into concerns that Morgan would soon be negotiating, whose interest in the political dimensions of 'Romantic' writing, and in senses of a 'real life still unseen' (CP p. 329) stayed with him, as did the surrealist techniques he often uses to make them visible, initially to find a viable voice and then transformationally in later work. But the writing was already on the wall as far as any wider movement was concerned. In *Poetry Scotland*'s first issue MacDiarmid's review of Hendry's collection *The Orchestral Mountain* described the style as 'apt to achieve a grotesque and dismaying incoherence' and stated his refusal: 'I dislike and disbelieve in Surrealism for the same reasons that I dislike and disbelieve in Spiritualism'.[42] In 1946, none the less, *Poetry Scotland*'s third issue carried W. S. Graham's adaptation of Lawrence's argument for an 'imaginative release into another vital world' as means of renewal.[43] 'Notes on a Poetry of Release' explores the idea of poem as transfer of energy through Graham's personalised excess: 'The most difficult thing for me to remember is that a poem is made of words and not of the expanding heart, the overflowing soul or the sensitive observer'. 'The poem is the replying chord to the reader. It is the reader's involuntary reply'.[44]

Morgan was by this time back in Glasgow and would doubtless have read Graham's essay, but not all neophytes made productive use of experimental opportunities. A young Norman MacCaig, one of the contributors to the 1940 apocalypse anthology, tried his hand; and Morgan looking back forty years later noted the 'thick, rich, but almost meaningless deployment of metaphor and simile, irrational, undirected', in MacCaig's earliest published work. MacCaig's struggle to free his voice would produce the 'small-scale cat-like precision of movement and imagery' that came to characterise a later poetry Morgan felt lacking in 'the wonderful sense of letting go, of continuous long-distance spiritual drive and energy, which you get in Shelley'. He might almost be describing the different path he took out of the 1940s, since thickness and richness in his own post-war writing coexist with pressurised transmission of distant possibility; and insofar as they helped him find the measure of his selfhood he would take up whatever 'Romantic', apocalyptic or surrealist strategies proved useful. For his part, Hendry couldn't have been clearer about local specifications for urgency of purpose in constructing the New Jerusalem: 'Nowhere is the struggle keener than in Scotland, between individual and society: man and mechanistic environment: liberty and regimentation. From the Religious Wars until the Class Wars Scotland has nourished in her soul an apparently insoluble conflict, yet one that needs to be solved if she is to achieve her Identity in the Company of Nations'.[45] The fourth *Poetry Scotland* collection in 1949 firmly closed the door on this nascent dynamic. With MacDiarmid guest-editing the issue, Maurice Lindsay declared that *Poetry Scotland* 'aims at reviving the Scots and Gaelic cultures', not at developing what he was now calling 'Anglo-Scottish literature'. Apocalypse writers are 'the most obvious absentees' from this fourth anthology because 'whatever may be the value of their work to English literature, it is hardly concerned with the revival and restoration of our national tradition'.[46]

The New Apocalypse co-founder Henry Treece associated what he called 'the most militant movement seen in Britain for the last hundred years' with 'the form of Anarchism laid down by Herbert Read': 'an anarchism which substitutes equity and law for man-made justice and moral code'.[47] J. F. Hendry warmed to Read's 'intense awareness of man's mysterious journey through space and time', and so could Morgan. Before he left for army service he had read Read's *English Prose Style* (1931), *Collected Literary Criticism* (1938), and *Poetry and Anarchism* (1938).

He also knew Peter Kropotkin's *Mutual Aid* (1908).[48] In 1991
Morgan's copy of the essays that Read brought together as *Surrealism* in
1936 needed an elastic band to hold it together. 'Obviously I was interested', he recalled: 'at that time, around 1937-38, surrealism was at its
height, really; it was in the air and being discussed. So yes, there's something there'.[49] To identify the thought world and field of reference he
was bidding for, Hendry had asked: 'what could be more apocalyptic
than Shelley's "Mask of Anarchy"?' and quoted its first two stanzas. 'And
what is more apocalyptic than Blake's "America", or his "Proverbs of
Hell"?'. Blake's early impact on Morgan also stayed with him: 'the
method he has of often turning ideas inside out or casting a very strange
light on accepted ideas appealed to me very strongly. So I did go out to
Blake, I'm sure of that'. Similarly with Shelley: 'both the political element in "The Mask of Anarchy", which I remember enjoying as a student, and also "Prometheus Unbound" which moves right out into the
universe and asks serious questions about where power really resides'.[50]
In 1949, when apocalypticism was under erasure and before he translated either *Beowulf* or Mayakovsky, Morgan wrote '"The Triumph of
Life": A Conclusion to Shelley's Poem', continuing the incomplete text
on which Shelley was working at the time of his death, where Rousseau's
shade and changing times shed disenchanted light on power and subjection for an England gripped by political reaction: 'where'er // The char-
iot rolled, a captive multitude / was driven'.[51] Both poems inscribe a
global canvas for conflicted cultures, and both focus on manipulative ideologies. Shelley's terminal 'Triumph', in some ways a re-visiting of the
space- and time-travelling journey made in his youthful 'Queen Mab',
opens on a new day but disposes gloom, as far as its unfinished narrative
develops. Although it holds on to 'the wondrous story / How all things
are transfigured except love', 'The Triumph of Life' also represents submission to belief-systems mediated through priesthoods as an historical
encroachment of darkness on light: 'Till that eclipse, still hanging over
heaven, / Was worshipped by the world o'er which they strode', and calls
up a range of historical characters to emphasise the necessity for a continuing struggle towards self-knowledge.[52] In a post-atomic and cold-
war environment Morgan's conclusion could legitimately re-indict
'savage force and statecraft,' as well as 'the servile scientist, sophist in evasion' who expedite their designs; and its 'dark cavalcade' through mid-
century Scotland includes stinging reference to religious hate-mongers
who divide 'Where they should brighten into love, and hold' (CP p.
544). 'A Conclusion' sets astronomy against theology to resolve time 'in
the immensity of light' shed 'among the starry and immeasurable shires'

by Antares, one of the largest known stars with a diameter vastly greater than the sun's. With this luminous materiality in play, and seeking 'surer histories' for future possibility wherever 'the light of thought can strike', Morgan develops Shelley's refusal of 'thought's empire over thought' into a critique of proselytising theisms ('where God by every voyager is found') as primary alienations of the human imagination. In the Scottish context of a mid-century social order divided by ecclesiastical jurisdictions, beliefs and antagonisms, Morgan's Rousseau witnesses the 'Triumph' of these primary alienations. The poem's remembering speaker on the other hand, draws strength by internalising large dimensions: 'Some sea within me breathed in perfect rest' (CP p. 549). In 1822 Rousseau's ghost suggested that Shelley's thoughtful figure should 'from spectator turn / Actor or victim in this wretchedness'; in 1949 Morgan reactivates for a questing speaker the *terza rima* Shelley adapted from Dante:

> 'If you now lead,'
> I said, 'my eyes as you have led my steps'
> O let them into every quarter speed
>
> Where to your clearer sight the world reflects
> Images of that tranquillity surmised'. (CP p. 542)

Although tranquillity would be a fugitive mood and clearer sight the product of much labour, he was already identifying the scale of his ambition.

Notes

1   Antonio Gramsci, *Selections from the Prison Notebooks*, eds Quinton Hoare and Geoffrey Nowell Smith, London, 1986, p. 333.
2   Interview in Nicholson, *Poem, Purpose and Place*, p. 60.
3   I partly rely for information here on McCarra, 'Edwin Morgan: Lives and Work', and Hamish Whyte, 'Edwin Morgan: A Checklist', in Crawford and Whyte (eds), *About Edwin Morgan*, pp. 2–5, 185–7.
4   Edwin Morgan, 'The Beatnik in the Kailyard', *New Saltire* 3, 1962, p. 65.
5   Edwin Morgan, 'A Mirrear Dance Mycht na Man See', *Times Literary Supplement*, 20 March 1998, p. 26.
6   *Glasgow Herald*, 8 November 1946.
7   MacDiarmid's 'plastic Scots' letters to the *Glasgow Herald* are included in Alan Bold (ed.), *The Letters of Hugh MacDiarmid*, London, 1984, pp. 784–91.
8   *Glasgow Herald*, 11 November 1946.
9   *Ibid.*, 25 November 1946.
10 Hugh MacDiarmid (ed.), *The Golden Treasury of Scottish Poetry*, London, 1946, pp. ix, xii.

11 Maurice Lindsay (ed.), *Modern Scottish Poetry: An Anthology of the Scottish Renaissance, 1920–1945*, London, 1946, p. 18.
12 James Fergusson (ed.), *The Green Garden: A New Collection of Scottish Poetry*, Edinburgh, 1946, p. xiv.
13 MacDiarmid, *Golden Treasury*, p. 360.
14 *Times Literary Supplement*, 1 June 1946.
15 MacDiarmid, *Golden Treasury*, p. 353.
16 Bernard Fergusson, *Hubble Bubble*, London, 1978, p. 47; Bold (ed.), *Letters of Hugh MacDiarmid*, pp. 858–9.
17 *Glasgow Herald*, 16 November 1946; MacDiarmid, *Golden Treasury*, p. 359.
18 *Glasgow Herald*, 19 November 1946.
19 Douglas Young, *Glasgow Herald*, 16 November 1946; *Golden Treasury*, p. xxi.
20 *Ibid.*, pp. 353, 376.
21 Daniel Jones, *Everyman's English Pronouncing Dictionary* [1917], London, 1964, p. xv.
22 MacDiarmid *Golden Treasury*, pp. 362–3.
23 Edwin Muir, *Scott and Scotland: The Predicament of the Scottish Writer*, London, 1936, cited in MacDiarmid *Golden Treasury*, p. xvi.
24 *Glasgow Herald*, 15 November 1946.
25 *Glasgow Herald*, 26 November 1946.
26 Douglas Young, *'Plastic Scots' and the Scottish Literary Tradition*, Glasgow, 1946, pp. 10–11.
27 Edwin Morgan, 'Modern Makars Scots and English', *Saltire Review*, 1:2, 1954, p. 75.
28 'Auld Man's Coronach', Morgan's translation into Scots of lines 2444–62 from *Beowulf*, appeared in the *Glasgow Herald*, 8 August 1953.
29 Edwin Morgan: *Crossing the Border: Essays on Scottish Literature*, Manchester, 1990, p. 79.
30 Edwin Morgan, 'W. S. Graham: A Poet's Letters', in *Crossing the Border*, p. 263.
31 *Ibid.*, p. 260.
32 Michael Snow and Margaret Snow (eds), *The Nightfisherman: Selected Letters of W. S. Graham*, Manchester, 1999, p. 12.
33 Edwin Morgan, 'When the Blind Dream'; 'Twilight'; and 'Maya: Dream-Reality/Reality-Dream', *Glasgow University Magazine*, 2 February 1938, pp. 189, 190; *ibid.*, 4 May 1938, p. 300.
34 Dylan Thomas, *Collected Poems: 1934–53*, eds W. Davies and R. Maud, London, 1993, pp. 7–29, 58–63.
35 J. F. Hendry (ed.), *the new apocalypse: an anthology of criticism, poems and stories*, London, 1940, pp. 9, 11.
36 D. H. Lawrence, *Apocalypse, and the Writings on Revelation*, ed. Mara Kalnins, Cambridge, 1980, pp. 102–3.
37 Andrew Crozier, 'Thrills and Frills: Poetry as Figures of Empirical Lyricism', in Alan Sinfield (ed.), *Society and Literature 1945–1970*, London, 1983, p. 228.
38 G. S. Fraser, 'Apocalypse in Poetry', in J. F. Hendry and Henry Treece (eds), *the white horseman: prose and verse of the new apocalypse* London, 1941, p. 15.
39 J. F. Hendry, 'Myth and Social Integration', *the white horseman*, pp. 158–9, 176.
40 Maurice Lindsay, 'Editorial', *Poetry Scotland*, Glasgow, 1943, p. 3.

41 J. F. Hendry, 'The Apocalyptic Element in Modern Poetry', *Poetry Scotland*, Glasgow, 1945, p. 61.
42 Hugh MacDiarmid, 'Six Scottish Poets of To-Day and To-Morrow', *Poetry Scotland*, Glasgow, 1943, p. 68.
43 Lawrence, *Apocalypse*, p. 47.
44 W. H. Graham, 'Notes on a Poetry of Release', *Poetry Scotland*, Glasgow, 1946, pp. 56–7.
45 Hendry, 'The Apocalyptic Element in Modern Poetry', p. 65.
46 Maurice Lindsay, *Poetry Scotland*, Glasgow, 1949, p. 1.
47 Henry Treece, *How I See Apocalypse*, London, 1946, p. viii, p. 14
48 Edwin Morgan, 'Books I have Read (1927–1940)', in Crawford and Whyte (eds), *About Edwin Morgan*, pp. 270–1.
49 Interview in Nicholson, *Poem, Purpose and Place*, p. 66.
50 *Ibid.*, p. 61.
51 'The Triumph of Life', in *The Complete Works of Percy Bysshe Shelley*, eds Roger Ingpen and Walter E. Peck, New York, 1965, vol. 4, pp. 167–85 (p. 171).
52 Richard Holmes, *Shelley: The Pursuit* [1974], London, 1994, pp. 717–24.

2 A self-fashioning Scot

The process of perception is an aesthetic end in itself and must be prolonged. (Victor Shklovsky)[1]

Defiance of society includes defiance of its language.

(Theodor Adorno)[2]

The 'plastic Scots' dispute took place towards the end of 1946, the year in which Dylan Thomas's *Deaths and Entrances* appeared and New Apocalypse prospects still looked promising. During March of that year Morgan wrote 'Dies Irae' and 'The Vision of Cathkin Braes', the latter's couplets comic and celebratory, the former's blank verse highly charged and sombre. W. S. Graham told Morgan that as a whole 'Dies Irae' was not successful: 'To start off at such a high pitch of rhetoric ... is imprudent ... there are too many highly associated words in too short a space'. He also thought the poem 'very moving', described it as 'like nothing in contemporary poetry', and was impressed by its 'strong physical action language'. Morgan was already being drawn by 'Anglo-Saxon words and language with that basic strong feel about it'.[3] He was also going back to familiar biblical sources, where 'clothed with a vesture dipped in blood', the white horseman of *Revelation* 'in righteousness doth judge and make war'; and he whose 'name is called The Word of God' descends from the ether to 'smite the nations' and 'rule them with a rod of iron' (19, 11–15). Associating a solitary, ship-wrecked survivor with the atomic devastation recently visited on Japan, 'Dies Irae' turns New Testament rhythms to contemporary account by secularising a medieval hymn about the last judgement, part of which Walter Scott had built into his *Lay of the Last Minstrel*: 'On that day, that wrathful day, / David and the Sybil say, / Heaven and earth shall melt away'. Morgan combines biblical and alliterative phrasing to project Jehovah as destroyer in a visionary jeremiad fearful at 'God's grinding reef of chiding and condemnation, / His maelstrom threatening for mortal retrogression' (CP p. 21). With mortality under such threat, it is to the point that 'Dies Irae' changes *Revelation*'s 'sea of glass' commanded by the 'wrath of God' (15, 1–2) into a fragile vessel making uncertain headway:

I saw and heard in the gazing of a dream
Within my mind, and tempest there beheld.
So thought has wave in wave, deep behind deep,
Sea beyond sea stretched out far over the world,
Where we set sail, and founder, or to haven tremble,
A ship of glass among the bluffs to gamble. (CP p. 22)[4]

The straits of a singular navigation in 'Dies Irae' produce a troubled and troubling dreamworld where forms of the unconscious achieve forms of definition. Morgan would develop different delivery systems; but 'Stanzas of the Jeopardy' uses similar rhetoric for the biblical Paul to voice cold war fears of atomic annihilation: 'when space is rolled away / And time is torn from its rings, and the door of life / Flies open on unimaginable things – / At noon, at midnight, or at no time, as you receive these verses, O Corinthians' (CP p. 25). While nuclear apocalypse would become a recurrent frame of reference, biblical phrasing in these early poems derives from what Morgan called a 'fairly strict' upbringing:

My parents weren't really what you would call religious, but they were churchgoing, with a strong sense of right and wrong, and I [went] both to church and to Sunday school every week. You had to do it, and I got to know the Bible very well because I had to learn large parts of it by heart. Bible-imagery stays in your mind, whatever your beliefs eventually become, and when I was writing these apocalyptic things, like the one about the atom bomb, it came out in terms of religious imagery[:][5]

'Shall the trumpet sound before the suns have cooled?
Shall there not be portents of blood, sea-beds laid bare,
Concrete and girder like matchwood in earthquake and whirlwind?
Shall we not see the angels, or the creeping icecap, or the moon
Falling, or the wandering star, feel veins boiling
Or fingers freezing or the wind thickening with wings?'
The earth may spin beyond apocalypse;
Long before entropy the worlds may stop. (CP p. 25)

The earth spins into a different beyond when the speaker of 'The Vision of Cathkin Braes' turns to kiss his partner and spirit worlds erupt in a transhistorical carnival of desire and its discontents. Staged as a pantomime *walpurgisnacht*, the poem echoes Langland and plays games with Dunbar's 'Dance of the Sevin Deidly Sins' when an initially love-threatening display of political and cultural icons develops into partnerships unlikely enough to be at once transgressive and liberative. 'Cathkin

Braes' has fun with cultural mythology, in a reference to Jenny Geddes, when its startled lovers catch a fleeting glimpse of someone who hurls past them her three-legged stool in warning against their 'tongue-tip-kiss'. It seems that as symbol of popular resistance to an anglicising king, Geddes was largely an invention of nineteenth-century religious ideologues in search of historic defenders of the Scottish Kirk's continuing independence. In continuing disagreements between Presbyterian factions, Geddes is one of those invoked to establish true representatives of the Reformation and the Covenants. 'She was alive in 1637, when the stool was hurled in [Edinburgh's] High Kirk of St Giles to spark off a revolt against Charles I, but there is no evidence that she threw it'.[6] It is part of its contemporary charge that 'Cathkin Braes' gives not a fig for such argument except insofar as it misdirects energy; and before John Knox makes his entry into this midsummer night's dream, William McGonagall appears astride a two-horned beast that gives promise of carnal if not pneumatic bliss. Laughed at in his own lifetime by public house audiences he took seriously, McGonagall was an impassioned declaimer of Shakespeare, so is here identified by reference to the 'poet's eye, in a fine frenzy rolling' as spoken by a duke himself having trouble with midsummer night things more strange than true reported by Shakespeare's lovers (V, 1, l.12).

Glancing from earth to heaven and back again, the narrative brings on Knox who anathematises our couple as 'Jezebel and your minion' before departing 'to prick the infamous'; a phrase that becomes differently suggestive when he reappears. But not before Lauren Bacall, whose screen partnership with Humphrey Bogart had recently cast her as prominent figure of desire (1945 with 'To Have and Have Not', and a year later in 'The Big Sleep'), puts in an appearance as femme so fatale and seductive 'that my dear love was jealous for her skill / and slew her on the spot, if looks could kill'. Bacall, singing a pastiche of Donne and Burns, plays American comic havoc with both Scottish and English voices: at which point enters a Queen of Scots to a nursery-rhyme jingle that in popular tradition recorded the contrariness of Mary's French and Popish inclinations so displeasing to Knox. Morgan makes mischief with the dynastic and genealogical schemings in which Mary was both player and plaything, not in terms of the rhyme that conventionalised her fate but according to what have been described as the best-known four-line stanzas in the English language (and originally produced by a mid-nineteenth-century American), 'Mary had a Little Lamb'.[7] When the 'lamb a smiling saint' makes its exit with Scotland's most famous Mary the poem resurrects a nineteenth-century explorer as drunken Glaswegian

street busker, 'stumbl[ing] on with his strange minstrelsy'; then introduces Salome, whose 'creamy thigh and quick feet made her fame / In
divers lands'. With desire, power, possession and manipulation thus
brought into Morgan's *bricolage* of personality and period, there then
appears a comically unkempt Wordsworth speaking assorted echoes of
his published lines and blithely unaware of the misery inflicted on the
young girl he has in tow. When Wordsworth and she quit the scene our
two lovers, thinking this night's haunting over, set to their original purpose – at which intention of fulfilment emblematic border-crossings
dance their comic-grotesque transgressions. Bacall and Mungo Park get
the music going; Wordsworth (having 'disposed' of the accompanying
child elsewhere in the wood) partners Jenny Geddes. In the flower of her
maidenhood, Salome seduces John Knox (his 'eyes half-closed, no doubt
on heavenly vision'); and after Mary and MacGonagall bring different
Scotlands into unlikely rhythm the poem includes another dig at Knox
and leaves Mary with her cocktail soubriquet, singing the Scot Henry
Lyte's nineteenth-century hymn appropriated for twentieth-century
believers as traditional and English largely through its annual association
since the early 1930s with the Wembley Cup Final:

> the last we saw of these blithe spirits was
> The horse of KNOX nosing the hoary grass,
> While MUNGO took fair LAUREN on his knee,
> And BLOODY MARY sang Abide with Me. (CP p. 49)

Unlikely syntheses constitute a continuing resource for Morgan's
craft. It now seems a feature of his writing, part of the politics of his
technique that there is always an alternative, another form to engage
and voice to adopt; another theme to vary or further way of looking
waiting to be tried in words. At this early stage 'The Vision of Cathkin
Braes' mobilises diverse and multicultural elements including improb-
able pairings and Dionysian promise in the permissive parameters of a
distinctively social text. If the couplings and doublings it subversively
proposes are culturally transformational, the techniques it incorporates
are evolutionary and developmental. Morgan would soon be describing one of Dunbar's poems as 'a late-flowering growth of a very old
tradition, which pleases by showing what it sprang from – and its
author's awareness of this: the ghostly prevalence of Anglo-Saxon rhyth-
mical types' (*Essays*, p. 95). Something similar might be said of the
alliterative phrasing in parts of 'Cathkin Braes'. Morgan refers to the
'disequilibrating infusion of forthright zestful topsyturvydom' in
medieval Scots verse, and his staging of contemporary iconoclasm

through medieval and serial historical precedent becomes visible in the
line-spacings specified for Mungo Park's nineteenth-century roaring of
a 'most anciently designed / Rank drunken mongering of crambo-clink
[= doggerel]', begging the price of another drink in Harry Lauder's
strains, but opening with a phrase from 'Tam o' Shanter':

> O it gars me greet when Glasgow . drouthy is of drink
> After adventures in Africa . I pine for a pint
> Lusty lovers if ye be at all . I call ye unkind
> If ye blow me not a bawbee . for a half and a half
> Glasgow to go round and round . I stir it with my staff
> On Saturday at the Saltmarket . or at bloody Brigton
> You may behold it belongs all . to me Mungo Bigtoun. (CP p. 46)

Anarchic comedy would find other fields and multiple variations: meanwhile different resources were being tapped and their technical possibilities tried out. Between May and June of 1947 Morgan translated 'The
Seafarer' and 'The Wanderer' from Anglo-Saxon into modern English,
both of them to do with voyaging and voyagers and both of them voicing an isolated subject. He later commented that 'The Wanderer' dealt
with a figure 'put into exile, somebody who is not part of the society he
enjoyed so much'; and reflected that 'the state of mind of this isolated
figure ... is probably related to some of the themes recurring in my
poems.'[8] Refracting personal stress through the stoical rhythms of 'The
Wanderer', Morgan uses that character's isolation – 'there is none now
alive / To whom I might dare reveal in their clearness / The thoughts
of my heart' – to filter an existential discontent.

   During a moment of crisis between August and September in 1950
Morgan wrote 'The Cape of Good Hope', addressing what he has since
called the alienation of solitude, the difficulty of social adjustment and
problems about creative direction (NNGM pp. 47, 70).[9] 'The Cape' was
not published until 1955, but it belongs with other poems scheduled to
appear in 1952, where similar pressures are disclosed. 'What river-growl
appals my flesh?' asks 'A Warning of Waters at Evening' (CP p. 26), and
'The Sleights of Darkness' wonders 'What would suffice of it all // To
my friend in his fleshly desolation?' (CP pp. 27–8). 'Memory and phan-
tasmagoria of memory' trigger 'The Sleights of Time':

> Lust was lifted like a torch
> And rebellious shame in ruffled hair
> Surrendered laughing to the bloodrace ways
> Of hallucinating touch. (CP p. 28)

'Sleight-of-Morals' opens with 'A death in the ditch of libertinism!', includes a 'wounded ganymede glow[ing] like Gabriel', and ends hoping that 'cold juries' as well as 'judge and witness' may 'see through the Braille of good and evil' (CP p. 29). Judgement is as threatening when Morgan's version of Edward II's 'Courtly Overture' to Gaveston brings illicit love into the personal orchestration of a private rhythm still fragile as glass, but seizing the day and dancing on (CP pp. 49–50). If elliptical shifts, tenuous logic and a sometimes-inflated rhetoric in these early poems relate them to a fashion of the time, they also, Morgan later agreed, have 'lots of troubled feelings at the back of them':

> They must be connected with some kind of repression or frustra-
> tion, and possibly a bit of guilt too; I don't think that was large,
> but it was probably there, probably part of it. It wasn't repression
> in the sense that nothing was happening physically, sexually, but
> nothing satisfactory was happening; there was still a sense there of
> great frustration and unhappiness because the things that were hap-
> pening were not giving me any real feeling of fulfilment at all.[10]

'The Cape of Good Hope' journeys out to where 'everything that is is nature' and navigates 'my leviathan / Libertinism' through a symbolic order more threatening than sustaining. At the end of its second movement, sea-storm imagery shifts to moonlight in readiness for part three's dream-sequence presentation of artists and scientists (and artist-scientists) whose creative and sexual lives clashed and combined to different, but for this harried speaker cumulative, effect. A manuscript version in Glasgow University Library carries a dedication to Hart Crane, who jumped to his death in the Gulf of Mexico in 1932; and the first of the artist-scientists called up in 'A Dream at the Mysterious Barricades' is Leonardo da Vinci 'abhorring / the work of his hands. / Woman to man to / Androgyne'. Similarly Michelangelo 'abhorred his power / to paint Eve harridan / And in Adam's slumber / And the faces of youths / plant gratifications / to his eternal guilt'. For Michelangelo 'lust and suppression' are the contraries that produce creative movement; whereas Newton's pioneering attempts to displace chaotic feeling on to the 'abstract tranquillity' of physical laws ran aground in final madness. Herman Melville sees all too clearly 'the vortex and the revenge / And the ambush laid for man's valour / And man's love that is dashed bitterly / Away like tears from the eyes of the soul'; and Vladimir Mayakovsky, artist and satirist of the Russian Revolution, is here seen behind 'more mysterious barricades' asking painful questions:

> And when men turn to
> Men, or the sea, or phantom images
> Of art, or science with its secret face
> Unmoralled and terrible, or music,
> Whose vaults, whose vaults burst with that pain and cost? (CP p. 71)

At these unforgiving barriers between desire and social permission, Beethoven's Jacobin energies offer 'rapturous release' to a persisting speaker. Though it ultimately looks towards the hope of its title the poem's stresses more immediately relate to a voice of large capacity frustrated. Morgan came to think 'The Cape' did not work as well as he once believed (NNGM p. 47), but its rhythms effectively deliver conflict between fulfilment and denial.

The textual personality taking shape in this early work is already engaging in an alternative cultural archaeology that would entail a continuing negotiation with Scotland's leading poet. Between his 'Modern Makars' essay of 1954 and a piece on 'James Joyce and Hugh MacDiarmid' in 1982, Morgan wrote about MacDiarmid's work on several occasions, earning guarded praise in 1975 from a subject who described the essays to date as 'among the best things so far written about my poetry – welcome oases on the desert of literary journalism. That's not as you know,' MacDiarmid added, 'to say I agree with them – only that I am glad to encounter high intelligence anywhere'.[11] In 1976 Morgan wrote a monograph on MacDiarmid for the British Council's *Writers and their Work* series, describing poems in *Sangshaw* (1925) and *Penny Wheep* (1926) as 'one of the peaks of his achievement':

> [MacDiarmid's] poetry changed so fundamentally during the thirties and forties that comparison is difficult, but there seems no doubt that these early lyrics, miniatures though they are, retain an extraordinary freshness and strangeness.... It should be impossible to deny the force, vividness, and illumination of his best poetry.... His methods are his own, and he is a model for no one, but he is one of the great twentieth-century writers, and a writer whose individuality it will take the next century to sift and define.[12]

Morgan is already historicising MacDiarmid's work, and if the latter had felt able to respond positively to 'Modern Makars' and to Morgan's sympathetic 1959 review of 'The Battle Continues' – written to controvert Roy Campbell's celebration of Franco's victory in the Spanish Civil War – he may not have been cheered by Morgan's suggestion that MacDiarmid places little trust in satire partly because 'he himself lacks the sophistication of mind required for continuously sparkling satire'.[13] Morgan also acknowledges that when in 'The Battle Continues' MacDiarmid moves away from a poetry of statement and 'permits himself a spare Brechtian image, [he can be] brilliantly successful':

> Anywhere you go in Britain today
> You can hear the people
> Economising consciousness,
> Struggling to think and feel as little as possible
> Just as you can hear a countryside in winter
> Crepitating in the grip of an increasing frost.[14]

Morgan's summary of MacDiarmid's drift on Spain catches a sense of his own political allegiance: 'The doomed struggle of the Republicans and the International Brigade shines like a good deed in a naughty world, and although they failed in a material sense they will only have failed in a spiritual sense if we refuse to take up their challenge'.[15] A 1966 poem 'To Hugh MacDiarmid' praises him for generating breadth of vision from 'a cottage / in a small country' by taking 'that hazard of naming, letting the drops / fall on the desert of uninterest for those with / "a taste for Frontiniac" but not for the glass of Esk water' (CP pp. 153–4).[16] More critically, in a BBC Third Programme broadcast for MacDiarmid's seventy-fifth birthday, Morgan identified 'an enormous gap of ordinary human experience' in the poetry; the truth of which MacDiarmid privately acknowledged.[17] Quoting MacDiarmid's disgust with 'almost all modern Scottish poetry that gives off a great sense of warmth and offering, like a dog when it loves you,' Morgan suspects 'an inadequacy as well as a polemic ... behind this rejection of warmth' (Essays p. 221).

The promotion of a Lallans sound world as an appropriate medium for cultural and political self-identification that effectively radicalised perceptions in the 1920s came to emphasise division as time passed. MacDiarmid's powerful reactions could produce a reactionary power, and a sense developed that his standard bearing for the earlier renascence movement had itself become an entrenchment against which others were impatient to measure innovation. During the 1960s MacDiarmid was flying high: the chorus of approval that greeted his Collected Poems in 1962 secured a degree of recognition whose absence hitherto he had cause to resent. With that body of writing gathered in print, The Guardian was now telling its readers, 'there can be no doubt that MacDiarmid is one of the major poets of this century'.[18] This was an already established Scottish opinion, to the extent that writers looking for alternative space thought MacDiarmid inflexible about what should or not be encouraged. There had, for example, been a sometimes-acri-monious correspondence arising from the publication in 1959 of *Honour'd Shade*, a commemorative anthology (using three of Morgan's poems) for the Burns bi-centenary.[19] Edited by Norman MacCaig, *Honour'd Shade* was not felt by *The Scotsman*'s reviewer to be sufficiently representative (19 November 1959). The review dubbed the anthology 'The Muse in Rose Street' (sometimes called Edinburgh's amber mile for the number of public houses it contains, including 'The Abbotsford', then a favoured haunt of MacDiarmid, MacCaig and Goodsir Smith). Within months, seven excluded poets – Tom Buchan, Stewart Conn, Ian Hamilton Finlay, Shaun Fitzsimon, Anne Turner, W. Price Turner and Tom Wright, issued a tape-recording of their poems called *Dishonour'd Shade: Seven Non-Abbotsford Poets*. Over the next couple of years things simmered and flared until the *Scottish Field* published early in 1962 an attack by Tom Wright on the 'attitudes and dogmas of the older poets'. Because the 'Lallans boys' held most of the critical and editorial positions of influence, younger poets were finding 'a massive road block in their way'.[20] MacDiarmid's letter in reply referred dismissively to 'Scotland's self-pitying *jeunes refusés*'; and a month later *The Scotsman*, 'having become aware that in younger Scottish poetic circles it was believed that there was a kind of literary establishment sitting on the aspirations of younger Scottish poets … asked Edwin Morgan to speak for them.'[21]

'Poet and Public' lays blame for difficulties in poetry reaching an audience on the scarcity of Scottish publishing outlets (in the previous November Morgan's essay 'Who will Publish Scottish Poetry?' appeared in *New Saltire*).[22] His *Scotsman* piece also shares an opinion that estab-lished writers 'have not been notably sympathetic towards the changes now taking place in Scottish poetry', and levels a specific charge: 'Mr MacDiarmid will have to find other grounds for his opposition: in partic-ular, he will have to come to terms with the criticism that his own kind of aggressive, dogmatic, proprietorial Scottishness may not be the best for Scotland, and may in fact be the very thing that is holding Scotland back at the present time'.[23] MacDiarmid responded by describing as 'a group of teddyboy poetasters' writers associated with the Wild Hawthorn Press, whose broadsheet *Poor, Old, Tired, Horse* Morgan thought attractive and MacDiarmid 'utterly vicious and deplorable'.[24] A month earlier Morgan's 'Beatnik in the Kailyard' essay had set against a subsequent evolution the real if contradictory breach with tradition signalled by the 1920s move-ment: 'the language problem, the problem of Scottishness' had now turned into 'something of an incubus'. Because Scottish speech is 'still very fluid in the range from broad Scots to standard English, even among individual speakers', Morgan was now seeing it as 'a real and unavoidable incubus (shake it off, and you leave scars and puncture marks)'. All of which 'makes it all the more difficult for the Scottish writer to develop integrally':

> I am certain that Scottish literature is being held back … not only because of publishing difficulties but also because of a prevailing mood of indifferentism and conservatism, a desperate unwilling-ness to move out into the world with which every child now at school is becoming familiar – the world of television and sputniks, automation and LPs, electronic music and multistorey flats, rebuilt city centres and new towns, coffee bars and bookable cinemas, air travel and transistor radios, colour photography and open-plan houses, paperbacks and water-skiing, early marriage and larger fam-ilies: a world that will be more fast, more clean, more 'cool' than the one it leaves behind. (*Essays* pp. 174–5)

If the list now sounds dated its openness to current phenomena does not, and Morgan is clear: 'I make no apology, in the present context, for emphasising the contemporary aspect of things. "Scotland's heritage" is hung about our necks like a taxonomical placard. Conform or depart! Well, there is a time for gathering up one's history and traditions, and there is a time for showing the face of the present and looking forward. The second of these is what we need now' (*Essays* pp. 175–6).

Morgan sees another provincialism superseding MacDiarmid's avowed internationalism – the MacDiarmid who had recently recalled his earlier intention to 'escape from the provincialising of Scottish litera-ture'.[25] 'Almost no interest', Morgan goes on, 'has been taken by estab-lished writers in Scotland in the important postwar literary developments in America and on the Continent. Ignorance is not apologised for. The Beat writers are dismissed as a throwback to the 1920s' (*Essays* p. 174). MacDiarmid's initial response was a squib called 'Question to Edwin Morgan', carefully worked over as Hamish Whyte has shown:

> Is there even ane o' thae Beatnik poets
> Wi' which the place is sae raji rife
> Da'en mair than juist feelin' a lassie's bloomers
> And thinkin' he's seein' Life?[26]

MacDiarmid traced what he called 'the germs of this near nihilism' in 'the present generation of beat poets' back to 'the late French Symbolism', and claimed to find 'those germs … in Marinetti's "Futurism", in the German Expressionists, in the Surrealists, in Kafka who wanted his work destroyed, and in Paul Klee, who said: "I want to be as though new-born, knowing nothing, absolutely nothing of Europe"'.[27] Morgan, who appreciated William Burroughs's fiction for opening up 'the full horror of the world which De Quincey and Baudelaire more tentatively explored', responded more generally to American Beat writing's breach with conventions whose English variants he found uninspiring and whose Scottish openings were being so imperiously policed. His 1962 essay, called 'The Beat Vigilantes', praises jazz for refusing the cultural priorities of an academic establishment and describes the Beat movement as 'in one sense an act of protest or dissent, made within the general 1950's context of the H-bomb, the cold war, the McCarthy investigations, and the problems of the "affluent society" with its "planned obsolescence" and "hidden persuaders"'. 'I would be happier,' Morgan concludes, 'about our critics' rejection, or *de haut en bas* head-patting, of the Beats if I could see either criticism or literature in this country showing an equally vigorous, risk-taking contact with human issues'.[28] A couple of weeks after 'The Beat Vigilantes' appeared, MacDiarmid used the *Scottish Daily Express* to attack literary conference-goers who reject 'the high traditions of great literature' and who believe that 'the central issues of life today, with which literature should deal are sexual perversion, and the vicious habits of beatniks and layabouts'.[29]

MacDiarmid sometimes associated his work with modernist practices developed by Ezra Pound: as a step towards reconstruction, Morgan published in the summer of 1963 an essay whose lunar setting came from 'Stony Limits', MacDiarmid's elegy for the geologist Charles Doughty. 'A Glimpse of Petavius' fashions out of moonscape metaphor an alternative evolution for science and poetry by associating MacDiarmid with a line of practitioners including Walt Whitman, John Davidson and William Carlos Williams, but not Yeats, Pound, Eliot or Stevens. 'I think this', Morgan argued, 'is a much needed corrective, especially when we are asked to look on a man like Eliot as "speaking for his generation" or "expressing the anguish of a period," as we often are' (*Essays* pp. 5, 14). Quoting Carlos Williams approvingly – 'one must be at the advancing edge of the art: that's the American tradition' – Morgan responded to 'subtle speech-movements of the verse' in *Paterson*, and referred to Dylan Thomas's successful tours, and readings and recordings by Ginsberg and Kerouac as evidence of the advances recently made by poetry in public performance (*Essays* pp. 7, 12). In a local direction that summer, *New Saltire* carried Morgan's comments on Robert Garioch's 'The Muir', a poem taking much of its energy from developments in sub-atomic physics, the outcome, Garioch noted, of his 'attempt to understand the 1953 Reith

Lectures on *Science and the Common Understanding*, by J. Robert
Oppenheimer.'[30] Whereas MacDiarmid found very little of value in
Garioch's work and thought it 'not only dull but vulgar in the worst sense',
Morgan acknowledges MacDiarmid's lyric gift but considers Garioch 'our
most persuasive user of [Scots], at any rate in poems of any length':

> He has a fine ear for what remains of spoken Scots, and has had
> more success than most modern Scottish poets in building unob-
> trusively on this speech basis, though not without some archaism:
> but at least the archaism is constantly being corrected by a nice col-
> loquial accuracy, and the over-all tone is usually acceptable. (*Essays*
> p. 17)[31]

Morgan was tapping into different experimental modes, and in the
year that Morgan's first concrete collection was published, MacDiarmid
was 'absolutely frank' to Maurice Lindsay about the set-up of *Scottish
Poetry*, an annual anthology that ran for ten years after 1966:

> I deplore Edwin Morgan's association with you and George Bruce
> in the editorship ... Morgan's prominence in connection with
> 'Concrete Poetry' and with Ian Hamilton Finlay rules him out
> completely as far as I am concerned. I will not agree to work of
> mine appearing in any anthology or periodical that uses rubbish of
> that sort, which I regard as an utter debasement of standards but
> also a very serious matter involving the very identity of poetry.
> These spatial arrangements of isolated letters and geometrically
> placed phrases, etc. have nothing whatever to do with poetry – any
> more than mud pies can be called architecture. And I feel so
> strongly about the need to fight this sort of thing *à l'outrance* that
> I, and I am happy to say several other poets, have refused to allow
> any poems of ours to appear in the Oxford anthology if stuff of that
> sort by Morgan or Finlay or anybody else is to be included.[32]

In 1967 Morgan's *Emergent Poems* was published, and in September
MacDiarmid voiced to Edinburgh University's Roman Catholic chaplain
Anthony Ross, then setting up the magazine *Scottish International*, what
he called 'the gravest suspicion' about why 'the Establishment [is] ready
now to help *Scottish International* if not just because it is designed to
betray the aims of the Scottish Renaissance':

> It is significant that two of the editors – Robert Tait and Edwin
> Morgan – have not only never taken any active part in Scottish
> Nationalist developments either literary or political, and are

associated with very questionable international developments like 'concrete poetry' and other pro-Beatnik and 'with it' tendencies. Nor are either of these gentlemen of sufficient weight as writers themselves to justify their appointment as editors unless the object is to serve undeclared ends at complete variance with the proclaimed purpose.

I think you will agree that I cannot lend my name and influence to a project which does not accept as of prime importance the encouragement of Scots and Gaelic, the necessity of Scottish Independence, and the recognition that in contradistinction to the situation in England a deep-seated Radicalism is the chief, and an irreversible, element of the Scottish political tradition and a prime requirement of Scottish conditions today and henceforth.[33]

A year later Morgan wrote a piece on concrete poetry for a collection called *Innovations: Essays on Art and Ideas*, followed in 1972 by a more detailed account called, 'Into the Constellation: Some Thoughts on the Origin and Nature of Concrete Poetry'.[34]

In the tropic melodrama of Freudian text-analysis, Morgan evidently confronted a difficult 'Father' – certainly MacDiarmid was a giant in the literary landscape who had become inextricably identified with influential conceptions of Scottish difference and political self-government. In actuality Morgan responded to each confrontation with argument in critical essays and with poetry that continued to reconfigure possibility. MacDiarmid identified with a cultural history of rivalry between north and south; Morgan elaborates both Scottish and English alterities, including a recognition of Scottish writing from the years preceding and following the Great War as 'only part of a wider twentieth-century movement, a peripheral Renascence of English poetry: the attempted stabilisation of an enfeebled English tradition by poets breaking into it from its boundaries – by Yeats and MacNiece from Ireland, by Pound and Eliot from America, by Dylan Thomas from Wales, by MacDiarmid and Graham from Scotland'.[35] 'We Scottish poets', MacDiarmid had announced, 'must needs travel back ... into Scots and Gaelic. Anglo-Saxon is not for us'.[36] With different ideas and commitments about reconstructed pasts and continuing development, Morgan set about redesigning the imaginative space of Anglo-Saxon epic. *Beowulf*'s most recent translator calls it 'one of the foundation works of poetry in English', and its 'first native epic': by first opening it to twentieth-century idiom Morgan extended its genealogy into Scottish writing.[37]

Drawn by what he calls *Beowulf*'s 'mixture of brooding melancholy and something heroic and stoical', Morgan has said how early and powerfully Anglo-Saxon appealed to him as 'the first really convincing heroic poetry' he read as a student (NNGM, pp. 44, 121). He responds by bringing alliterative measure and epic rhythm within speaking range of a modern readership. From Hrothgar's reminiscence addressed both individually to Beowulf and collectively to the assembled company:

> In this brief hour the flower of your manhood
> Blows, and then in a flash either sickness or the sword,
> Either the seizure of fire or the seething of the flood,
> Either battle-blade's bite or battle-spear's flight
> Or terrible decrepitude shall deprive you of life[38]

to the elegy of the last survivor for whom:

> There is no harp-pleasure
> And no happy minstrelsy, there is no good hawk
> To swoop through the hall, there is no swift horse
> with hoofbeats in the courtyard (B p. 62)

technique translates poignancy of feeling as unobtrusively the original carries it. Seamus Heaney's reference to 'another, outer rim of value' in the poem suggests a fitness for Scottish perception of cultural interface in *Beowulf* where an alien Christian ideology gains influence over and within a pagan environment. With an eye to conflict between a 'British' Northern Ireland and the independent state of Eire, Heaney identifies 'a circumference of understanding ... within which the heroic world is occasionally viewed as from a distance and recognized for what it is, an earlier state of consciousness and culture, one that has not been altogether shed but that has now been comprehended as part of another pattern [arising] from the poet's Christianity'.[39] 'Woven from two such different psychic fabrics', Heaney suggests, '*Beowulf* perfectly answers the early modern conception of a work of creative imagination as one in which conflicting realities find accommodation within a new order' (p. xvii). With an eye to Scotland's changing relationship with England as well as to internal dispositions Morgan in 1971 considered that *Beowulf* 'gets its values very often, its poetic or aesthetic values' from the clash between a strongly felt Christian narrator and heroic pagan contexts:

> though I think in the end that maybe the stronger things do come from the pagan part of it. It does have parallels with later situations, perhaps with our own situation today, and maybe subconsciously I felt that this was what it was all about, and perhaps it attracted me because of this. (NNGM p. 44)

An opening epigraph from Mayakovsky strikes appropriate terms for combative memory by connecting twentieth-century experiment with ancient text, and Russian modernist tragedy with Anglo-Saxon precedent:

> Rifling by chance some old book-tumulus
> And bringing into light those iron-tempered
> Lines of its buried verse – never be careless
> With ancient but still formidable weapons!

'What literary activity is more purposeful than translation?' is the opening question of Morgan's Introduction, which argues his intended distance from the ideological reinforcement that previous translations provided for 'the long-hallowed ballad-cum-Spenser-cum-Authorized-Version fixative from which *Beowulf* during the last century has been faintly gleaming like a dragonfly under an inch of amber' (B p. x).

England's nineteenth-century restoration to prominence of a seed-bed script by Anglo-Saxon progenitors invented an effective tradition in support of claims to cultural supremacy, both over colonised territories and among burgeoning European nationalisms. In Morgan's reading of them, previous modernisings have stalled on a deployment of archaic style and turns of phrase he associates with 'relics of a rule of English' to be kept at a distance: 'If it is a case of losing an archaism or losing the poetry, the archaism must go'. In support of the metre he develops as an equivalence for the flexibility of Anglo-Saxon measure, Morgan quotes A. D. Wackerbarth, who produced the first full translation of *Beowulf* in 1849: 'if the literary bent of this country should continue for some few years longer the course it has of late years pursued, it will be time to give this poem to the English people in English alliterative metre, and I shall be thankful to see it done'. Morgan extends that possible audience by quoting Edward Fulton's 1898 promotion of technical improvements he would operate himself: 'What we want, and there seems no reason why we should not get it, is an adaptation of the English, irregular, four-accent measure sufficiently like the Anglo-Saxon to suggest it at once and inevitably, yet not so unlike the English line as to sound strange to the modern ear' (B pp. xiv, xix). The Eliot elsewhere resisted on ideological grounds is here acknowledged for his development of a four-beat rhythmic line. *Sweeney Agonistes* (1927) provided a 'perfect instance of the old 4-beat stress metre adapted to modern needs', which subsequently constituted the predominant rhythm of *Murder in the Cathedral* (1935) and came to serve, in Helen Gardner's phrase, as 'the norm to which [Eliot's] verse constantly returns'; thereby helping to establish a pattern of accentually rather than syllabically organised writing, followed as occasion prompted by Auden, Day Lewis and Spender (B pp. xx, xxi).[40]

English-language reconstructions of selfhood with Scottish specifications were proceeding on other fronts. Six months before his translation of *Beowulf* appeared, Morgan's essay on 'Dunbar and the Language of Poetry' was recovering a shared possession of Anglo-Saxon measure in Scottish historical rhythms. His contention that 'our stubborn alliterative tradition ... influenced Dunbar', suggests a northern pedigree for his own modernisation of Anglo-Saxon script.[41] Like some of his medieval contemporaries, Dunbar's practice 'proves that the older tradition was very pervasive and very congenial to the Scottish spirit, and they pay it that debt of exemplification which is often more revealing than their addresses to Chaucer' (p. 82). Morgan had already (in 1949) published a translation of 'The Ruin' that was to have been collected along with 'The Seafarer' and other poems in 1952, the year Ezra Pound's version of 'The Seafarer' was re-issued.[42] Morgan knew Pound's version and was not sympathetic to it, thinking it 'a strange old-fashioned kind of translation';[43] and the effectiveness of his challenge to a high priest of canonical modernism is made evident by setting Pound's:

> Not any protector
> May make merry man faring needy.
> This he little believes, who aye in winsome life
> Abides 'mid burghers some heavy business,
> Wealthy and wine-flushed, how I weary oft
> Must bide above brine (p. 77)

against Morgan's:

> what prince
> Could shield or comfort the heart in its need!
> For he who possesses the pleasures of life
> And knows scant sorrow behind town-walls
> With his pride and his wine will hardly believe
> How I have often had to endure
> Heartbreak over the paths of the sea. (CP p. 32)

Beowulf becomes speakable as twentieth-century idiom moves out into difference and acclimatises to its textual other in mutually developmental ways. It now seems as evident that Morgan during the 1950s was testing his voice in a variety of ways and often through translation, such that the Seafarer's words: 'Again and again the mind's desire / Summons me outward far from here / To visit the shore of nations unknown' prescribe journeyings still at some distance in Morgan's future work. He has often said, and the evidence is there, that the 1960s gave him a second life. As far writing is concerned he associates this with the Beat movement. But Kenneth White recognised that it is with 'The Whittrick: a Poem in Eight Dialogues', the first of which appeared in 1955 (opening a sequence not published as a whole until 1973 but begun in 1954 and completed in 1957), that Morgan began the break-out from what he has since called 'a rather bleak and tight phase' of the effort to write (NNGM p. 114).[44] He had earlier, in 'Ingram Lake, or Five Acts on the House', devised out of a kind of charades in reverse an entertainment where five lightly disguised playwrights do not mime but versify their improvisations. Firstly a scene sketched by a well-known chronicler of Southern United States excess, William Tennissippi. Tennissippi's closing reference to 'the meagre chaos of cutlery and crockery' leads into Eliot's Anglo-American fastidiousness; followed in turn by Jean-Paul Sartre in 'l'enfer c'est les autres' mode; by Konstantin Semeonoff's promise of communist redemption, and finally by Christopher Fry's domesticity. Five dramatists in search of a plot neatly counterpoints Pirandello's absurdist pre-text and stretches monologue into dialogic relation. Morgan was flexing a mode that would develop as a favoured form, from the sometimes-grotesque realism of 'Stobhill' to the tape-recorded playbacks of 'Memories of Earth', or a voluble sperm over-coming danger and finding fit partner.

Published in the same year as MacDiarmid's 'In Memoriam James Joyce' (1955), the first of 'The Whittrick' dialogues, 'James Joyce and Hugh MacDiarmid' designs a high-spirited spoof of the poem MacDiarmid opened by directly addressing the Irishman: 'I remember how you laughed like Hell / When I read you from Pape's 'Politics of the Aryan Road': / "English is destined to become the Universal Language!"'[45] That is a fictional scenario: MacDiarmid never met Joyce and if he had, his biographer suggests, 'it is doubtful if the Irish master would have tolerated a reading from a man MacDiarmid described as "A. G. Pape, whose ancestors on either side embraced almost all the great diplomats of France and of Great Britain and with whom, for a time, I had a good deal to do in Edinburgh"'.[46] Joyce shadows 'In Memoriam' comprehensively, and Morgan's first 'Whittrick' dialogue reconfigures a modernist relationship. 'We have MacDiarmid's word for it', he comments, 'that Joyce knew his poetry and in particular "A Drunk Man Looks at the Thistle" (1926), but the influence that can be documented goes in the other direction'. 'A Drunk Man' appeared while Joyce was working on *Finnegans Wake* and the likely impact of that book on MacDiarmid's

writing has been recognised.[47] In Morgan's view it was Joyce's 'bold and
innovative use of language in *Ulysses* that encouraged [MacDiarmid] to
take equal risks in giving new life to what had become the effete tradition of writing in Lowland Scots'.[48] Reminding us that MacDiarmid
identified a 'moral resemblance' between Joyce's *Ulysses* and Jamieson's
Etymological Dictionary of the Scottish Language, Morgan quotes a
remark from *The Scottish Chapbook* edited by MacDiarmid in the early
1920s:

> A *vis comica* that has not yet been liberated lies bound by desue-
> tude and misappreciation in the recesses of the Doric: and its poten-
> tial uprising would be no less prodigious, uncontrollable, and
> utterly at variance with conventional morality than was Joyce's
> tremendous outpouring.[49]

With extensible recesses, here was an uprising to which Morgan
could lend unstinting support: 'a liberation through language and, inter-
estingly, a liberation that will please the spirit of comedy: MacDiarmid
... like Joyce sees an effect of moral catharsis in comedy'.[50] Effects of
moral catharsis in comedy are a continuing dynamic for Morgan, who
was by this time reading MacDiarmid with a sometimes appreciative but
as often critical assessment of extracts from 'The Kind of Poetry I want',
from 'Cornish Heroic Song' and from parts of 'In Memoriam James
Joyce' that had already appeared in print:

> [MacDiarmid] has been paying more and more attention to sub-
> ject matter, and less and less attention to style; his poetry is becom-
> ing, as he describes it, 'a poetry of fact and science', a poetry that
> will teach rather than entertain. It is also true, though he has to
> admit it indirectly, that in this process he has found Scots lacking,
> and English (or English internationalised, English bejoyced) his
> natural medium.[51]

'English bejoyced' says Morgan; and supports his claim that
MacDiarmid's poetry in Scots makes his 'one of the distinctive voices of
our period' by quoting from 'Water Music', a uniquely Joycean poem in
MacDiarmid's output, whose opening epigraph uses Irish stream of consciousness associations to ground a Scottish sound world:[52]

> *Wheesht, wheesht, Joyce, and let me hear*
> *Nae Anna Livvy's lilt,*
> *But Wauchope, Esk, and Ewes again,*
> *Each wi' its ain rhythms till't.*

I
Archin' here and arrachin there,
Allevolie or allemand,
Whiles appliable, whiles areird,
The polysemous poem's planned.[53]

[Archin = flowing smoothly; arrachin = tumultuous; Allevolie = volatile; allemand = orderly; appliable = compliant; areird = troublesome]

Morgan reads this as MacDiarmid's enthusiastic response to the fragments of Joyce's 'Work in Progress' that had appeared during the 1920s: 'a lyrico-musical, alliterative, onomatopoeic recognition' of Joyce's dexterity.[54] By relying on a vernacular lexis mainly derived from the first letters of the alphabet, MacDiarmid was also indicating the initiatory aspect of his attempt to forge a native modernism in the smithy of his craft.

Soon after 'In Memoriam James Joyce' (and 'The Whittrick's opening dialogue) appeared, Morgan was advising readers that together with a 'wilderness of parentheses and long sentences', MacDiarmid's addiction to lists and catalogues has 'a cumulative comic effect' of which he seems to be unaware, 'and this is interesting, because here he and Joyce begin to diverge':

> Joyce is precisely one of the writers who have taught us to laugh at the very things MacDiarmid is so painstakingly proliferating: all the Alexandrian pedantries and ramifications of modern specialized scholarship. Parts of *Finnegans Wake* read like a proleptic parody of the poem that celebrates their dead author.[55]

When they meet in 'The Whittrick' over a bottle of whisky, the Irishman's mellifluous speech serves as perfect foil to the conversational address of MacDiarmid's dialectal toast to the creator of Stephen Daedalus:

> Fill yir gless, Icarus! Thae nichts'll no revert!
> The warld, for aa that it's gruppen wi sair decreets
> O physics, stound and steid, will preeve to you and me
> Yon auld camsteerie ghaistlie place Lucretie thocht
> He had exhilit fae the nature o things. Nicht
> Will dwine and flee and leave anither you and me
> Happit in relativitie's raggit yestreen.
> Let aa we were and aa we sall be ming and mell
> In this ae lowe o the unfremmit hours, my freen! (CP p. 79)

[revert = return; gruppen = in the grip of; sair = difficult; stound and steid = time and space; camsteerie = perverse; dwine = fade; happit = wrapped; ming and mell = blend and mingle; ae lowe = single flame; unfremmit = familiar]

W. N. Herbert suggests that Morgan's very personal and fluid voice is
unlike MacDiarmid's, and that this whittrick poem 'speaks in a language
formed when standard English collides with spoken Scots', and that collision is part of the poem's point.[56] Certainly this first dialogue has fun
with radically unlike protagonists: 'two men could hardly be more different in fundamental outlook than Joyce and MacDiarmid', Morgan has
commented, 'all they have in common is [that] they are virtuosos of language',[57] and he measures this distance by quoting Joyce from 1907:

> The old national soul that spoke during the centuries through the
> mouths of fabulous seers, wandering minstrels, and Jacobite poets
> disappeared from the world with the death of James Clarence
> Mangan.... It is well past time for Ireland to have done once and
> for all with failure. If she is truly capable of reviving, let her awake.[58]

Set that against MacDiarmid's recurrent perception in *Lucky Poet*
and elsewhere of Ireland as a Celtic motherland and his claim that 'a
Scottish Scotland must be a Gaelic Scotland', and we have some sense of
the differences out of which Morgan's dialogue makes pantomime from
incomprehension and mishearing.[59] After MacDiarmid's hope for 'an all-
embracing language, an interpenetration of all languages' – 'Let aa we
were and aa we sall be ming and mell' – Joyce's reply can be read as a
bemused assumption that whatever MacDiarmid may have been saying
was convivial: 'Friendly and propitious be the salutation' (CP p. 79).[60]
Joyce then launches into a display of punning that imagines reason into
a variety of circumstances and, via Jack London's *White Fang*, transforms
the yellow fog curling around houses and gutters that Eliot's Prufrock
visualises as feline, into a canine whiskey drinker that 'leaps / Upon the
dusty curtain, slinks by the candles, / Snuffs at the crystal and laps at the
fire-water'. In full tilt at the ghosts of a cultural past, Morgan's Joyce rolls
a space-time continuum into vivid simultaneity where surreal stream of
consciousness connects discursive difference: Hannibal's legendary triumph with mathematics ('elements have crossed the Alphs'); Coleridge's
imagined 'Kubla' with the colonising Khanate established by a Tatar
'Golden Horde'; Arthurian legend and Celtic myth surrounding a semi-
historical king of the Britons with an ancient tribal queen's resistance to
Roman occupation; and with war in The Crimea.

Joyce introduces the motifs of the sequence; flickering candlelight,
the jinn of Arab demonology and the weasel-like whittrick that flits too
quickly to be caught in focus. Once 'the jinn are out of the candles, [to]
flicker-flacker / Up the walls and across the ceiling', and with the con-
cretion of a bottle of blended whisky out of which Joyce refills his glass,

the 'guthering shadies' of spirit worlds past and future are conjured as both legendary and historical figures:

> Finn MacCool
> Fifing on a bollard, Arthur at his truffle,
> Diving Grendel and a gun-grey dragon. Bottles
> Have jinn as well as candles, and as I uncork
> This gentle johnny, watch the shadows. – How they jumped!
> Something we hardly saw leaped out – animal or
> Vegetable lamb or mineral spring: what sprang?
> A drink to all the unknown jinn of history.
> Whisky always makes me think about history. (CP p. 80)

Joyce, who as far as origin-myth was concerned believed that 'the river flowed to the sea, the rain fell on the hills, and the river flowed to the sea, and that was all', was singularly underwhelmed by the idea of a Gaelic revival as Ireland's literary salvation.[61] But its imaginative appeal was 'by no means alien to Joyce's concerns': 'both Finn and Finnegan, after all, to say nothing of that rex futurus Arthur, were chosen by Joyce as chief exemplars of reawakening and all are Celts'.[62] MacCool, Irish folk-hero, descendant of a Druid and raised in the forest, was legendary father of Ossian, and so part of a narrative genealogy reinvented by eighteenth-century Scottish seekers after space for cultural difference in the aftermath of political union with England.

If Joyce comes to play with ghosts as he buries them, MacDiarmid both praises them and raises them. Mishearing the final line of a tipsy author of *Finnegans Wake*, a tipsy Scot plunges into a whittrick's wake as gothic as anything Tam o' Shanter stumbled across on his way home. Here the great Grieve is no longer looking at a thistle, but fallen among ten mourning whittricks who speak his language and toast his continuing health: 'ten o the friskiest dustifit shennachies / This side o Ardnamurchan'. Shennachie once signified a professional recorder and reciter of family histories and genealogies but now refers to a teller of traditional Gaelic tales; and that shift from relayed linkage to recycled myth and legend is an interface of archive and fable that constitutes this dialogue's narrative. Speaking a strange argot, Morgan's MacDiarmid dramatises a wake in the animal kingdom that seems and does not seem to relate to *Finnegans Wake*, compounding Finn MacCool, whose return to life will secure Ireland's redemption, with Tim Finnegan the music-hall ballad hero who sprang to life in the middle of his own wake. 'Surely no Christian tongue,' says the listening Joyce – 'Choctaw, Chukchaw? Glesgaw?'. Nothing daunted, MacDiarmid elaborates his tale, taking the hazard of naming in a confused and confusing context and describing how whisky confounded the dead whittrick's mourners by making it 'cry / Like its ain Frankenstein for metamorphosis'. When he passes out and everything vanishes like a broken spell, mutual incomprehension is again signalled by Joyce picking up on 'history', the word with which he had earlier finished, as though nothing has intervened. Except that as a night's drinking passes into dawn, 'wake' shifts from noun to eye-opening verb: Joyce metamorphoses at will, MacDiarmid sees the grave still 'green [longing] for the gleg [quick] whittrick that loups by the whins [gorse]', and Joyce accurately describes their drinking session as 'our nocturnal circumcolloquy'.

Recurrent reference to jinns released from bottles, to candle-flame flickerings and to whittricks, installs an appropriately floating signifier across the sequence. Applied most commonly to the weasel, but also to the stoat, the ferret and the polecat, even as a Scots noun 'whittrick' is vanishing, existing only as a variant of 'whitrat'; and in 'Dialogue VI: The Brahan Seer and Lady Seaforth', appearing in further variant form as 'futtret'. Apart from MacDiarmid dropping in on a whittrick wake, across the eight dialogues the creature is only partially seen and mostly glimpsed, compromising perception and teasing the reader out of thought. One effect of the Sots sound-world that Morgan invents for his contrapuntal comedy prefigures his later suggestion that the 'MacDiarmid "renascence" of a general synthetic Scots fifty years ago can still be felt, and learned from, but the move should now be towards the honesty of actual speech'. (*Essays* p. 178).

That was looking back over the sixties. In the early 1950s, and from another direction, Morgan's pursuit of speech rhythms and conversational forms might have found Charles Olson's 'Projective Verse' essay congenial. Morgan's modes are distinctive, but Olson's injunctions have a prognostic if quirky relevance to technique in 'The Whittrick', where an expanding and contracting syllable count controls the line in a diversifying non-sequential sequence:

> Let's start from the smallest particle of all, the syllable. It is the king and pin of versification, what rules and holds together the lines, the larger forms of a poem.... In any given instance, because there is a choice of words, the choice ... will be, spontaneously, the obedience of [the] ear to the syllables. The fineness, and the practice, lie here, at the minimum and source of speech.[63]

Morgan will 'imitate' Olson's Black Mountain colleague Robert Creeley and, given the opening of the field he was developing in 'The

Whittrick', would find supportive Olson's emphatic repetition of Creeley's ordinance: 'FORM IS NEVER MORE THAN AN EXTENSION OF CONTENT'.[64] Another signifying dimension of Morgan's first 'Whittrick' dialogue (and the sequence generally) develops from its relation prospectively to the next dialogue – 'Hieronymous Bosch and Johann Faust' – and to those that follow; and retrospectively as an accumulating re-reading. In the second apocalypse anthology of 1941, the art critic Robert Melville described Bosch as an apocalyptic painter whose revelatory images are 'so potent that it is still difficult to assess their aesthetic value'.[65] Morgan opens up a poetry of process where prescriptive structures of belief are tested and found wanting in a conversation between the painter whose bizarre and sometimes demonic representations continue to haunt a European imagination, and Faust of the legendary deal with the devil: 'But neither then nor in sleep is the soul sold / Unless you believe it sold, and act the rest' (CP p. 83). As a foretaste of what he might enjoy, Faust dreams of pleasure: 'but at the end is hell'. When Bosch then describes a painting he calls 'God creating the World of Hell', the verse includes elements from Bosch's 'The Garden of Earthly Delights' to accuse both God and men of constructing contexts for agony: what the angels 'fall down into is being made / Hell'. 'Some men say', Bosch reports, incorporating legend into art history, 'that I in my imagination have dreamed / What only a devil-elect could gaze on / Sane, and paint as a tale is told'. Morgan displaces doom-laden prophecy with redemptive friendship.

In the final dialogue, where the whittrick has transmuted into a genetically engineered evolution of machine intelligence: 'a quick thing, / A brain and a voice', it has to contend with a programmed adaptation of 'Machina speculatrix' to 'Machina docilis'. So Morgan's metaphor of movement is associated with 'the flash of imagination' whose 'logic allows the leap of thought'. We enter 'a Cybernetic Unit' (the poem was written in the 1950s before the term had any general currency), 'linking research / By engineers, linguists, mathematicians / And neurophysiologists', to hear Jean Cocteau discuss science and art with W. Grey Walter in a dialogue that includes Scots speech, and where the whittrick first speaks. Walter's *The Living Brain* (1953) publicised new information generated by electroencephalograph (EEG) measurements of electrical impulses in the brain. This whittrick has been programmed to find the 'end of every beginning, the probable / Haystack in the open field of the possible'; and logic leaps on its own account when Morgan's Walter links entropy and writing:

The poem you write is already foreshadowed
When you pencil the first warm phrase, and every word
Is a choice that lessens choice, till the anxious voice
Picks one last possibility out of silence. (CP pp. 114–15)

Pairing Walter with Cocteau reciprocates Walter's literary chapter headings. Chapter 4 of *The Living Brain*, called 'Revelation by Flicker', opens with lines from Eliot's 'The Hollow Men': 'Between the conception / And the creation / Between the emotion / And the response / Falls the shadow'.[66] In the flickering intertextual mind-games played across 'The Whittrick', Bosch has already described how 'fantasy / And reality, the energies of work / And the energies of imagination / Swirl in [him] so hauntingly', and as the sequence encodes the work of writing, so it inscribes desire. A playful phallocentrism in dialogue III, where 1001 Arabian Nights reach 1002, projects narrative reversal from queen talking for her life on to king postponing pleasure under the guise of 'love, / Trust, reconciliation', and finally moving to consummation. A conversation between 'Charlotte and Emily Brontë' then plays narrative crossover from past fiction to fictionalising present. As Charlotte puts it: 'This house / Is thick with phantoms, sick with the past, / Littered with our childish brain-children.... Imagination looms through this rain / Like a great message – a dead rider / with his cold fingers on a letter'. When she asks 'What would imagination matter / If we looked out on reality?' Emily's two-syllable reply justifies the line's measure. Cultural reconfiguration is operating here too: MacDiarmid's Introduction to his *Golden Treasury* anthology reinforced a twentieth-century mythic strain for Scottish chauvinism by associating what he called 'the depotentization of human intelligence' with 'that early matriarchal control which ... delayed the coming of civilisation for thousands of years' (p. xx). In a singular departure from mainstream criticism, Morgan's 1950 essay 'Women and Poetry' described Emily Brontë as 'our greatest woman poet. ... at once powerful and exact, intense and restrained'. In her whittrick dialogue, Emily's cryptic replies to a chattering Charlotte enact a 'bareness and economy' that Morgan admired in her verse; where he also reads 'the cry of a mind which earthly experience has lacerated so harshly that it puts on armour against any hope and promise of happiness', and sees her poetry as 'projections of a personality trying to materialize its inward wars and loves'.[67] He knew whereof he spoke.

As he executes his polysemous poem Morgan engages in projections and materialisations of his own, foregrounding both structures of self-presentation and systems of cultural representation. Meetings of East and

West in 'The Whittrick' include Marilyn Monroe swapping modes of perception with Galina Ulanova, who doesn't understand Marilyn's justifi-
cation of sheer nylon stockings, and then does; and a conversation
between Hakuin the Japanese Bhuddist teacher described as a founder
of modern Zen, and his fellow countryman and contemporary,
Chikamatsu, a puppeteer known as the Japanese Shakespeare. Conflict
between freethinking art and religious prescription that is European
between Bosch and Faust now has an oriental inflection: 'Keep the inef-
fable on the prayer-mat, / With rice and chopsticks, but neither brush
nor ink'. When their attitudes coincide over ritual tea-drinking ('this too
is Zen') the poem discloses Zen doing what it does successfully across
historical time and cultural space – adapting to unfolding circumstance.
Still 'kick[ing] the paradoxes around [his] memory' (CP p. 110),
Morgan tests his versatility as presenter of spoken circumstance by ventriloquising forms of self-making uninhibited by discursive conventions
governing fact and fictionality, and unconstrained by periodicity, cultural
location or custom and practice.

   Opening the field of invention as it closes 'The Whittrick' sequence,
the figure of Conneach Odhar, a prophetic speaker who knew the ends
of several beginnings long before Walter's whittrick became a laboratory
possibility, resurrects a Celtic myth of second sight and a tale that has
entered Scottish folklore. Traditionally it was Conneach's skill as a Seer
that first attracted the attention of Kenneth, third Earl of Seaforth, who
gave him a place at Brahan Castle where he offended the Countess
Isabella, Lady Seaforth, when at her insistence he 'saw' the Earl's infi-
delity while in Paris on Charles II's business. She had the Seer arrested
for witchcraft and burned in a spiked barrel of tar on the Ness at Fortrose,
and the story goes that before he died he foresaw the downfall of the
Seaforth Mackenzies, whose line eventually came to an end in the
manner he foretold:

> I see into the far future, and I read the doom of the race of my
> oppressor.... I see a chief, the last of his house, both deaf and dumb.
> He will be the father of four fair sons, all of whom he will follow to
> the tomb.[68]

Historians can find no support for this well-known tale. In contrast with
the sixteenth, the seventeenth century is a well-documented period in
Scottish history yet there is no evidence of the Brahan Seer's existence,
let alone his death, in contemporary writings or records of the day. In
Morgan's handling legend is repetition; tradition is narrative invention;
writing their transforming mode of continuity.

Notes

1 Victor Shklovsky, 'Art as Technique', in *Russian Formalist Criticism: Four Essays*, trans. L. T. Lemon and M. J. Reis, Lincoln, 1965, p. 11.
2 Theodor Adorno, *Prisms*, trans. S. Weber and S. Weber, London, 1967, p. 225.
3 Snow and Snow (eds), *The Nightfisherman*, pp. 94–6.
4 It is also possible that Morgan was playing a variation on the image of a ship in a bottle in W. S. Graham's poem 'My Glass World Tells of Itself', published in *2nd Poems* a year before Morgan wrote 'Dies Irae', and an image that recurs throughout Graham's work as a 'personal symbol of the timeless and motionless work of art'. (See Damian Grant, 'Walls of Glass: The Poetry of W. S. Graham', in Peter Jones and Michael Schmidt (eds), *British Poetry since 1970: A Critical Survey*, Manchester, 1980, p. 23.)
5 Nicholson, *Poem, Purpose and Place*, p. 58.
6 Michael Lynch, *Scotland: A New History*, London, 1992 edition, pp. xv–xvi.
7 Iona and Peter Opie (eds), *The Oxford Dictionary of Nursery Rhymes*, Oxford, 1992, p. 301, 300.
8 Marco Fazzini, 'Edwin Morgan: Two Interviews', *Studies in Scottish Literature*, 29, 1996, p. 54.
9 Edwin Morgan, *Papers*, Glasgow University Library, MS Morgan 69.
10 Interview with Morgan, 17 August 1998.
11 Edwin Morgan, 'James Joyce and Hugh MacDiarmid', in W. J. McCormack and Alistair Stead (eds), *James Joyce and Modern Literature*, London, 1982, pp. 202–17; Bold (ed.), *Letters of Hugh MacDiarmid*, p. 675.
12 Edwin Morgan, *Hugh MacDiarmid*, London, 1976, pp. 7, 11, 28, 33.
13 Edwin Morgan, 'MacDiarmid Embattled', *Lines Review*, 15, 1959, pp. 17–25, [*Essays*, pp. 194–202].
14 Hugh MacDiarmid, *Complete Poems*, eds M. Grieve and W. R. Aitken, Manchester, 1993, vol. 2, p. 938. Cited by Morgan in 'MacDiarmid Embattled', *Essays*, p. 199.
15 'MacDiarmid Embattled', p. 200.
16 Mention of Frontiniac indicts indifference to Scotland's cultural spaces by reference to Wordsworth's early advocacy of verse rooted in a living and knowable community, and his disdain for people who 'talk of poetry as of a matter of amusement and idle pleasure; who will converse with us as gravely about a *taste* for poetry, as they express it, as if it were a thing as indifferent as a taste for rope-dancing, or Frontiniac or Sherry'. See the 1802 'Preface' to *Lyrical Ballads*, in William Wordsworth, *The Prose Works*, W. J. B. Owen and J. W. Smyser, Oxford, 1974, vol. 1, p. 139.
17 Bold (ed.) *Letters of Hugh MacDiarmid*, pp. 674–8.
18 Duncan Glen, *Hugh MacDiarmid (Christopher Murray Grieve) and the Scottish Renaissance*, Edinburgh, 1964, p. 227.
19 Norman MacCaig (ed.), *Honour'd Shade: An Anthology of New Scottish Poetry to Mark the Bi-centenary of the Birth of Robert Burns*, Edinburgh, 1959.
20 Tom Wright and Hugh Rae, 'Burns and the Poets of Today', *Scottish Field*, 109:709, January 1962, p. 19.
21 Bold (ed.) *Letters of Hugh MacDiarmid*, p. 808.

22 Edwin Morgan, 'Poet and Public', *The Scotsman*, 12 March 1962; 'Who Will Publish Scottish Poetry?', *New Saltire* 2, 1961, pp. 51–6.
23 Morgan, 'Poet and Public'.
24 Bold (ed.) *Letters of Hugh MacDiarmid*, p. 814.
25 'MacDiarmid on MacDiarmid', *The Guardian*, 22 February 1962.
26 Bold (ed.) *Letters of Hugh MacDiarmid*, p. 810. See Hamish Whyte, 'MacDiarmid and the Beatniks', *Scottish Literary Journal*, 13:2, 1986, pp. 87–90.
27 Hugh MacDiarmid, *The Ugly Birds Without Wings*, Edinburgh, 1962, p. 12.
28 Edwin Morgan, 'The Beat Vigilantes', *New Saltire*, 5, 1962, pp. 75–80.
29 Cited in Glen, *Hugh MacDiarmid and the Scottish Renaissance*, p. 226.
30 Robert Garioch, *Complete Poetical Works*, Edinburgh, 1983, p. 298, n. 54.
31 Bold (ed.) *Letters of Hugh MacDiarmid*, p. 703.
32 *Ibid.*, pp. 627–8.
33 Bold (ed.) *Letters of Hugh MacDiarmid*, pp. 872–3.
34 Edwin Morgan, 'Concrete Poetry', in Bernard Bergonzi (ed), *Innovations: Essays on Art and Ideas*, London, 1968, pp. 213–25; 'Into the Constellation: Some Thoughts on the Origin and Nature of Concrete Poetry' [1972], *Essays*, pp. 20–34.
35 Edwin Morgan, 'Modern Makars, p. 80.
36 MacDiarmid, *Golden Treasury*, p. xvii.
37 Seamus Heaney, *Beowulf: A New Translation*, London, 1999, pp. ix, xii.
38 Edwin Morgan, *Beowulf: A Verse Translation into Modern English*, Berkeley, 1952, p. 48. Hereafter B.
39 Heaney, *Beowulf*, p. xvi.
40 Helen Gardner, *The Art of T. S. Eliot*, London, 1949, p. 29, cited in Morgan, B, p. xxi.
41 Edwin Morgan, 'Dunbar and the Language of Poetry', *Essays in Criticism*, 2:2, 1952, included in *Essays* to which page numbers refer.
42 The intended collection was published in *Poems of Thirty Years*, Manchester, 1982, pp. 3–24. Pound's 'The Seafarer', from *Ripostes* [1912], is included in *Personae: Collected Shorter Poems of Ezra Pound*, London, 1952, pp. 76–9.
43 Fazzini, 'Edwin Morgan: Two Interviews', p. 51.
44 White, 'Morgan's Range', p. 32. The dates of 1955–1961 given in the *Akros* [1973] publication of the *Whittrick* sequence refer to the publishing of individual poems in magazines. Morgan confirmed the earlier dates of composition.
45 MacDiarmid, *Complete Poems*, vol. 2, p. 739.
46 Alan Bold, *MacDiarmid: A Critical Biography*, London, 1988, p. 357.
47 See for example Carl Freeman, 'Beyond the Dialect of the Tribe: James Joyce, Hugh MacDiarmid, and World Language', in Nancy Gish (ed.), *Hugh MacDiarmid: Man and Poet*, Edinburgh, 1992, pp. 253–73.
48 Morgan, 'James Joyce and Hugh MacDiarmid', pp. 202, 207, 213.
49 Hugh MacDiarmid, 'A Theory of Scots Letters', *The Scottish Chapbook*, 1, 1922, pp. 180–4, cited by Morgan in 'James Joyce and Hugh MacDiarmid', pp. 207–8.
50 Morgan, 'James Joyce and Hugh MacDiarmid', p. 208.
51 Morgan, 'Modern Makars, p. 78.
52 Roderick Watson, '"Water Music" and the Stream of Consciousness', *Scottish Literary Journal*, 5:2, 1978, p. 6.

53 MacDiarmid, *Complete Poems*, vol. 1, p. 333, cited by Morgan in 'Modern Makars', p. 78.

54 Morgan, 'James Joyce and Hugh MacDiarmid', p. 209.

55 Edwin Morgan, 'Jujitsu for the Educated: Reflections on Hugh MacDiarmid's poem "In Memoriam James Joyce"', *The Twentieth Century*, 160:955, 1956, p. 228.

56 W. N. Herbert, 'Morgan's Words', in Crawford and Whyte (eds), *About Edwin Morgan*, pp. 71–2.

57 Morgan, 'Jujitsu for the Educated', p. 230.

58 James Joyce, 'Ireland, Island of Saints and Sages', in Ellsworth Mason and Richard Ellman (eds), *The Critical Writings of James Joyce*, London, 1959, pp. 173–4, cited by Morgan in 'James Joyce and Hugh MacDiarmid', p. 205.

59 Hugh MacDiarmid, *Lucky Poet. A Self-Study in Literature and Political Ideas*, London, 1943, p. 201.

60 See the epigraph from Vladimir Solovyov, for 'In Memoriam James Joyce', MacDiarmid, *Complete Poems*, vol. 2, p. 737.

61 Morgan, 'Jujitsu for the Educated', p. 230.

62 'James Joyce and Hugh MacDiarmid', p. 206.

63 Charles Olson, 'Projective Verse' [1950], in D. M. Allen and W. Tallman (eds), *The Poetics of the New American Poetry*, New York, 1973, p. 149.

64 See Morgan's 'Unpublished Poems by Creeley', in 'Newspoems: 1965–1971', (CP p. 129); Olson, 'Projective Verse', p. 148.

65 Robert Melville, 'Apocalypse in Painting', in *the white horseman: prose and verse of the new apocalypse*, London, 1941, p. 135.

66 T. S. Eliot, *The Complete Poems and Plays*, London, 1969, p. 85, cited in W. Grey Walter, *The Living Brain* [1953], Harmondsworth, 1961, p. 80.

67 Edwin Morgan, 'Women and Poetry', *Cambridge Journal*, 3:2, 1950, pp. 648, 650–2.

68 Alexander Mackenzie, *The Prophecies of the Brahan Seer* [1877], Essex, 1977, p. 109.

3 From Glasgow to Mayakovsky

I tend to use Scots where it would be used naturally in a poem, in speech. I'm very much aware that this leaves the whole position in the air – whether one should use Scots as a deliberate political act – this is clearly a possibility. (Edwin Morgan, NNGM p. 49)

In the case of a signifying practice such as 'poetic language,' the *semiotic disposition* will be the various deviations from the grammatical rules of the language: articulatory effects which shift the phonemative system back towards its articulatory, phonetic base and consequently towards the drive-governed bases of sound-production ... and that capacity is, for the *subject*, the capacity for enjoyment. (Julia Kristeva)[1]

J. F. Hendry described Mayakovsky as 'apocalyptic in his fervour'.[2] At the same time MacDiarmid was promoting Scots as appropriate medium for cultural mobilisations; and by the 1950s Morgan was feeling his way into a poetics of the spoken word. At a later time Julia Kristeva remembered listening to Roman Jakobson's recorded readings of Mayakovsky and Velimir Khlebnikov: 'He ... imitat[ed] their voices, with the lively, rhythmic accents, thrust out throat and fully militant tone of the first; and the softly whispered words, sustained swishing and whistling sounds ... constituted by the 'trans-mental' ('zaum') language of the second'.[3] Twenty years before Kristeva published *La Révolution du langage poétique* (and thirty before its English appearance) Morgan was using Russian intertext to explore what Kristeva would call 'the sociality in which the (speaking, historical) subject is embedded'. On behalf of semiotic theories of meaning she also sought to transform, Kristeva would argue for language as a mobile and not a static signifying system, and the terms of her assault on structuralist practice seem retrospectively relevant:

Either it will remain an attempt at formalizing meaning-systems ... on the basis of a conception (already rather dated) of meaning as the act of a *transcendental ego*, cut off from its body, its unconscious and also its history; or else it will attune itself to the theory of the

speaking subject as a divided subject (conscious/unconscious) and
go on to specify the types of operation characteristic of the two sides
of this split ... exposing them on the one hand to what Freud
labelled 'drives', and, on the other hand, to social constraints.[4]

'Language', Kristeva insists, must be treated as 'either system of signs or
strategy for the transformation of logical sequence'.[5] 'I don't think of
language as in any way static', Morgan has commented:

> I know it's an ordered system in the sense that we can all use it and
> understand each other; but in writing, particularly in poetry, I see
> it as a very extensible and explorable system. Some of the experi-
> ments you undertake if you are dealing with language will turn out
> not to be useful, may be cul-de-sacs. But you have to take that risk,
> and other things you discover will be useful, and will extend your
> instrumentation. Hugh MacDiarmid used to speak about the
> human brain being largely unused. I'm sure that's quite true, and
> I think language is like that too.[6]

Morgan also explores what Kristeva would call 'functions between the
signifying code and the fragmented body of the speaking subject'; functions which presuppose 'a frontier ... and the transgression of that frontier'.[7] His reassembly of literary modernism against an established canon
and through a reconfigured subjectivity qualifies as both transgression
and renewal, where crossing frontiers is habitual.

For Kristeva part of the value of hearing Jakobson read Mayakovsky
and Khlebnikov lay in its opening up a way of reconsidering the aesthetic
and always political battles of Russian society on the eve of revolution
and during its first years of victory. The politics degenerated into a ruthless domination, but the promise of economic self-management and
redistributive justice continued to concentrate the energies of diverse
individuals. Jakobson and Mayakovsky knew each other, debated poetics hotly, and in the year after Mayakovsky's suicide Jakobson wrote: 'The
poet catches the music of the future in an insatiable ear, but he is not destined to enter the Promised Land. A vision of the future is present in all
the most essential pages in Mayakovsky's work'.[8] That was in 1931, by
which time Trotsky's obituary had described Mayakovsky as the greatest
poet of Soviet Russia, a latter-day futurist and 'not only the singer but
also the victim of the epoch of transformation'. Trotsky charged 'the current [Soviet] ideology of "proletarian literature"' with 'a total lack of
understanding of the *rhythms and periods of time* necessary for cultural
maturation'. 'In recent years', he went on, 'it has become simply a system
of bureaucratic command over art and a way of impoverishing it'.[9] In

1943, portions of MacDiarmid's 'The Kind of Poetry I want' published in *Lucky Poet* called for:

> A Communist poetry that bases itself
> On the Resolution of the C. C. of the R. C. P.
> In spring 1925: 'The Party must vigorously oppose
> Thoughtless and contemptuous treatment
> Of the old cultural heritage
> As well as of the literary specialists....
> It must likewise combat the tendency
> Towards a purely hothouse proletarian literature.[10]

Mayakovsky might have responded to the latter sentiment, but he had been a signatory of the 1912 manifesto *A Slap in the Face of Public Taste* which declared: '*We* alone are the *face of our time*. The horn of time blows through us in the art of words. The past constricts.... Pushkin, Dostoievsky, Tolstoy, etc., etc., must be thrown overboard from the ship of Modernity'.[11] Mayakovsky's personal style shakes up normal syntax, coins verbal forms and uses inventive rhyming to break influential stylisations in traditional Russian verse. Translators agree that neither his linguistic innovations nor his ingenious rhyming are easily rendered into English, and Morgan's choice of Scots responds to this by encoding cultural conflicts closer to home – within Scotland and in relation to England; reconstructing Mayakovsky to focus on language as the springboard for a permissive politics of subjectivity and a poetics centred on heterodox cognitions. The opening sentence of Morgan's introduction to *Wi The Haill Voice* praises Mayakovsky's 'springy and accessible vitality' to ideas and feelings about poet and society that are 'as relevant now as they ever were'; and the poems devise a proletarian Scots for Mayakovsky to speak a vanishing mode of cultural production in a transforming society.[12] By experimenting with revolutionary modernism during the mid-1950s and later, before the term 'Modernism' had achieved critical currency, when Scots language use was a highly politicised medium, when English poetry was becoming associated with the post-imperial conservatism of Movement poetry, 'no more than a marginal pleasure, a deliberately and self-confessedly *provincial* utterance', and with Mayakovsky's expansiveness as alter ego, Morgan makes necessary space.[13] Mayakovsky's version of Whitman's 'Song of Myself', 'A Cloud in Trousers' (1914–15), whose original title 'The Thirteenth Apostle' was censored, sets a young man against the universe: 'shak[ing] the world with the might of my voice, / and walk[ing] – handsome, / twentytwoyearold'.[14] Morgan, slightly built, several years older and having difficulty shaping his account, might identify with Mayakovsky's:

> I feel
> my 'I'
> is much too small for me.
> Stubbornly a body pushed out of me[15]

Writing in a society extensively influenced by religious thought-worlds, Morgan could as readily warm to Mayakovsky's iconoclasm: 'Swindlers with wings, / huddle in heaven! / Ruffle your feathers in shuddering flight! / I'll rip you, reeking of incense, / wide open from here to Alaska':

> Hey, you!
> Heaven!
> Off with your hat!
> I am coming! [16]

Mayakovsky completed his epic 'Vladimir Ilyich Lenin' in the year the first Soviet leader died. Morgan's 'Harrowing Heaven, 1924' records that passing in its own way: 'Tell the archangels in their cells of divinity / They must levitate like larks, for LENIN is coming'. Lenin's preference for actual over mystical transformation shapes a free-thinking eloquence in which Morgan displaces the ritual eating of a god on to an expanding materialism of the present, where measurable discovery mobilises a transubstantiating lexis:

> A vision of bread without theophagy,
> A handful of salt in the hands of humanity,
> And wine that makes but is not blood:
> Naked of sacrament, stranger to effigy,
> Food for the Magellans of nature's infinity:
> Such is the substance of my word.

Setting Lenin as Jesus harrowing heaven rather than hell brings promise of lower-case and temporal deliverance: 'When world's-dreamer is heaven's undreamer / Saints in their chains may murmur "redeemer"' (CP p. 30).

As 'troubadour of the Russian Revolution' Mayakovsky kept up a punishing schedule, explaining to workers and their new soviets how a slogan is effectively drafted, or a propaganda song or factory notice designed for maximum effect.[17] And drawing posters: his entry for 1920 in 'I Myself' includes 'made about 3,000 posters and 6,000 titles'. An entry for 1917 reads: '*October.* To accept or not to accept? For me (as for the other Moscow Futurists) this question never arose. It is my revolution'.[18] They didn't come more revolutionary than the soviets in and around Moscow at the time, and Mayakovsky's energy is only partly suggested by his published output. The writer whose epic '150,000,000', composed during international armed intervention in Russia's civil war, uses cartoon giganticism to send a peasant Ivan wading across the Atlantic for hand-to-hand combat with Woodrow Wilson, also figures the Eiffel Tower as lover and invites her to Moscow. Russia's sharpest satirist was an educator who used sound and rhythm to encourage a workforce out of subjection by accommodating it to feelings of ability and capacity individually organised – a poetics of empowerment for people in need of focused perception:

> This struggle to organise movement, to organise sounds around oneself, discovering their own proper nature, their peculiarities, is one of the constants of the work of the poet: laying in rhythmic supplies. Rhythm is the fundamental force, the fundamental energy of verse. A poet must develop just this feeling for rhythm in himself ... (all the time you ask yourself: is this the word I want? Who must I read it to? Will it be understood in the right way?)[19]

Mayakovsky did not follow his friend Khlebnikov into the arcane aurality of invented word-sound; Morgan, who translates both poets, did. In *Virtual and Other Realities* (1997), 'Ule Elye Lel Li Onye Kon Si An' is the first line of 'Zaum', a poem that refers to sound patterning as 'virtual poetry' for which 'not what it cannot, please, but what it can / is your criterion for its board and keep':

> I tell you its very duty is to be strange,
> it hits you and you don't know half its range,
> it leaves you with a world to rearrange.[20]

Khlebnikov's technical exuberance inspired Mayakovsky, and Morgan owes something to them both. Like Khlebnikov, and sometimes including the Russian's ingenious unintelligibility, he reaches towards a total immersion in, and an intricate play with, the word-roots of his native tongue.[21] In Morgan's case that could be Anglo-Saxon, or the play of English in 'The Computer's Second Christmas Card' (CP p. 142); of Scots in 'Canedolia' (CP p. 156); of pure sound in 'The Loch Ness Monster's Song' (CP p. 248) or nonsense becoming sense in 'Shaker Shaken, (CP p. 352); or of whatever the mixture is in 'Spacepoem 1: from Laika to Gagarin' (CP p. 194); and as parable of failed colonialism in 'The First Men on Mercury' (CP p. 267). Approaching difference as

an event in itself and often pursuing the most absurd possibilities and
audacious imaginings, in entertaining and sometimes crazy ways rhythmic sound-words become sufficiently substantive to constitute an *other*,
as Kristeva puts it, to the normative linguistic and/or social contract.[22]
She warmed to Bakhtin for identifying as social and political protest the
ways in which carnivalesque discourse 'breaks through the laws of a language censored by grammar and semantics'; and as she reviews what she
calls 'some of the themes or mythemes' in Jakobson's readings of futurists, Kristeva's 'silent causality and ethics' seem extensible to Morgan's
reconstructions of Mayakovsky's rhythms that predicate a desiring subject.[23] Desiring subjects are also speaking subjects and in a discursive
move Morgan would surely endorse, Kristeva enlists Jakobson's admiration for Mayakovsky in her argument to redress a shrinkage in the operational effectiveness of a professional linguistics significantly organised
within terms of reference laid down by Saussure; where the speaking subject becomes an irrelevance. Because of this abolition, neither conventional linguistics nor the structuralisms it generated 'can think the
rhythm of Mayakovsky through to his suicide or Khlebnikov's glosso-
lalias to his disintegration – with the young Soviet state as backdrop'.[24]
For Jakobson and Kristeva (as more scintillatingly for Mayakovsky,
Khlebnikov and Morgan) poetry remains a practice of communicative
orality, its language a site where the dialectic of subjectivity is inscribed.
The 'roar of basic rhythm' in Mayakovsky's phrase analogises historical
continuities within which, he argued, individual words might ease
themselves towards freedom.[25] Against this, Mayakovsky's suicide sets a
ruthless counter-acknowledgement – that on the eve of Stalinism
and Fascism: 'a (any) society may be stabilised only if it excludes poetic
language'.[26] Taking arms against that oblivion through a resurgent 'I',
and spelling out the constituting struggle of language in society, *Wi the
Haill Voice* speaks a form of Scots as vigorous as any in the twentieth
century.

   Mayakovsky had been for some time a footfall in Morgan's
memory, from the schoolboy Morgan hearing of the Russian's suicide
to the combined impact on his undergraduate reading of Baudelaire
and Rimbaud in French, Eliot in English and Mayakovsky in Russian.
Mayakovsky was 'a revelation ... a bit like the kind of Baudelaire/
Rimbaud thing, I think, because they were happening about the same
time too, in my first two years as a student'. Out of this cocktail of
contraries – when 'a whole world, or series of worlds, of which I had
not had the remotest inkling, began to explode in my mind' (NNGM
p. 192) – comes Morgan's engagement with 'a modernism that yielded

nothing to the Right, that avoided propaganda and retained its sense
of poetic adventure':[27]

> With Mayakovsky what attracted me particularly there – again it
> was something I hadn't seen before but had perhaps subconsciously
> been looking for ... was the combination of a very strong, com-
> mitted political content and a very adventurous style. He was a rev-
> olutionary poet as regards his style, but whereas in Anglo-American
> poetry the revolution had tended to go with a right-wing view of
> politics in Eliot and Pound and people like that, this, for the first
> time for me anyway, was a poet who was committed to the left but
> being revolutionary in language. (NNGM pp. 138–9)

Pound and Eliot's reactionary modernism developed as counterpart to
European versions it coveted technically but denied ideologically.
Stimulated by Mayakovsky's combination of 'high lyricism and a deep
grandeur of socio-political statement', Morgan uses Scots to specify alternatives to Anglo-American twentieth-century forms then being produced and privileged in resistance to pressure for political change.
Meanwhile, as Morgan starts to translate Mayakovsky, English descendants of that modernism with Philip Larkin, in Donald Davie's words, as
'the effective laureate of England', exercised provincial skills. 'And for
Larkin indeed this seems to be one of the rules of the game: there is to
be no historical perspective, no measuring of present against past'.[28]
Mayakovsky 'struggling at [an] extraordinary moment in history' made
him for Morgan 'a kind of legendary heroic figure', and he develops
alternative perceptions of modernity as an incomplete project through
the medium of a poet who had the carpet pulled from underneath him
by the very politics he served, who shot himself under the pressure of
events yet whose work remains 'in a deeper sense, optimistic':

> I think that was one of the things which drew me to him, in the
> sense that I had read people like T. S. Eliot whom I admire but
> didn't really like from the point of view of what he was saying; the
> pessimism, the very deep-rooted pessimism of Eliot and also the
> sense of, whatever he was doing in being avant-garde as regards the
> form of poetry, he was extremely conservatively traditional in other
> parts of his mind. Whereas, in Russian Futurism, perhaps especially
> in Mayakovsky, there's a sense that the experiment in art – the mod-
> ernistic experiment in art – is to be linked up with the future, not
> with the past and I'm drawn more, in that sense, to European mod-
> ernism, especially Russian modernism, than to the modernism of
> Eliot and Pound. (NNGM p. 106)

Russian futurism came to speak of itself as the art of a working class and its revolution: in the 1950s, using a poet whose suicide was provoked in part at least by the onset of what he later called 'the most iron days of Soviet anti-creativeness', Morgan tests relationship and alterity.[29] Mayakovsky's fizzy and anarchic individuality did not survive, but in the jungle of literary politics that developed in Moscow in the late 1920s he gave as good as he got. He campaigned against Proletkult doctrinaires in the Russian Association of Proletarian Writers (RAPP) over the political necessity for a proletarian art to be comprehensible to a wide and untrained readership; and when Morgan went to see a 1982 reconstruction of the exhibition Mayakovsky had put together shortly before his suicide, he noted that it had been arranged to continue the argument: 'as for instance in one section where the self-wounding heading "Mayakovsky is not intelligible to the masses" is attached to cuttings of his poems taken from popular newspapers with a circulation in towns all over Russia'.[30] Morgan had already quoted Mayakovsky's retort: 'Art is not born mass art, it becomes mass art as the result of a sum of efforts'; and Mayakovsky associated himself with what he called 'the individual infiltration into production'. The Russian had clear ideas about cultural leadership: 'I always said there is poetry of a technical kind and poetry of the masses armed with a different kind of weapon, weapons of the working classes'.[31] Those emphases and discriminations were important to him: 'we retain the name futurism because this word is for many a flag under which they can gather together ... . When our consciousness is also the consciousness of the masses, we shall give up this term'.[32] He was admired by French surrealists – several of whom had come through Dadaism, gone on to join the Communist Party, soon to reject its dogmatism with varying degrees of mutual vituperation. Just how corrupted things were already becoming can be seen in the Party newspaper's response to Mayakovsky's suicide: since no true socialist could conceivably contemplate self-destruction, the Russian must have been a bourgeois reactionary all along. André Breton was disappointed at finding this 'miserable sort of argument in the pages of *L'Humanité*, the one place in France where Mayakovsky might have expected to find defenders'.[33]

Morgan translated most of the Mayakovsky poems during 1959-60, but the first of them, 'Mayakonferensky's Anectidote', which appeared some years earlier in *Lines Review* (1954), had been the first of Mayakovsky's poems (called something closer to 'Re Conferences'), to be published in a Soviet national daily.[34] An absurdist comedy arising from the impossibility of the poem's speaker gaining access to a Bolshevik representative because of the latter's 'conference-crazy' participation in a never-ending round of committees and assemblies, the lines caught Lenin's eye. He announced in crowd-warming vein to one such assembly in 1922:

> 'Yesterday, I happened to read in *Izvestia* a political poem by Mayakovsky. I am not an admirer of his poetical talent, although I admit I am not a competent judge. But I have not for a long time read anything on politics and administration with so much pleasure as I read this. In his poem he derides this meeting habit, and taunts the Communists with incessantly sitting at meetings. I am not sure about the poetry; but as for the politics, I vouch for their absolute correctness.[35]

Lenin was generally unsympathetic to experimental writing, though as his widow Krupskaya tells it he came to make an exception in Mayakovsky's case after an encounter with young art students during the famine years of the revolution. They had blurted out their preference for Mayakovsky over Pushkin: 'after that Ilyich … whenever he heard [the] name it reminded him of those young art students, full of life and joy, ready to die for the soviets, and who, not finding in the contemporary language words to express themselves, sought this expression in Mayakovsky's rather obscure verse'.[36]

We can begin to gauge something of Morgan's approach by comparing the poem he calls 'Ay, but can ye?' which opens *Wi The Haill Voice* and whose Russian original first appeared in a futurist collection in 1913, with a 'more or less literal rendition' called 'But Could You?':

> I colour-smeared the chart of every-day
> Splashing paints on it from a drinking glass,
> On a dish of fish-jelly I showed
> The slanted cheekbones of the ocean.
> On the scale of a tin fish
> I read the message of fresh lips.
> And you –
> Could you play a nocturne
> On a downspout flute? [37]

Here is Morgan:

> Wi a jaup the darg-day map's owre-pentit –
> I jibbled colour fae a tea-gless;
> ashets o jellyteen presentit

> to me the great sea's camshach cheek-bleds.
> A tin fish, ilka scale a mou –
> I've read the cries o a new warld through't.
> But you
> wi denty thrapple
> can ye wheeple
> nocturnes fae a rone-pipe flute?[38]

[jaup = splash; darg-day = work-day; owre-pentit = over-painted; jibbled = spilled; ashets = dishes; jellyteen = gelatin; camshach = crooked; cheek-bleds = cheek-bones; ilka = each; mou = mouth; denty thrapple = delicate throat; wheeple = whistle; rone-pipe = downspout for rainwater]

Vivid demotic delivers a shock of difference as answerable configuration for what Morgan calls Mayakovsky's 'mind-bending imagery and juxtaposition'.[39] By ventriloquising into vernacular Scots the 'ego' constructions that Trotsky called 'Mayakomorphism', a voice which assumes the agency of alterity as correlative for the strangeness and impact of Mayakovsky's poem also satisfies Kristeva's desire for a poetic language making free with 'heterogeneity ... and the ensuing fracture of a symbolic code which can no longer "hold" its (speaking) subjects'.[40] At a reading in Moscow years after its first composition, Mayakovsky defended his poem's intelligibility by maintaining that only illiteracy would prevent anyone from understanding it. Perhaps: but the term 'cubo-futurist' was first applied to a group of Russian artists including Mayakovsky, and the poem makes its case for the transformation of workaday actuality into city music by splashing colour over daily labour. In Morgan's version 'the great sea's camshach cheek-bleds' presented to its speaker by 'ashets o jellyteen,' hardly yields meaning directly, at least to non-Scots speakers. So we have an interesting conjunction. Mayakovsky was accused of not being intelligible to workers and peasants; and Morgan translates into a vernacular as generally strange to mid-century rural and industrial workers as to most educated speakers in Scotland.[41] As he designs a Scots resonance for Mayakovsky's political poetics, vernacular usage revitalises a particular modernist strain, and *Wi the Haill Voice* tunes a language experiment in recognition and variation. We can adapt a remark Morgan makes in another context to see him here and across the Mayakovsky poems using Scots to 'resurrect the creative imagination through a development of that linguistic *ostranenie* ("dislodgement", "alienation", "making strange") which the Russian formalist critics of the 1920s saw as central to poetic vigour' (*Essays* p. 73). Morgan is entirely at home with the concept of defamiliarisation as proposed by Russian formalists, 'and he has gone on to pursue his own vision of verbal estrangement in many evocative and disturbing poems.'[42] In a textual movement elegising the death of an original speaker, a form of Scots that will always be a minority usage comes to speak the early twentieth century's golden-mouthed bid for social transformation.

Whatever we may not initially understand in Morgan's sequence is delivered by a speaker whose non-bourgeois status is announced with dramatic clarity. Exploiting a translation gap between standard English and this deployment of Scots, one aspect of the 'proletarian' requirement that caused Mayakovsky some distress is satisfied at a stroke: Morgan's 'denty thrapple' speaks a persuasive idiom that flexes metaphor and transforms perception. However we construe the poem's interpellated 'you', a lively Scots register installs difference to satirise the repression of history Fredric Jameson reads in 'the perfected poetic apparatus' of early twentieth-century Anglo-American practice; where the political, 'no longer visible in the high modernist text, any more than in the everyday world of appearance of bourgeois life' becomes 'a genuine Unconscious'.[43] As *Wi the Haill Voice* shifts Russian futurism into sometimes-surreal Scottish verse, the political is foundational and recurrently satirical. In 1923 when a debate was launched about the practice of satire in then-prevailing Soviet conditions, Mayakovsky's pamphlet *May One Become a Satirist?* called on writers to 'arm themselves with satirical skills'.[44] In transcultural response, whether focusing on economic enslavement, colonial and judicial oppression and intolerance in 'Hymn to a Jeddart-Justicer' [= pre-judging judge]; or levelling a broadside against depoliticised indulgence in 'Mandment [= Order] No. 2 to the army o the arts', Morgan's vernacular displaces a battery of assumptions.

In the poem that amused Lenin, called by Morgan 'Mayakonferensky's Anectidote', technique catches Mayakovsky's 'sense of a newly liberated popular speech which must find its way into art'. Facing the challenge of whether Scots could match 'the mixture of racy colloquialism and verbal inventiveness in Mayakovsky's Russian', Morgan finds precedent in medieval Scots poetry's 'vein of fantastic satire'. 'But satire', he adds, 'has also its secret and unacknowledged wellsprings, deep in the imagination, and in comedy, and in language'.[45] Wellsprings articulate differently when a poem that conventionally translates as 'Listen!' but is here called 'Forcryinoutloud!' uses starlight to undermine claims for a non-human cosmic designer:

The starns light up – aa richt:
does that prove some loon hud to hae it?
Does it prove some loon mun want their starnhuid?
Does it prove some loon mun caa it pairls – thon strawn o spit?

[Starns = stars; loon = fellow; strawn = sprinkle]

The Makar who speaks Mayakovsky's 'Brooklyn Bridge' bodily transcends other-worldly belief systems:

Like a cracked sanct
           hirplin
                  to his kirk,
   to some stere,
          semple
             Culdee wig-
 wam o stane,
        here
            in the grey dwam and mirk
  o gloamin   /
        I set fit doucely on Brooklyn Brig. (WHV p. 59)

[cracked sanct = crazy saint; hirplin = limping; stere = austere;
Culdee = eighth century Scoto-Irish religious order; dwam = swoon;
doucely = softly]

Stepping his lines eye-catchingly towards rhyme as his speaker sets foot softly on the bridge, Morgan re-maps ancient Celtic faith on to Native American space in praise of modern engineering. Resistance to star-struck alienation is developed as a constructive materialism of the present:

                     I trig-
  ger my sicht
          fae the airy
                starn-thrangsters
  doon
      through aa New York
           by Brooklyn Brig. (WHV p. 60)

Across the shifting borders of a speaking 'I' in translated texts where the positioning of the reader is structurally involved in the shaping of voice, alternative constitutions of subjectivity become both theme and medium. Specific context for these textual effects are foregrounded in 'Fine', a Mayakovsky poem not translated by Morgan:

> This is time
> > humming taut
> > > as a telegraph wire,
> My heart
> > alone
> > > with the truth,
> > > > whole and sole.
> This happened –
> > with fighters,
> > > with the country entire,
> in the depth
> > of my own soul.[46]

Mayakovsky lived a revolution on the pulse and thought its large thoughts as personal experience. *Wi the Haill Voice* fuses public with personal resonance, and constructs its speaking citizen accordingly, finding epic measure for a lyric impulse and dramatising a political alternative to the depersonalised poetic ego deemed appropriate in Eliot's contemporary formulations.[47]

Kristeva developed Jakobson's emphasis on immortality signifiers in Mayakovsky's verse by relating linguistic invention to a recurrently imaged sun against which the poet must struggle. But the poem Morgan translates as 'Vladimir's Ferlie' [= marvel, surprise] posits a speaker who demands that the sun, instead of setting, should sit down and join him 'for a cup o tea' – and is initially terrified when the sun does just that:

> till
> bit by bit
> I forgot my fear,
> fund my tongue, cam oot o my shill:
> I talk to'm
> aboot this and that;
> near deaved, says I, wi my agitprop (WHV p. 35)

> [deaved = deafened]

Demythologising by domesticating Apollo empowers Vladimir and the two set up a mutually illuminating alliance:

> To shine ay and shine aawhere, shine
> to the end o endmaist days –
> that's aa!
> This is the sun's slogan and mine! (WHV p. 37)

Morgan extends the reasons Jakobson and Kristeva give for remembering Mayakovsky into a class-conscious poetry of republican address. 'To be a bourgeois', Mayakovsky wrote in a draft of his poem '150,000,000': 'does not mean to own capital or squander gold. It means to be the heel of a corpse on the throat of the young. It means a mouth stopped up with fat'. Correspondingly, to be proletarian 'doesn't mean to have a dirty face and work in a factory; it means to be in love with the future that's going to explode the filth of the cellars'.[48] Enter an astute if rough and ready witness wandering around 'Versailles', relishing the fate of Louis and his partner, and as suspicious of superabundant statuary as he is unsympathetic to the regime it buttressed and adorned:

> Apollos aawhere,
> 　　　　　　and thae
> 　　　　　　　　Venus-susies
> 　withoot their airms –
> 　　　　　　　loads o them tae. (WHV p. 50)

Blinking in astonishment, this speaker looks forward to a future shaped by 'the new virr [energy] // and breenge [rush] o the machine.' Confronted by a palatial display of wealth and confidence, what most compels his attention is a deeply scarred table-top:

> Thon wadge
> 　　　　　　was druv in
> 　　　　　　　　by the bayonets
> 　o the revolution,
> 　　　　　　　to a dance and a sang,
> 　when
> 　　　　the queen-quyne
> 　　　　　　　was steery-fyked alang
> 　by sansculottes
> 　　　　　　to the widdy steps. (WHV p. 51)

[quyne = hussy; steery-fyked = bustled; widdy = gallows]

Morgan's shifting persona resonates a grounded and self-aware Scot to make the question of who is addressing whom, when and in what context a lively concern of the writing. Always a Scots sound world, it focuses now Russia, now Scotland, emphasising now Mayakovsky's circumstance, now his Scots interlocutor; now addressing the early years of the Bolshevik revolution, now recuperating Scottish attitude. 'My verse', says the speaker of the title poem:

                    will tyauve
                              and brak through Grampian time
             and shaw itsel – rouch,
                                        wechty,
                                                sichty,
                                                        like
             some aqueduct
                        survivit
                                sin langsyne
             when Roman slave-chiels
                                      biggit brick and dyke. (WHV p. 83)

[tyauve = struggle; rouch, wechty, sichty = rough, weighty, impressive; biggit = built]

If Mayakovsky bridges into future possibility, Morgan connects a different past and present to the narrative of struggle; in which perspective Mayakovsky's two-line poem 'To the Bourgeoisie', originally written mid-revolution, comes to sound appropriate for industrial Clydeside in the years before, during and immediately following the First World War:

    Stick in, douce folk, – Pineaipple, fesant's breist:
    stuff till ye boke, for thon is your last feast. (WHV p. 28)

In 1920, when Vladimir was chatting with the sun, John Maclean, described by MacDiarmid as 'the greatest leader the working class of Scotland have yet had', was confident that 'we on the Clyde have a mighty mission to fulfil', and looked forward to making Glasgow 'a Petrograd, a revolutionary storm-centre second to none'.[49] For MacDiarmid, Maclean was the culmination of a line of Scottish radical and republican thinkers to whom 'all sorts of living currents in the movement today can be traced back'.[50] In the palimpsest of sound and sense, speaker and space that constitutes *Wi The Haill Voice*, Russian history surfaces in Scottish sound, and Scottish memory stirs politically aware rhythms. The claim that Glasgow is the UK city most readily associated with radical politics derives in turn from a specific history of political and industrial organisation.[51] The activism and militancy soon mythologised as a 'Red Clyde' arose from actual conflict over material conditions and the shaping of recorded event. Some of that history's spin-offs are tailor-made for legend. In 1918, having been elected (together with Lenin, Trotsky, Karl Liebknecht and others) an Honorary President of the First All Russian Congress of Soviets, Maclean was appointed by Lenin as the first Soviet consul for Scotland.[52] Since the Soviet state was not then

recognised by Westminster, there was propaganda value in this, though
Maclean seems to have taken his consular responsibilities seriously. But
Lenin mistook him for an Englishman, and when the Communist Party
of Great Britain was founded Maclean set up instead the Scottish
Workers' Party. Morgan's poem commemorating the fiftieth anniversary
of Maclean's death begins with its subject's uncompromising refusal: 'I
am not prepared to let Moscow dictate to Glasgow'; and celebrates
Maclean's failure at 'Party' by echoing a personal endorsement:

> Maclean was not naïve, but
> 'We are out
> for life and all that life can give us'
>
> was what he said, that's what he said. (CP p. 351)

Michael Lynch refers to the '*annus mirabilis*' of 1919, 'when the
Red Flag was brandished during a demonstration of more than 100,000
in [Glasgow's] George Square', when the Secretary of State for Scotland
spoke of 'a Bolshevist rising', and when Maclean reckoned that 'we in
this country are moving in the rapids of revolution'.[53] Translating those
rapids into contemporary rhythms of technical innovation, Morgan
quotes Mayakovsky writing in 1918 ('post-Revolution but only just'):
'Revolution in content is unthinkable without revolution in form', and
adds 'for content [Mayakovsky] was thinking about "socialism-anar-
chism," and for form "futurism"'. Citing Mayakovsky's 1926 essay 'How
Are Verses Made' – 'Innovation, innovation in materials and methods, is
obligatory for every poetical composition' – Morgan warms to a poet of
large ideas conversationally based, whose commitment to social change
he considers 'one of the prerequisites for modern poetry' (WHV p.
10).[54] *Wi The Haill Voice* re-inscribes an autonomous republic as political prospect and, with Maclean as intertext encoding a localised return
of the history that Jameson sees repressed in the conventions of Anglo-
American modernism, develops a narration conspicuously lacking in sec-
tarianism; with colloquial speech uttering political desire. He could
develop this partly because social conflict inscribes its own continuities.
Morgan was translating Mayakovsky in the 1950s and he included what
would become his title poem 'Wi the Haill Voice' in *Sovpoems* (1961).
In June 1971, a year before *Wi The Haill Voice* was published, the public
space of Glasgow Green, venue for many of the meetings that helped give
form and definition to a 'Red Clyde' earlier in the century, saw tens of
thousands gathered in protest at the closure of Upper Clyde
Shipbuilders. In August 1971, when an estimated quarter of all Scottish

workers downed tools in solidarity, the George Square over which the
red flag fluttered, and into which a panicked government in 1919 had
sent troops and tanks to quash a feared Bolshevik insurrection, was
crowded with 80,000 people demonstrating their support for what was
left of the Clyde shipyards' work force. That work force intensified its
opposition to redundancy by organising a 'work-in' that became one of
the most remarkable events in late twentieth-century industrial history.
With high levels of local support the work-in was sustained for several
months until, early in 1972, financial backing was secured for the shipyard's continued survival.[55] What looked then like a triumph for political solidarity and community determination proved a temporary stay of
execution. Morgan's handling of Mayakovsky's optimism might, then,
be read as a willed survival of options for people at risk.

   Optimism of the will is balanced by realism of the intelligence.
Disclosing a grimmer political awareness of industrial decline, 'Glasgow
Sonnets' (published in this same year of 1972) imports pugilistic
rhythms into high cultural form. The 'Laura' sonnets with which
Morgan opened his translations of *Fifty Renascence Love Poems* (1975)
were a way of acknowledging that what he calls Petrarch's 'deadly glaze
of the ideal, which he most laboured to effect' and which 'must stand
between us and him' was also 'a truly beautiful glaze, and of the first
quality' for poems that retained some basis in experience. Since the
inventor of this extensible instrument had been 'interested in the whole
of Europe', Morgan comments, 'it was fitting that his influence should
be widely felt, from Scotland to Cyprus, from Portugal to Hungary'.[56]
When he uses Petrarch to frame urban dereliction as lived, twentieth-
century experience, Morgan is already shattering the glaze. 'Glasgow
Sonnets' preserves the outline of a Renascence practice but strips out
its conventional furniture and designs instead Scottish interiors; mobilising percussive metre against dominant practice. No sustaining faith
or reinforcing astrology operate in a city where 'glittering stars press
/ between the silent chimney-cowls and cram / the higher spaces with
their SOS':[57]

> A mean wind wanders through the backcourt trash.
> Hackles on puddles rise, old mattresses
> puff briefly and subside. Play-fortresses
> of brick and bric-a-brac spill out some ash. (CP p. 289)

In a prospect of loss rather than blissful bower, and decidedly non-
Mediterranean weather, the 'last mistresses' here occupy rooms in a tower
block 'condemned to stand, not crash', where the only roses visible are

'mould grow[ing] from ceiling to wall'. It is important to Morgan generally that poetics is about production (*poiesis*) and that like labour, language
is symbolically mediated interaction.[58] The technique 'Glasgow Sonnets'
secures by playing difference into traditional rhythm and scansion enacts
a claim of right to the occupation and altered operation of an established
mode of production of meaning.

Pulling no punches, the second sonnet opens with 'a shilpit
[starved] dog fucks grimly by the close' [entrance to a tenement build-
ing], and the hermetic symbols of urban street-gang graffiti undermine
a ground of Christian beseeching: 'No deliverer ever rose / from these
stone tombs to get the hell they made / unmade. The same weans
never make the grade'. Out in the social exclusion zones where the
only resurrecting spirit is whisky's delusory protection against a freezing winter, the urban demotic of sonnet three's tenement shark further shatters social solidarity in a miserable and predatory exploitation
of homeless people. The fourth poem introduces knowable community: a self-identifying 'we' in line seven responds to an idiomatic and
unspecified 'you' in the first, addressed by a speaker who echoes the
Communist Manifesto to cajole a continuing present: 'you have nothing to lose but your chains, / dear seventies'. Re-mapping 1930s
Depression on to 1970s Glasgow by setting the time-travelling speaker
of MacDiarmid's 'Glasgow 1960' (first published in 1935) against the
1848 Manifesto, Morgan revisits an understandably incredulous voyager into the then future of Glasgow's Ibrox Park football stadium
where record crowds are gathered not for soccer but a 'debate on "la
loi de l'effort converti"'; followed by a 'Turkish Poet's Abstruse New
Song'.[59] It is to this projected 'feast of reason and flow of soul' that
Morgan's poem responds: 'We never got an abstruse song that charmed
the raging beast'. As time frames are stretched, prospective difference
collapses into chronic sameness, and a closing trope implicates the creative destruction endemic to capitalist investment programmes.
Punning on a contrast between 'greeting' as welcome and as Scots
idiom for shedding tears, the poem shapes its elegy:

> Dalmarnock, Maryhill,
> Blackhill and Govan, better sticks and stanes
> should break your banes, for poets' words are ill
> to hurt ye. On the wrecker's ball the rains
> of greeting cities drop and drink their fill. (CP p. 290)

Extending the 'long unfinished plot / of heating frozen hands' in
this fourth poem, the fulcrum sonnet five invokes the figure whose fate

was recorded by Mayakovsky's Scots interlocutor in Morgan's version of 'Versailles'. Recalling the callousness of Marie Antoinette's imputed response to imminently pre-revolutionary Parisian crowds hungry for bread, the poem prefers her honesty over the deceptions attempted on Clyde-side shipyard workers before, during and after the occupation by workers fearing shut-down in 1972, when Morgan's sequence appeared. A first line complements her utterance by turning English idiom north of the border:

> 'Let them eat cake' made no bones about it.
> But we say let them eat the hope deferred
> and that will sicken them. We have preferred
> silent slipways to the riveters' wit.
> And don't deny it – that's the ugly bit. (CP p. 290)

Silent majorities are condemned in a poem involving the process of de-industrialisation that between 1950 and 1972 saw membership of the Clyde Shipbuilders' Association fall from twenty-nine to thirteen.[60] Large crowds assembled in August 1971 chanting the slogan: 'Launch UCS [Upper Clyde Shipbuilders] – sink Heath' [then Conservative Prime Minister], give topical urgency to the sonnet's contention that power brokerage might sooner have made the necessary policy adjustments and resource allocation had its dispensers lived and worked in the immediate aftermath of their priorities. In the 'bucking' tankers linguistically appropriate to stormy waters it is hard not to hear a suppressed expletive, as octet moves into sestet. At the start of the occupation James Reid, who would soon achieve international recognition as the representative of a willing work force, announced to press, radio and television journalists:

> We are taking over the yards because we refuse to accept that face-less men can make these decisions … . We want to work … . There will be no hooliganism, there will be no vandalism, there will be no bevvying [drinking]. It is our responsibility to conduct ourselves with dignity and maturity.[61]

In the conduct of Morgan's sonnet a sceptical awareness turns ultimate employee subordination to profit against the disregard of peripheries by centralised economic power. A cavalier erasure in the poem's last line mounts a chilling and reificatory enactment of Walter Benjamin's remark about Janus-faced documents of civilisation encoding simultaneously a barbaric progress:[62]

'There'll be no bevvying' said Reid
at the work-in. But all the dignity you muster
can only give you back a mouth to feed
and rent to pay if what you lose in bluster
is no more than win patience with 'I need'
while distant blackboards use you as their duster. (CP p. 290)

By which point the sequence has shed contemporary light on a city and
some of its inhabitants.

Since the interpretative community generally interpellated in Morgan's
poetry is nothing if not plural and permissive, it is to the point that in
'Glasgow Sonnets' it is also economically contextualised. A North Sea oil
bonanza that surrealistically skews Scotland by draining the Clyde in poem
six produces human waste on a local scale to the benefit of transnational
power: 'the images are ageless but the thing / is now'. This sixth sonnet is
mired in the dilemma identified as MacDiarmid's in the fourth; measuring a
widening gap between urban modernity and yesterday's styles: 'elegists can't
hang themselves on fled- / from trees or poison a recycled cup'. Knowing
the material inefficacy of his craft, this speaker sees hope postponed:

Without my images the men
ration their cigarettes, their children cling
to broken toys, their women wonder when
the doors will bang on laughter and a wing
over the firth be simply joy again. (CP p. 291)

Inner-city gentrification is represented in poem seven: 'Prop up's the
motto. Splint the dying age'; and Morgan registers both gains and losses
in the difficult narration of the eighth, where motorway access to the city
centre creates forms of excitement. Rhythmic energy sides with 'the bull-
dozer's bite' and, in Robert Crawford's words, with 'the energy of metamorphosis which will make it new in ways that might "displease the
watchers from the grave" yet still delight Charles Rennie Mackintosh'.[63]
A closing reference to Japanese *ukiyo-e* town and city prints reinforces
the poem's dedication to urban contexts; and in sonnet nine the city
reacts to modernisation with a music for its own continuance: 'dig[ging]
its pits to a shauchling refrain'. Balancing human agency against cycles
of prosperity and decline, this penultimate sonnet weighs an evident law
of uneven development:

The west
could still be laid with no one's tears like dust
and barricaded windows be the best

to see from till the shops, the ships, the trust
return like thunder. Give the Clyde the rest.
Man and the sea make cities as they must. (CP p. 292)

In the closing poem's connection of housing provision with life opportunities, a schoolboy on the thirtieth floor of a tower block, reading *King Lear* and looking out of the window, remembers Edgar's invention of a landscape to forestall his father's suicide. The allusion implicates Lear's belated attention to 'houseless poverty' (III, iv, 26), and may connect with sonnet nine's representation of the city as drunken Scot enduring 'squalls of pain' and 'hoist[ing] a bleary fist at nothing then at everything, you never know'. 'Stalled lifts generating high-rise blues' can still activate a schoolboy's imaginings: against which stand cramped, one-room family accommodation ('single-ends') that typified slum tenements now displaced by improved (if 'vertiginous') living space. But 'Stalled lives never budge' wherever they are, and the final sonnet measures a 'they' against an 'us' in terms of contrasting horizons. In a difficult negotiation, modern schemes are set against sonnet two's tenement children who generationally 'never make the grade' and are left to 'linger in the single-ends that use / their spirit to the bone':

and when they trudge
from closemouth to laundrette their steady shoes
carry a world that weighs us like a judge. (CP p. 292)

Notes

1 Julia Kristeva, 'The System and the Speaking Subject', in Toril Moi (ed.), *The Kristeva Reader*, Oxford, 1986, pp. 28–9.
2 Hendry, 'The Apocalyptic Element', p. 63.
3 Julia Kristeva, 'The Ethics of Linguistics', in *Desire in Language: A Semiotic Approach to Literature and Art*, ed. L. S. Roudiez, trans. T. Gora, A. Jardine and L. Roudiez, Oxford, 1984, p. 23; *La Révolution du langage poétique: l'avant-garde à la fin du XIXe siècle: Lautréamont et Mallarmé*, Paris, 1974.
4 Kristeva, 'The System and the Speaking Subject', pp. 25–6, 28.
5 Kristeva, 'The Ethics of Linguistics', p. 24.
6 Nicholson, *Poem, Purpose and Place*, p. 63.
7 Kristeva, 'The System and the Speaking Subject', p. 29.
8 Roman Jakobson, *Selected Writings*, The Hague, 1962–82, vol. 3, p. 50; vol. 5, p. 415; 'On a Generation that Squandered its Poets', in E. J. Brown (ed.), *Major Soviet Writers: Essays in Criticism*, Oxford, 1973, p. 13.
9 Leon Trotsky, 'The Suicide of Vladimir Mayakovsky' [1930], in P. N. Siegel (ed.), *On Literature and Art*, New York, 1970, pp. 175–6, 177.
10 MacDiarmid, *Complete Poems*, vol. 1, p. 615.

11 E. and C. R. Proffer (eds), *The Ardis Anthology of Russian Futurism*, Michigan, 1980, p. 189.
12 Edwin Morgan, *Wi The Haill Voice: 25 Poems by Vladimir Mayakovsky*, Oxford, 1972 (hereafter WHV), p. 7, included in *Collected Translations*, Manchester, 1996, hereafter CT, pp. 105–54.
13 Morgan confirmed that his first translations of Mayakovsky were completed in 1953. Donald Davie, *The Poet in the Imaginary Museum*, ed. Barry Alpert, Manchester, 1977, p. 47.
14 Vladimir Mayakovsky, *The Bedbug and Selected Poetry*, ed. P. Blake, trans. M. Hayward and G. Reavey, London, 1961, p. 61.
15 Mayakovsky, *The Bedbug*, p. 71
16 *Ibid.*, p. 109
17 Herbert Marshall, *Mayakovsky*, London, 1965, p. 18.
18 Herbert Marshall (ed.), *Mayakovsky and his Poetry*, London, 1942, p. 27.
19 Vladimir Mayakovsky, *How Are Verses Made*, trans. G. M. Hyde, London, 1970, p. 38.
20 Morgan, *Virtual and Other Realities*, p. 87.
21 Victor Erlich, *Modernism and Revolution: Russian Literature in Transition*, Massachusetts, 1994, p. 40.
22 Kristeva, 'The Ethics of Linguistics', p. 30.
23 Kristeva, 'Word, Dialogue, and Novel', in *Desire in Language*, p. 65.
24 Kristeva, 'The System and the Speaking Subject', p. 24
25 Mayakovsky, *How Are Verses Made*, p. 36.
26 Kristeva, 'The Ethics of Linguistics', pp. 31, 34.
27 Robyn Marsack, 'Edwin Morgan and Contemporary Poetry', in Crawford and Whyte (eds), *About Edwin Morgan*, p. 33.
28 Donald Davie, *Thomas Hardy and English Poetry*, London, 1973, p. 65.
29 Bengt Jangfeldt, *Majakovskij and Futurism, 1917–1921*, Stockholm, 1976, p. 93; Edwin Morgan, 'Diabolical Experiment', *Times Literary Supplement*, 7 December 1967, p. 1181.
30 Edwin Morgan, 'Some Classical Ephemera', *Times Literary Supplement*, 5 February 1982, p. 133.
31 Vladimir Mayakovsky, 'The Workers and Peasants Don't Understand You', in *Selected Works in Three Volumes*, ed. Alexander Ushakov, trans. Dorian Rottenberg, Moscow, 1985, vol. 3, p. 215, cited in WHV, p. 9; Mayakovsky, 'Twenty Years', in Marshall, *Mayakovsky and his Poetry*, p. 132.
32 Mayakovsky, 'Speech at the Dispute "Futurism Today"', in *Selected Works*, p. 175.
33 Cited in Helena Lewis, *Dada Turns Red: The Politics of Surrealism*, Edinburgh, 1990, pp. 90–1.
34 '21 poems by Vladimir Mayakovsky (1894–1930) translated from Russian into Scots', National Library of Scotland, MS 27493.
35 Cited by Alexander Ushakov, 'Vladimir Mayakovsky, Poet of a New World' in VM, *Selected Works*, vol. 1, p. 273, n. 66.
36 Herbert Marshall, *Mayakovsky and his Poetry*, p. 3, n. 1.
37 Edward J. Brown, 'Mayakovsky's Futurist Period', in George Gibian and H. W. Tjalsma (eds), *Russian Modernism: Culture and the Avant-Garde, 1900–1930*, Ithaca, 1976, p. 119.

38 Morgan, WHV, p. 19.
39 Ibid., p. 10.
40 Kristeva, 'The System and the Speaking Subject', p. 30.
41 See Vladimir Mayakovsky, 'The Workers and Peasants Don't Understand You' [1928], in *Selected Works*, vol. 3, pp. 214–19.
42 Roderick Watson, 'Internationalising Scottish Poetry', in Cairns Craig (ed.), *The History of Scottish Literature: vol. 4, The Twentieth Century*, Aberdeen, 1987, p. 324.
43 Fredric Jameson, *The Political Unconscious: Narrative as a Socially Symbolic Act*, London, 1989, p. 280.
44 Cited in Mayakovsky: *Selected Works*, vol. 1, p. 22.
45 Edwin Morgan, *Scottish Satirical Verse: An Anthology*, Manchester, 1980, p. xix.
46 Mayakovsky: *Selected Works*, vol. 2, p. 209.
47 T. S. Eliot, 'Tradition and the Individual Talent', in *The Sacred Wood: Essays on Poetry and Criticism* [1920], London, 1960, pp. 47–59.
48 Cited by Jakobson, 'On a Generation that Squandered its Poets', p. 13.
49 Hugh MacDiarmid, *The Company I've Kept: Essays in Autobiography*, London, 1966, p. 125; John Foster, 'Red Clyde, Red Scotland', in Ian Donnachie and Christopher Whatley (eds), *The Manufacture of Scottish History*, Edinburgh, 1992, p. 115.
50 MacDiarmid, *The Company I've Kept*, pp. 125, 189.
51 Sean Damer, *Glasgow: Going for a Song*, London, 1990, pp. 107–39.
52 Nan Milton, *John Maclean*, Bristol, 1973, p. 155.
53 Lynch, *Scotland, A New History*, p. 427; Milton, *John Maclean*, p. 220.
54 Korney Chukovsky, 'Akhmatova and Mayakovsky', in Brown (ed.), *Major Soviet Writers*, p. 50.
55 Jack McGill, *Crisis on the Clyde: The Story of the Upper Clyde Shipbuilders*, London, 1973, p. 7.
56 Edwin Morgan, 'Fifty Renascence Love Poems', in CT, pp. 161–2.
57 Edwin Morgan, 'Glasgow Sonnets', in CP p. 289.
58 Marc Shell, *The Economy of Literature*, Baltimore, 1993, p. 9.
59 MacDiarmid, *Complete Poems*, vol. 2, p. 1039.
60 John Foster and Charles Woolfson, *The Politics of the UCS Work-in*, London, 1986, pp. 21–69; Frank Herron, *Labour Market in Crisis: Redundancy at Upper Clyde Shipbuilders*, London, 1975, p. 13.
61 McGill, *Crisis on the Clyde*, p. 102.
62 Walter Benjamin, *Illuminations*, ed. Hannah Arendt, trans. Harry Zohn, New York, 1969, p. 256.
63 Robert Crawford, '"To Change/ The Unchangeable" – The Whole Morgan', in Crawford and Whyte (eds), *About Edwin Morgan*, p. 18.

4 A cognitive mapping

Here is another paradox; at times when states are anxious to establish their national identity and to prove the virtues of their language, they have very often in history indulged in widespread
translation from other cultures; yet in the process of doing this they
subtly alter their own language, joining it in many unforeseen ways
to a greater continent of almost undefined and non-specific human
expression. (Edwin Morgan, NNGM p. 234)

'The Scottish air', Morgan said in a reprise of its 1960s poetry, 'tends to
be thick with advice and assertion, much of it hectoring, strident, uncon-
sidered. Vehemence, and various sorts of fierceness, we have; but reason
and thought and justice, and the stillness out of which a personality can
grow to its full stretch without spikiness and shoulder-chips – these are
harder to come by, and much to be desired'.[1] While he was projecting a
form of Scots as Mayakovsky's activist medium, Morgan was simultaneously exploring the stillnesses out of which a personality might grow in
structures of feeling developed by Eugenio Montale partly as a way of
surviving the enforced silences of Mussolini's state. Through Montale,
and also Salvatore Quasimodo, who developed a socially committed
poetics out of private resonance, Morgan fashions a role as transla-
tor/historian of specific strands in a European evolution.[2] He had doors
to open: the Hermetic tradition drew his attention and Montale makes
private places out of public spaces to preserve an enigmatic integrity in
the face of a repressive and hostile politics. Morgan explores an agnostic
mysticism:

> Little I knew but what I saw in a rune,
> A vision of the divine Unconcern:
> There by the statue in the drowsy sun
> At noon, and the cloud, and the heaven-climbing hawk.[3]

In more stringent vein, 'shiverings / Of a life that runs like water /
Through the fingers' (CT p. 10) call up a bleak transcendence:

> Come back north wind, tomorrow, come colder,
> Break up the ancient power of the sandstone,
> Scatter about the books of hours in garrets,
> And let all be a still lens, a dominion, a prison
> Of the undespairing sense! (CT p. 21)

Morgan's reading of Montale's non-cooperation and withdrawnness as 'the sort of commitment he endorsed in the days of Fascism' (CT p. 5), produces phrases like 'a gloom charges the air / Over a flickering world' ('Sarcophagi III', CT p. 7); 'I feel the garment / Of my immobility laid on me today like a torment' ('Sirocco', CT p. 10); 'one single moan and roar / Rises from lacerated lives' ('Tramontana', CT p. 11); 'Evil's victorious … The wheel never stays' ('Eastbourne', CT p. 19). Morgan has related Montale's verse to 'the anguish of Italy under Fascism' and acknowledges that although 'he doesn't write about Fascism very much … it is there and I think this gives a tenseness and an edge to a lot of his writing that is not immediately obvious'. When he adds 'I reacted to Montale very strongly and I am sure I learned from him' (NNGM, p. 72), he opens up the attraction of translated alterity: 'to be as various / As vast, yet fixed in place' (CT p. 9).

Poems from Eugenio Montale appeared in 1959.[4] During the late fifties Morgan first encountered in Italian translation the left-wing Hungarian poetry of Attila József: 'and made my own translations from that, out of sheer excitement and delight at coming across a poetry of such deep urban pathos and concern – it was almost like finding a kind of poetry I had been half-searching for (in Baudelaire, in "B.V." Thomson, in early Eliot) but never truly experienced till then' (NNGM p. 115). If Morgan had discovered in Baudelaire what Marshall Berman called 'modernism in the streets',[5] József helped fertilise an intention to redress a political and ideological imbalance by 'open[ing] the door slightly on a world which political (and in part linguistic) considerations have kept too remote from Western writers and readers', when Morgan put together a collection of translations he called *Sovpoems*. The translations were made between February 1959 and January 1961, when a political climate of public fear and international intimidation included an American Secretary of State declaring (in May 1958) in Berlin that any Soviet attack on the city would be regarded as an attack on the West. Two months later Britain and America publicly agreed to shared weapons development, which was a way of saying England could purchase selected nuclear hardware; in September a Russian leader announced that any attack on China would be regarded as an attack

on the Soviet Union; China was refused admission to the United
Nations and the USSR resumed nuclear testing. In May 1959 Russia
offered to act as co-guarantor of Japanese neutrality in return for the
removal of American bases; England and Canada made agreements with
the United States for defence cooperation. In the following month the
USA agreed to provide Greece with nuclear information and to supply
ballistic missiles; and Cuba expropriated American-owned sugar-mills
and plantations. In March 1960 Soviet delegates walked out of disar-
mament talks; in May an American spy plane was shot down over the
Ural mountains; another one in July over the Barents Sea; and America
published its proposals to equip West Germany with Polaris missiles.
In October the United States imposed a trade embargo on Cuba; a
year later the Berlin Wall went up. As 'The Flowers of Scotland' would
make clear, Scottish territory had its share of the 'cancer of monstrous
installations of a foreign power' (CP p. 203), and a poem that became
one of the *Sonnets From Scotland* (1984) grew out of the perception
that the area just north and west of Glasgow contained 'the largest
concentration of nuclear weapons and installations in these islands, so
that in the event of a major conflict the Glasgow conurbation, with
about two and a half million people, would be a prime target' (NNGM
p. 220):

> Lucky seemed those at the heart of the blast
> who left no flesh or ash or blood or bone,
> only a shadow on dead Glasgow's stone,
> when the black angel had gestured and passed.
> Rhu was a demon's pit, Faslane a grave;
> the shattered basking sharks that thrashed Loch Fyne
> were their killer's tocsin. (CP p. 452)

So the voices in *Sovpoems'* alternative commonwealth have much to
contend with, not least a withering knowledge that 'socialist-bloc' aspirations to economic and social justice had been and were being system-
atically and repeatedly suborned. When Morgan was translating
Mayakovsky's last major work, he could not help but be aware that
beyond Mayakovsky's grounding identification with revolution there
was another 'indissoluble combination of motifs' in his work, involving
revolution and the destruction of the poet.[6] 'At the Top of My Voice'
(1930) concedes that 'Agitprop / sticks / in my teeth too' and recognises the effect of 'setting my heel / on the throat / of my own song'
for the sake of political mobilisation. Morgan updates some of
Mayakovsky's references:

I'm fair stawed
          agitprop,
                    ye ken,
and naethin
          wid be nicer –
                    or mair profitable –
nor I sud screeve ye True Romances,
                              hen. (WHV pp. 81–2)

In the obituary he wrote for his friend in 1922, Mayakovsky commented 'I know living people who are not [Khlebnikov's] equal, perhaps, but who are in for a similar fate'.[7] His own was cruel enough. In 1935 Stalin pronounced Mayakovsky 'the best and most talented poet of our Soviet epoch' and by adding 'indifference to his memory and to his work is a crime', consigned them both to the pedagogy of a brain-numbing orthodoxy. In 1959, when Morgan was bringing Mayakovsky back to vernacular life, Boris Pasternak recalled that from the mid 1930s Mayakovsky began to be 'introduced forcibly, like potatoes under Catherine the Great. This was his second death. He had no hand in it'.[8] Knowing that, and concerned to remember a fragmenting idea, *Sovpoems* proposes a republic of voices as inclusive as it is reconstructive.

Pasternak's sympathies inform an extract from 'Leitenant Schmidt' here translated as 'Sevastopol 1905', to mark the year when a general strike in Russia led to the formation of the first soviet ('council') composed of delegates in St Petersburg. The Czar was forced to issue an 'October Manifesto' granting legislative powers for the Duma (parliament) called into being in August: also conceded was a wider franchise for its election as well as a measure of guaranteed civil liberties. Pasternak's blizzard that 'shatters all earthly connections' speaks encouragement 'to the howling land':

> 'The unborn watch. Don't flinch,
> Not one inch back! Swear this!'
> 'We swear! Not an inch!' (CT p. 32)

Mayakovsky had called on the Gosplan (State Planning Commission, responsible for drawing up the national economic programme) 'to sweat / in debate, / assigning me / goals a year ahead'.[9] Pasternak's 'To a Friend' – 'I too am measured by the five year plan. / I fall and rise as that plan draws its breath' – uses personal address to justify expropriation as redistribution: 'Only a monster would not prefer the delight / A million win, if an hundred idle are sloughed' (CT p. 33). The pending extinction of these hopes gives an edge to the voices Morgan resurrects; but for the elective affinities of *Sovpoems'* intertextual republic, Leonid Martynov's declaration makes an appropriate epigraph:

> Poems are not composed in a cringing position,
> Nor is it possible to write under any man's supervision,
> Contempt, it's said, can act as your ignition:
> No!
> Poetry's dictated only by clarity of vision. (CT p. 51)

Morgan mobilises Brecht against 'Those Who Deprive The Table of Meat' and who 'Teach men to be content with their lot' (CT p. 43); and in support when 'A Worker Reads, and Asks These Questions'. Also remembered is Brecht's 'Conversations Rowing':

> It is evening. Two folding-boats
> Glide past, with two young men in them,
> Naked. Rowing side by side
> They talk. Talking
> They row side by side. (CT p. 45)

Making space for Marina Tsvetayeva's semi-surreal refusals of capitalism's predatory freedoms ('I say no – who'd go free / With wolves in a market-place?') and of any tyranny:

> I say no – I'll not howl
> With the sharks of the plains.
> I say no – I'll not sail
> Down streams of human spines (CT p. 36),

Sovpoems celebrates the heterodox and spontaneous. 'We didna need,' says the speaker of 'Wi the Haill Voice', 'the readin to see / whase camp to fecht in, and which wey to choose. / It wisna Hegel lernt us dialectic' (CT p. 40). Standing 'At the Partisans' Graves' and looking back to immediately post-revolutionary Russia, Yevtushenko's speaker makes a similar point as he returns Communist symbolism to its supposed owners:

> Marx, I am sure, was a closed book to these souls,
> who reckoned God still walked about the earth,
> but went and fought and brought the bourgeois down,
> and gained the name of marxists which they own...
> Destroyed in the first years of their new world
> They lie here, peasants of Siberia,
> with crosses on their breast, but none overhead –
> above them the red star of the proletariat. (CT pp. 53–4)

Pablo Neruda's 'The Heights of Macchu Picchu', pre-Columbian city of
the Incas in the Peruvian Andes, became a centrepiece of his *Universal
Song* from where, says Morgan, 'surveying the vast mountain-top ruins
of an almost forgotten empire, [Neruda] asks his great question':

> Stone on stone: but where was man?
> Air on air: but where was man?
> Time on time: but where was man?
> Were you too the shattered relic
> of unfinished man, that empty eagle
> that the streets of today, the footprints,
> the leaves of lifeless autumns, watch
> crushing the soul right into its grave? (CT p. 48)

As part of its display of alternatives to Ezra Pound's imperial conspectus,
Neruda's *Universal Song* celebrates love in a cold climate:

> in my country they throw miners in jail
> and judges hang on general's lips.
> And yet I love to the very roots
> this freezing meagre land of mine. (CT p. 50)

Sovpoems reads an East–West split in the different uses made of technical innovations by on the one hand a largely American-influenced
anglophone poetry and on the other a Russo-European modernism, and
Morgan describes a preferred landscape for his commonwealth:

Symbolism, futurism, imagism, and surrealism, to say nothing of free
verse, were available to all; but I would venture to claim that what
Blok did with symbolism, what Mayakovsky did with futurism, what
Neruda did with surrealism, holds a lesson for us which we don't
learn from Yeats, Stevens, Pound or Eliot. The lesson – without
trying to spell it out – is related to the fact that literary movements
should serve the ends of life as well as the ends of art. And this, with
all respect to Pound, means something more than merely 'maintaining the cleanliness of the tools.' Clean tools can kill as well as make.
If Western writers will not take this from a Mayakovsky, will they at
least take it from a Pasternak who said: 'Much of the work of the
twenties which was but stylistic experimentation has ceased to exist.
The most extraordinary discoveries are made when the artist is over-
whelmed by what he has to say. Then he uses the old language in his
urgency and the old language is transformed from within.'[10]

Coolly retrieving Wordsworth's locally democratic emphasis – 'a poet must
be seen to be a man, and the man must be seen to speak' – Morgan reads

together 'With The Whole Voice' and Eliot's 'Ash Wednesday' to ask why, of these 1930s productions by writers who had both experienced the modernist upheaval, Mayakovsky's poem still 'crackles with a fierce life', while Eliot's has 'a dying charm'. Quoting as typically western John Peale Bishop's view that whereas 'Present evils are for men of action, / Art has the irremediable ones', Morgan reminds us that for 'the non-bourgeois part of the world ... there is no greater aesthetic heresy'. Turning to an English provenance and reading Larkin's 'Church Going' against Yevtushenko's 'At the Partisans' Graves', he finds in the first 'a fear of statement and commitment, a form of studied self-deprecation, a desperate disbelief in the power of poetry to speak out on man and society': not a receptive temper for the articulations that *Sovpoems* valorises. There remains, Morgan suggested, something to be learned from Neruda's and Pasternak's 'poetry with a sense of history'; a poetry that is 'suffused – ironic lesson to the West – with an awareness of the individual's place in history'.

A parallel though seemingly different reinforcement was coming from across the Atlantic. Since it constituted what Morgan termed 'a new amalgam of liberation towards the end of the 1950s', it is clear that American Beat poetry signalled a series of ways forward:

> In Ginsberg it was equally a freedom of spirit and of form. I am thinking of 'Howl' in particular ... the long swinging lines, the extraordinary juxtapositions of imagery, the sexual explicitness – all these things appealed.... The Beats came as I was struggling out of a rather bleak and tight phase of my own poetry, but whether I liked them because I had begun to loosen up and liberate myself, or began to loosen up and liberate myself because I liked them, I shall never know.... From the Beats I got into Williams, and Creeley, and Bukowski. I learned, really learned for the first time, however much I may have thought I believed it intellectually, that you can write poetry about anything. You really can! The world, history, society, everything in it, pleads to become a voice, voices. More and more of 'the world' came into my poetry from that time. By 'that time' I mean that from 1956 to 1961 I was throbbing like a chrysalis but not quite out. In 1962 a new phase began. (NNGM p. 114)

It is clear that San Francisco about to launch into the 1960s was not Glasgow in the middle and late fifties, and as evident that Morgan's voice needed tailoring to meaningful context; a process in which 1962 evidently marks something of a watershed. In that year he published his 'Beatnik in the Kailyard' essay, issued his 'Poet and Public' challenge to MacDiarmid, recommended the San Francisco poets in 'The Beat

Vigilantes' and let 'the world' into such poems as 'The Death of Marilyn Monroe' (CP p. 146), 'Je ne regrette rien: in memory of Edith Piaf', and through the specifying Glaswegian associations of 'Linoleum Chocolate', 'Good Friday' and 'The Starlings in George Square' (CP pp. 163–6). By the time he wrote 'The Second Life' in May 1963 (not published until 1965), redesigning the cliché about life beginning at forty as what would become the title poem of his 1968 collection, Morgan was associating a resurgent vitality with both celebratory desire and urban renewal. In 1963 he met his partner John Scott to whom almost twenty years later he would dedicate *Poems of Thirty Years*. As the exuberance of 'The Second Life' charts a resurrecting spirit in the city of his birth – 'a great place and its people are not renewed lightly' – it intimates a coming out for a love learning to speak its name:

> Many things are unspoken
> in the life a man, and with a place
> there is an unspoken love also
> in undercurrents, drifting, waiting its time.

Now, 'The old seeds are awake. // Slip out of darkness, it is time' (CP p. 181). Three months later 'Glasgow Green' (written in August 1963, not published until 1967) sought to reclaim the night and blow away both Presbyterian propriety and social complacency by focusing on a homosexual rape in a city park. Its adopted terms of cinematic representation – 'cut the scene' – transform realist perception by subverting domestic routine:

> This is not the delicate nightmare
> you carry to the point of fear
> and wake from, it is life, the sweat
> is real, the wrestling under a bush
> is real, the dirty starless river
> is the real Clyde, with a dishrag dawn
> it rinses the horrors of the night
> but cannot make them clean,
> though washing blows
> > where the women watch
> by day,
> > and children run,
> > > on Glasgow Green. (CP p. 168)

In December 1963 'The Unspoken' speaks its absence; and in May 1964 'From a City Balcony' utters a 'silent love'. In the same year Morgan

publishes 'Strawberries' (CP pp. 184–5) and in October writes 'One
Cigarette' (CP p. 186). A string of lyrics over the next few years –
'Absence' (January 1965), followed by 'The Picnic', 'Without It', 'When
You Go' and 'The Witness' (written January, March, September and
November 1966 respectively) – shows a second life demonstrably in the
making.

We can trace a technical path for this making by jumping forward to
Morgan's 1972 essay on concrete poetry and reading it back into work
of the mid and late 1960s. To explain its contention that as a conscious
movement in the art of language concrete poetry can be dated from the
mid-1950s, 'Into the Constellation' outlines a history that takes us back
again but differently to the European crucible where modernist techniques were forged by writers and artists busily making traditions of the
new. One of them, the painter Kazimir Malevich, whose 1916 booklet
From Cubism and Futurism to Suprematism Morgan also cites (and who
is reported to have described Mayakovsky's poem 'From Street to Street'
as a successful experiment in 'versified cubism'), is here quoted for his
concretist declaration that: 'Economy [is] to be the new fifth dimension
which evaluates and defines the modernity of the arts and creative works.
All the creative systems of engineering, machinery, and construction
come under its control' (*Essays* p. 23).[11] Recovering classical dimensions
of *oikonomia* as a principle of ordering, distribution and dispensation in
literary construction, Malevich's discursive economy constituted a radically permissive republic of letters. Khlebnikov's experimentalism,
described by Roman Jakobson as a 'poetry of the bared medium', has
been translated by Morgan; as have poems by Eugen Gomringer.[12] In
the essay that is Morgan's springboard, Gomringer saw concrete principles as a way of returning poetry to an organic (i.e. instrumental) function, and thus 'restated the position of poet in society … . The
Constellation is an invitation' (*Essays* p. 25). Morgan quotes (p. 33) lines
by Mallarmé 'from whom Gomringer derived the word and idea', and so
suggests Mallarmé as a precursor of concrete poetics:

A CONSTELLATION

cold from neglect and disuse
yet not so much
that it does not count
on some empty and superior plane
the next collision
sidereally
of a final reckoning in the making

The lines may also have triggered a response in Walter Benjamin, for whom ideas came to represent 'timeless constellations' because they 'are not represented in themselves, but solely and exclusively in an arrangement of concrete elements in the concept; as the configuration of these elements'.[13] In collaboration with Benjamin, Theodor Adorno developed the notion of constellation as a configuration in which various concepts, ideas or other materials take shape, so that 'cognition of the object in its constellation is cognition of the process stored in the object'.[14] As part of a determined resistance to traditional notions of totality Adorno would argue that 'Constellation is not system': 'Everything does not become resolved, everything does not come out even; rather, one moment sheds light on the other, and the figures that the individual moments form together are specific signs and a legible script'.[15] 'Into the Constellation' endorses the idea that the tighter the construction the better the poem, lays out an inclusive schema for the developing moment of concrete, and establishes some of Morgan's idiosyncrasies by recognising that it is 'easier to apply a constructivist aesthetics to sculpture and painting (and architecture and industrial design) than to an art working in language'. Because 'one cannot brush aside moral, social, and psychological values so long as the medium in question is linguistic', it is to be expected that 'expressionisms, individualisms, and romanticisms move in and out of concrete poetry and have to be reckoned with'. It follows for Morgan that wit, satire and direct social comment' are 'not to be denied to the concrete poet' (*Essays* pp. 23–4). Although his work in this area testifies to a generally high-spirited acceptance of the invitation, the title poem for his first concrete collection, elegising victims of the Sharpeville massacre of demonstrators against South Africa's pass laws, is an activist intervention in the form.[16] Composing its threnody around the first letters of Sharpeville's two syllables, and alternating compound words with monosyllabic lines, 'Starryveldt' turns its concluding Latin tag 'woe to the conquered' into both lament for the African dead and threat to continuing white rule. Punning on 'southvenus' as invented variant of 'parvenus,' the poem names the then South African Prime Minister and architect of a strict apartheid policy and, with the word-line 'scattervoortrekker' urges victory over descendants of the original Dutch emigrants into the Transvaal by implicating Boer history in ruling South African brutality (CP pp. 157–8).

Resonating out from its bared medium, but in good constructivist fashion, the solidity on the page of the column structure of 'Archives' (CP p. 140) becomes a self-evident effect of its own typographical engineering; its lexical units either regressively disintegrating as the eye falls down the print-column or condensing into outlined shape as perception rises from incoherent beginnings. Either way, a semantic gesture, building a block of signification out of discrete and uncertain elements, satirises genealogies as built on sand while evolutionary structures persist. If 'Archives' develops a perception that such work is thing-like, immobilised in visual space and subject to backward and forward scanning, 'Construction for I. K. Brunel' energises its visually static delineation of a print-bridge by punning on metaphor's etymology in transfer, bridging, carrying over. 'Canedolia, an off-concrete Scotch fantasia', has fun with place-sounds and pastimes; or Morgan's concrete sets symmetry against permutation with 'The Computer's First Christmas Card' (CP p. 177). Morgan was convinced of a relationship between some aspects of European concrete poetry and the development of computer technology: 'The element of combination or re-combination of elements is quite strong in concrete poetry and it began to be written at the very time when computers began to be used.'[17] It is also quite possible that he shared Jonathan Raban's sense of anti-authoritarian aesthetic potential in the 'impersonal randomisation of the computer'.[18] 'Into the Constellation', at any rate, makes clear Morgan's hopes for the transcultural communicative possibilities of concrete writing, even to the extent of forming 'the nucleus of the future universal common language' by tapping 'a Chomskian deep universal structure' (*Essays* p. 27). Playing with notions of language as a system of signs that expresses ideas, and challenging assumptions about both the nature of linguistic signs and our understanding of structural relationship between them, 'Spacepoem 1: from Laika to Gagarin' pushes syllable-repetition over the edge of sense to connect technology with Dadaist subversion – from 'dada' to 'dagaga' (CP p. 194).

Varying the concretist display of print mechanics, Morgan's textual mosaics focus single words or parts of words as contributors to systems of pattern and design disconnected from their usual or accepted semantic field. In this dispensation 'even individual isolated letters, and especially the spaces (or absences) between them, become an eloquent expressive force in their own right ... in order to liberate phrases, words, morphemes, and ultimately phonemes from their conventional semantic sequences'.[19] Customarily transgressing the relative structural purity concrete called for, Morgan links disruptive specificity with narrative, percolating image into concrete to connect visual effect with semantic transmission. Though it is not immediately obvious from the scattered leaping around the page of their grapheme embodiments, we do eventually see 'The Fleas' making love (CP p. 553). Alternatively, the shark-fin slicing out 'Warning Poem' (CP p. 554) relates visual shape to a self-fulfilling prophecy resolving its top into its bottom line.

Morgan teases typeface graphics into signification such that his concrete sequence *The Horseman's Word* (1970) presents a cross-cultural miniature of his practice, from the phonic shift that elicits place from repetition by transforming 'a man' into 'Amman' and 'a mane' into 'immane' (of great size or strength) in the opening poem 'Arabian Nights Magic Horse', to the syllabic variations chronicling a blue roan's life and death in 'Elegy'. 'Clydesdale' patterns its plosives and obstruents to image field workhorses and forge unlikely links between Sicily and a village outside Edinburgh. The graphemes in 'Newmarket' combine idiomatically to encourage a winner past the post; and 'Centaur' – 'a kind of dramatic monologue ... it's "Thoughts of a Centaur" if you like' (NNGM p. 61) – reaches towards linear poetry as it swings a plea for metamorphosis from equine to human on a colon substituted for a comma. Whereas 'Eohippus', oldest known genus of the horse family, traces its emergent nominalisation from a soup of unpromising phonemes, 'Kelpie', a Lowland Scots water-spirit usually appearing as a horse, bears surprised but naturalistically onomatopoeic witness to an appearance of splashing, heaving animal from surrounding loch; plays variations on a distinctively Scottish fricative, and pants at its own exertions:

> och och
> laich loch
>   hoch heich
>   moch smeuch
>   sauch souch
>   rouch pech
>   teuch skreich
>   each oidhche
>   stech eneuch (CP p. 211)

[laich = low-lying; hoch = hindquarters; heich = high; moch = misty atmosphere; smeuch = energy; sauch = tough; souch = sound of rushing water; rouch = untamed; pech = panting; teuch = vigorous; skreich = screech; oidhche = (Gaelic) night; stech = gorged; eneuch = enough]

Connecting with Scottish fable and sound-world, the radically stripped syntax of 'Hrimfaxi', Old Norse for 'frost mane', coaxes entry into Scandinavian myth via single-word imaging of its legendary horse of the night from whose bit fell the 'rime-drops' of dew. Then, given the

way its Mexican lexis enriches American topography, 'Zane's' probably
refers to Zane Grey (1875–1939), author of numerous 'western' novels
and whose *Riders of the Purple Sage* (1912) sold over two million copies.
'Hortobágy' occupies its space by naming a Hungarian region known for
horse-raising and composing itself out of 'ló', Hungarian for horse,
strung diagonally across the page like a cropped mane. In his catalogue
note on concrete for a 'Between Poetry and Painting' exhibition at the
ICA in 1965, Morgan referred to tensions between the visual impact of
shapes on a page and his 'strong sense of solidarity with words as parts
of a semantically charged flux':

> Insofar as I isolate or distort them I do this in obedience to imag-
> inative commands which come through the medium of language
> and are not disruptive of it. This means that each of my poems has
> a 'point' and is not just an object of contemplation, though it is also
> that. I like to hear the semantic mainsheets whip and crack but not
> snap…. Abstract painting can often satisfy, but 'abstract poetry' can
> only exist in inverted commas. In poetry you get the oyster as well
> as the pearl, and the pursuit of purity is self-defeating. The best con-
> crete poems, as it seems to me, acknowledge this fact inversely; their
> anatomy may be rigid and exoskeletal, but there is something living
> and provocative inside. (NNGM pp. 256–7)

Concrete was only one aspect of Morgan's exoskeletal probing into
living interiors. Four *Emergent Poems* written in 1966 trace a transformational semiotics in sentences eclectically gathered from Brecht, Burns,
Dante and the *Communist Manifesto*. Perhaps he was remembering, with
the Burns-derived 'Dialeck Piece', that during the 'plastic Scots' controversy of 1946 MacDiarmid had allowed that contemporary writing 'may,
like Burns, use an occasional phrase even many Scots do not understand
without recourse to a dictionary – e.g., "a daimen icker in a thrave"'.[20]
In Morgan's restructuring Scots phrase multiplies English idiom, rather
as 'workers of the world unite' proliferates terms of struggle and resistance and ends by restating its main theme. A year later *Newspoems* cut
from newspapers, pasted on to sheets of paper and photographed, dissolve context to surprise meanings which articulate everyday possibility.
'Most people', Morgan commented:

> have probably had the experience of scanning a newspaper page
> quickly and taking a message from it quite different from the
> intended one. I began looking deliberately for such hidden mes-
> sages and picking out those that had some sort of arresting quality,
> preferably with the visual or typographical element itself a part of

the 'point', though this was not always possible. What results is a series of 'inventions' both in the old sense of 'things found' and in the more usual sense of 'things devised'. (CP p. 118)

Between pictorial stasis and syntactic linkage, Morgan makes space to develop concrete principles into forms of narrative. Lines 'To Ian Hamilton Finlay' catch 'the pleasure / of made things', where 'the construction holds / like a net; or it / unfolds in waves / a certain measure, / of affection' (CP pp. 154–5); and even 'Summer Haiku' tells a story:

P o o l.
P e o p l
e   p l o p!
C o o l.

As do expanding and diminishing font sizes for the two letters (and common Magyar phoneme) that represent 'Siesta of a Hungarian Snake' (CP p. 174). Other work from the sixties, including *Gnomes* (1968), shows Morgan developing semantic mobility by playing with assumed separations. 'Visual Soundpoem' (CP p. 130) requires oral response to release the text's printed sign into acoustic space: 'Sick Man' also needs orality as signifying medium. Playing on ear-eye and oral-textual relationships to emphasise sound as dynamic production inside living organisms, these poems weigh a shift from orality to literacy and print and then, with various computer-based poems, to electronic media. 'Message Clear', 'supposed to be a monologue spoken by Christ on the cross' (NNGM p. 59), reconstructs a gospel triangulation of word, beginning and godhead (John, I, 1) by going forth and multiplying spatialised forms for one of Jesus' most remembered utterances:

i am   r   ife
            i n
        s   ion and
i   d   i e

Or, in a transformation involving Egyptian gods of art, science and the sun, yet closer to Hindu reincarnation than either non-Judaic middle-eastern or biblically derived theocracies:

i am th   o   th
i am   r   a

The end effect is a poem that seems to assemble itself as it goes along, and a text that calls for active decipherment and reconstruction by the reader: 'It is as if we are witnessing some interrupted or static-ridden communication, only gradually patching itself together. Perhaps the sender is having difficulty; perhaps the receiver is faulty; perhaps the atmospheric conditions are unpropitious'.[21]

Variable conditions for semantic transmission are topic and theme when two poems written on the same October day in 1973 alter the position and perspective of a speaker who remains situated within the field of the given utterance, and play classificatory closure into comic deconstruction and differential dissemination. 'Levi-Strauss at the Lie-Detector' (CP p. 354) opens with a logic-breaking reversal of dictionary procedure to have fun with Levi-Strauss's determination that 'any classification is superior to chaos':

> an   is   p rior to   a

Dissolving procedural dogma generates plural permission:

> any class   cat   is superior to   o;

or:

> class fic tion is s p   or t

so that in its newly formatted context a concluding reconstruction of the reasonable-seeming logic in the original quote seems as reasonable: 'any class fiction is superior   chaos'. Intertextual relations enact the notion that while we make our sentences we do not make the contexts in which we make our sentences: circumstance and syntax are both shaping and shaped.

On the lookout for random or unpredictable space in systems governed by determining laws, Morgan places 'Wittgenstein on Egdon Heath' (CP p. 355), as concentrating a sense of period and place as any in English fiction. Opening up the first proposition of Wittgenstein's *Tractatus* complicates some of his grounding assumptions: that a sentence that says something (i.e. a proposition) must be 'a picture of reality'; that 'we picture facts to ourselves'; that such a picture 'is a model of reality'; that 'a picture is a fact'; that 'the fact that the elements of a picture are related to one another in a determinate way represents that things are related to one another in the same way'; and in consequence of that determinate relationship, 'logical pictures can depict the world'.[22] 'Wittgenstein on Egdon Heath' runs rings around its quoted assumption, pluralising it then pluralising that plurality by personalising the categorical act to undermine its status as universal imperative. When Morgan's poem produces its variant 'the wor d is everything that is the case', Wittgenstein's celebrated propositions that 'the limits of my language are the limits of my world', and that because 'logic pervades the world, the limits of the world are also its limits' (p. 56), are implicated in a turn from logical-seeming certitude to inevitable circularity. And Hardy's imagined heath still localises a determining place: 'the wo ld is everything that is the case'.

After the events of May 1968, Morgan noted, French practitioners either rejected concrete poetry: 'or they have tended to employ collage, photomontage, fragments of newsprint ... in such a way as to fall back on concrete's secondary sources in Dada and Futurism, and hence to become involved in more expressionistic data than constructivist-minded critics would allow' (*Essays* p. 25). Morgan's *Newspoems* (1965–71), and his *Instamatic Poems* (1972) fragment and reassemble newsprint and photographs in seeming accord with Jean-François Bory's conviction that 'the next artists will not write in a pre-concrete manner, just as it is impossible to write today as though surrealism never existed' (*Essays* p. 27). If concrete poetry in its early forms took inspiration from Dada and surrealism, surrealism had already taken over Dada's radical rejection of bourgeois norms. Morgan retained 'a very strong interest' in surrealist painting (NNGM p. 94), and comfortably associates with developments in art that Herbert Read thought constituted 'not so much a revolution, which implies a turning over, even a turning back, but rather a break-up, a devolution, some would say a dissolution [towards] the birth of a new body, or bodies, distinct in character and incapable of fusion with the old body'; except that Morgan might be temperamentally unwilling to discount random fusions between old and new.[23] He plays with the semiotic aspect of poetry – 'the poem as sign, first of all' (NNGM p. 62) – by undermining rule-bound systems of discursive closure. Together with the visual signature of his concrete work, the sign-writing element in *Newspoems* relates to this form of attention; as do the errors built into 'Interferences' (CP pp. 253–7). 'Often,' he has suggested, 'the best parts of a poem are those lightning discoveries that fly into the mind, unplanned, from sources that may seem remote from the ongoing discourse of the poem. Doubtless everything in the universe has a cause, but in the heat of composition the causes, the concatenations, are like a chain that melts *into* being instead of out of it. And there are few things stranger than that. If we lose sight of the strangeness, we lose sight of poetry' (NNGM p. 222). 'Seven Headlines' satirises an interface between writing and print through serial variation on Rimbaud's theme (from *Un saison en enfer*) – 'il faut être absolument moderne':

```
              n   o
   f   et           t    er
   f          o           r
         absolu     t    e
            m       odern
            men              (CP p. 176)
```

Two 'Computer's Christmas Card' poems (CP pp. 142, 177) generate
their comic printouts from technological error; and 'Unscrambling the
Waves at Goonhilly' (CP p. 191), commemorating the first transatlantic
telecommunications signal, sends its transmitting satellite through an
ocean of marine life before identifying it by name. 'The Computer's First
Code Poem' (CP p. 277) locks its information delivery away from immediate access and thus serves as metaphor for poem as coded message
(NNGM p. 259).

Registering the reality of Scotland keeps Morgan attentive to the
fact that despite an increasingly globalised production and distribution
of image and information in the exercise and service of powerfully
homogenising motives: 'language riots, whether in Canada, Belgium,
or India, continue to testify that the global village is in no mood yet
to plug itself into a universal circuit' (*Essays* p. 153). But the universal
circuit continues to develop, and a 'craving for extraordinary incident
which the rapid communication of intelligence hourly gratifies' that
bothered Wordsworth on the threshold of the first industrial revolution has become an instantaneous delivery of graphic immediacy: 'actuality pictures' filmed, photographed or computer-generated anywhere
on the planet (or beyond) are routinely attached to headline encapsu-
lations and/or sound-bites tailored to momentary transmission and
adaptable to local requirements. Wordsworth worried about 'a multitude of causes unknown to former times which are now acting with a
combined force to blunt the discriminating powers of the mind', reduc-
ing them to 'a state of almost savage torpor'.[24] He should be living at
this hour. Or perhaps in 1967 when Guy Debord on France's anar-
chist wing published *The Society of the Spectacle* to raise an international
profile for a group of artists and intellectuals descended from Dada and
surrealism who had founded the journal *Situationiste internationale* ten
years earlier. Debord substituted for *Capital*'s opening assertion that
'the wealth of societies in which the capitalist mode of production pre-
vails appears as an immense collection of Commodities' his preferred
amendment: 'The whole life of those societies in which modern
conditions of production prevail presents itself as an immense

accumulation of *spectacles*.[25] Instead of the *Communist Manifesto*'s 'all that is solid melts into air', Debord suggests 'all that was once directly lived has become mere representation'.[26]

Alert to these contexts, and combining an 'interest in something that is very far from ordinary experience' with 'an equally strong interest in what actually has happened' (NNGM p. 33), Morgan develops a 'documentary myth' in *Instamatic Poems*, begun in March 1971 and written over the next two years. *Instamatic Poems* tailors economy of presentation to a camera-eye rendition of things reported in the press: 'in this grainy slanting picture'; 'the camera catches'; 'at the edge of the picture'; 'a low-angle shot along a parapet'; 'the flash reveals'.[27] Many of the cuttings Morgan gathered for this purpose had to be thrown away, because he 'couldn't get them into one camera shot' (NNGM p. 75). As a way of contextualising the *Instamatic* tactic of making news reports 'stand out in living art' (IP p. 12), it helps to read the last poem first. 'Heaven September 1971 AD' brings an increasingly obsolescent Gutenberg galaxy into focus by figuring God 'lying on a cloud / watching the teleprinter', delighted at the carnage in creation documented in the preceding poems, and reading a 'new version of the Lord's Prayer' that has:

> come through from earth
> And fills the large white screen.
> HOLY BE YOUR NAME YOUR
> KINGDOM COME.

While 'his son in blue / smiles tightly, shrugs politely' and 'the little holy ghost / chokes on his hubble-bubble', a dragonfly covers the screen's AMEN so that the poem withholds endorsement. There is much not to be endorsed in a sequence whose serial violence includes 'two dozen Picasso engravings' destroyed in a 'hyperfascist' raid by 'the Guerrillas of Christ the King' in 'Madrid November 1971' (IP p. 16).

The opening freeze-frame of 'Glasgow 5 March 1971' operates in grim parody of actuality pictures by representing criminally violent effect on unsuspecting victims who register 'surprise, shock, / and the beginning of pain' at being pushed through a shop window by single-minded perpetrators whose 'faces show no expression' as they loot the premises: 'in the background two drivers / keep their eyes on the road'. Adjusted tolerances for violent event in the second of two poems dated 'Glasgow 5 March 1971' – 'One feature / of this picture of the Central Police Court / is the striking absence of consternation' (IP p. 8) – are as

evident in a 'youth who sharpens his knife / nonchalant on the tomb-
stone' after stabbing in the back 'a woman kneeling at her mother's
grave' (IP p. 28). On the same March day that a Glaswegian magistrate
ducks to avoid a knife thrown in court, and '[a] Pakistani plunges his
knife / into the throat of a seventeen-year-old boy / on the M1', snow
falls on the Riviera and a bus burns in Belfast's Falls Road:

> Light flickers on the vizors of a frieze
> Of charging soldiers, and on their rifles.
> On a roof behind the burning bus
> One sniper kneels in silhouette.
> Your eye travels in rage from the classic frieze
> To the classic silhouette. (IP p. 9)

Use of a human corpse to test the safety of car air bags in 'Germany
December 1970' produces the initial illogic of 'A dead man [...] driving
an old Mercedes' (IP p. 11); which compounds as uneasily with the
absolute poverty of 'Bangaon India July 1971' (IP p. 28) as that poverty
does with the brutal stripping of an Indian prince in 'London March
1971'. The family horror of 'Campobasso Italy Undated Reported
March 1971', contrasting with an eerily emptied crime scene in 'Glasgow
November 1971', insinuates a global theatre for murderous intent (IP
pp. 32–3, 38). And theatre is operative term for a sequence whose present tense dramatises a compulsive voyeurism stimulated by reported
event; against which stands 'an old poet' witnessing the gondola cortège
of Igor Stravinsky's funeral in 'Venice April 1971', and who 'without
expression / watches the boat move out / from his shore' (IP p. 17). In
the same month, at Fort Benning in Georgia, the 'chubby but not ami-
able' American soldier responsible on the ground for the massacre of
some hundreds of Vietnamese men, women and children in the village
of My Lai three years earlier signs a publishing contract for one hundred
thousand dollars.

As far as formal economy is concerned, Morgan's selection and placing of detail is itself 'a kind of direction to the reader', with the aim being
to 'present just a picture of something that happened without comment'
(NNGM p. 73):

> I suppose they are a kind of documentary poetry.... It wouldn't be
> absolutely strictly documentary because I do use a certain amount
> of imagination, but it's documentary in a sense that all the poems
> relate to something that did happen at a certain place and time and
> ... they could be checked.... I began this by taking a number of

events that happened on the same day, and ... gradually building
up a kind of picture of a certain period. So far [August 1971] it's a
period of ... a few months but it probably will become a lot longer
than that. (NNGM pp. 27–8)

There are moments of comic relief: Rudolf Nureyev 'hurriedly stuff-
ing a rabbit's foot / into his jockstrap, for that / virility effect. Or perhaps it is a trick of the light' (IP p. 14); a snapshot taken inside a pillar-box
of four snails stoned on envelope glue (IP p. 23); a Hungarian hippy
aiming 'the weapon of her neat bare bottom / at the arriving police' (IP
p. 30). But optimism elsewhere in Morgan's work is generally compen-
sated for here. The thesis that all that was once directly lived has become
mere representation is satirised in a scene from the opening night of
Eduardo Paolozzi's crashed car exhibition where conspicuous consumption generates a waste-maker's art, and the poem produces a self-
enclosed circularity for image-making processes:

> And in the front left corner
> a noted art critic nailed down
> by a topless girl is slowly being
> interviewed.
> The interview is being viewed
> in the back right corner slowly
> on live closed-circuit TV.
> The art of dying
> is in the cars. (IP p. 20)

A 'crowded image of the dedication' at the Kennedy Centre for the
Performing Arts ('Washington September 1971') constitutes the theatre
of state as state theatre in a public order of conspicuous display, where a
drama of opposites sets opulence against racial exclusion, and in a figure
of the person who shot an alleged presidential assassin in front of television cameras, blurs riches into blood: 'Only outside is the black capital.
/ Splashes of red are only rubies, Ruby'. 'London November 1971'
opens different doors on to Moslems who have taken vows of poverty
and austerity. The rhythmically discrete dancing of dervishes at an Islamic
festival intimates a notional structure for the sequence: 'Pattern and no
pattern, / alone and in union / without unison'. If 'Mougins Provence
September 1971' (IP p. 15) foregrounds image-construction by coding
the poem as palimpsest – 'A picture of a picture of a picture. / Sort out
the splendid lights'; 'London November 1971' suggests a returning concern with suspended orality. Since the effect aimed at, Morgan has

commented, is 'a kind of snapshot', it follows that 'there are certain things you cannot do, you cannot talk about sound effects or people talking' (NNGM p. 27): yet here, as the dervishes dance, 'the drum measures / flutes and strings', and Quaker hosting Moslem enacts a separation overcome.

Notes

1 Morgan, *Crossing the Border*, p. 177.
2 Morgan, CT, pp. 3–24, 212–21.
3 Morgan, CT p. 8.
4 Edwin Morgan, *Poems from Eugenio Montale*, Reading, 1959.
5 Marshall Berman, *All That is Solid Melts Into Air: The Experience of Modernity*, London, 1983, pp. 131–71.
6 Jakobson, 'On a Generation that Squandered its Poets', p. 13.
7 Mayakovsky, *Selected Works*, vol. 3, p. 171.
8 Boris Pasternak, *An Essay in Autobiography* [1959], cited in Mayakovsky: *The Bedbug*, p. 50.
9 Mayakovsky, *The Bedbug*, p. 187.
10 Edwin Morgan, 'Introduction' to *Sovpoems* [1961]; reprinted in CT, pp. 27–31.
11 Malevich cited in Brown, 'Mayakovsky's Futurist Period', p. 117.
12 Brown, 'Mayakovsky's Futurist Period', p. 110; Morgan, CT, pp. 335–7, 423–7, 293–300.
13 Walter Benjamin, *The Origin of German Tragic Drama* [1963], trans. John Osborne, London 1998, p. 34.
14 Theodor Adorno, *Negative Dialectics* [1966], trans. E. B. Ashton, New York, 1973, p. 163.
15 Theodor Adorno, *Hegel: Three Studies* [1963], trans. S. W. Nicholsen, Massachusetts, 1993, p. 109.
16 Edwin Morgan, *Starryveldt*, Switzerland, 1965. In March 1960 the Pan-African Congress invited 20,000 supporters to court arrest by demonstrating without their passbooks near a police station in the black township of Sharpeville. When the crowd threw stones at police and their armoured cars the police fired on them with submachine guns, killing some 69 Africans and wounding 186 others with 48 women and children among the victims. A state of emergency was declared across South Africa under which 1,700 people were detained; the place and event coming to symbolise African resistance to white rule and a focus for international criticism of the apartheid regime.
17 Fazzini, 'Edwin Morgan: Two Interviews', p. 48.
18 Jonathan Raban, *The Society of the Poem*, London, 1971, p. 92.
19 Roderick Watson, 'Edwin Morgan: Messages and Transformations', in G. Day and B. Docherty (eds), *British Poetry from the 1950s to the 1990s: Politics and Art*, London, 1997, pp. 175, 177.
20 *Glasgow Herald*, 13 November 1946. The Burns phrase translates as 'one ear of corn in 24 sheaves'; thus, a very meagre supply of corn.
21 Watson, 'Messages and Transformations', p. 175.

22 Ludwig Wittgenstein, *Tractatus Logico-Philosophicus* [1921], trans. D. F. Pears and B. F. McGuinness, London, 1974, pp. 5, 8, 9, 10, 19.

23 Herbert Read, *Art Now* [1993], London, 1948, pp. 57–8.

24 William Wordsworth, 'Preface' to *Lyrical Ballads* (1800), in *The Prose Works*, Oxford, 1974, vol. 1, p. 128.

25 Karl Marx, *Capital*, vol. 1, Harmondsworth, 1976, p. 125.

26 Guy Debord, *The Society of the Spectacle* [1967], trans. D. Nicholson-Smith, New York, 1994, p. 12.

27 Edwin Morgan, *Instamatic Poems*, London, 1972, pp. 9, 10, 17, 18, 19, 20. Hereafter IP.

5 Out, in space

We would therefore propose the following revised formulation:
that history is *not* a text, not a narrative, master or otherwise, but
that, as an absent cause, it is inaccessible to us except in textual
form, and that our approach to it and to the Real itself necessarily
passes through its prior textualisation, its narrativisation in the
political unconscious. (Fredric Jameson)[1]

> greater power's
> in stories than in story.
> (Edwin Morgan)[2]

Personal as well as social and space fantasy themes in *From Glasgow to
Saturn* (1973) include singular representations of sexuality. Erotic displacement in 'The Apple's Song' (CP pp. 237–8) reaches out to find its
reader, and the lyric poise of 'Drift' assumes but does not specify gendered
response (CP p. 238). Like the lonely rememberer looking for comfort in
momentary contact 'After the Party' (CP pp. 239–40), a sense in 'At the
Television Set' (CP pp. 240), of 'moving out through stars / and forms
that never let us back' in quest of a stable relationship is not explicitly gendered. Morgan typically offers a spectrum of possibility: the note of regret
in 'Estranged' (CP pp. 241–2) intimates a personal haunting, and homosexual context implied in a treatment of promiscuity 'From the North'
(CP pp. 240–1) is radically specified in the unsettling memory of danger
missed as well as run in 'Christmas Eve' (CP pp. 283–4). Morgan's development of expressive instrumentality includes translation of *Fifty
Renascence Love-Poems* (1975) from the European canon to explore ideas
of the self as product of performance, and of gender as a central context in
which individuals are fashioned.[3] In the following year he called a selection of translations *Rites of Passage*, and there is room for considering his
work with Renaissance love poetry under the same rubric. Necessarily
aware that subjects are produced in and through the discursive practices
of sexuality, and unable to accept areas of his domestic culture's restric-
tions on self-representation, Morgan's versions of subject-formation in
lyrics of love and intimacy also include translating (in 1978) August Graf

von Platen-Hallemunde (1796–1835), whose 'more or less unhappy homosexual affairs', a note suggests, 'are often dealt with in his poetry in a surprisingly lightly coded way' (CT p. 308). By which time *The New Divan* (1977) had largely dispensed with coding for sexual encounters during military service in the Middle East. The range of Morgan's attention socialises by opening out homoerotic experience, and he is not attracted by the idea of writing for an exclusive readership:

> I've always tended to feel that in writing poetry you're just writing for human beings, you're writing for everybody, although there maybe are some poems which you know are going to be read differently by people who are in a minority.... I'd probably just say I'm a writer, I write poetry, it's meant for anybody who takes it up to get what he or she can out of it. I'm not trying to say I'm writing for a gay audience, although I know that in so far as it's realised then that audience will be there, will react differently.... You may have a gay subject matter, and that will appeal to people who are inclined in that direction, and it may cause offence or problems with a different kind of audience. But a great many things seem to me to have a general appeal, even though they have a special appeal as well. I think that would be the kind of thing that I would probably prefer. (NNGM pp. 185–6)

In the year he made that comment (1988), Morgan published 'Stanzas' (CP pp. 507–11), whose exact curves of emotion trace one-sided desire in a divided relationship: 'for you go home to him, and I to me'. Reflecting on a 'half-charted under-world of love', 'Stanzas' exercises a conviction that: 'we know / the truth's in feeling, and the openness / feeling must give at last'. The voice in 'Dear man, my love goes out in waves' (written 1987, published in *Collected Poems* three years later) is expressively 'out', extending the openness feelings give to speak a singular longing:

> Better to shake unseen
> and let real darkness screen
> the shadows of the heart,
> the vacant part-
> ner, husband wife. (CP p. 513)

The provocative appearance of 'Head' in *Sweeping Out The Dark* (1994) leaves nothing to the imagination, not even its transgressive and calculated act of represented recall; and by 1997 with *Virtual and Other Realities* Morgan is producing finely turned elegies ('The Glass', 'The Dead', 'Someone') that both invite and extend gendered readings.

Context-specific poems like 'For Love' ('not implied or inferred'); 'Not that Scene' – 'we've nothing hidden now, I know, you know' – 'Real Times' and 'In a Bar' open contours of experience hitherto, for this reader, unfamiliar.[4] Indexed over a life of writing that includes a personal record of love and loss, these entries in Morgan's encyclopaedia negotiate change in post-war attitudes and trace the difficult emergence of a self-aware gay strain in Scottish poetry.[5]

From Glasgow to Saturn's poems about people in relationships are one of several interests in a collection of voices that includes an unnervingly rational figure of death speaking 'Hyena' (CP pp. 246–7); and a comic-nonsense 'Loch Ness Monster's Song' that approaches without quite managing self-identification as diplodocus (CP pp. 248). When he was asked about the different environments the collection brings together, Morgan went back again to the 'kind of poetry ... which excited me most at the end of the 1930s', including the surrealist poet and campaigner David Gascoyne, whose 1935 book on surrealism Morgan knew (NNGM p. 54).[6] 'Because it is not a dogma,' Gascoyne was then arguing, 'because its principles have always demanded the maximum amount of freedom in every field, surrealism has been able to develop to the extent that its external features as they present themselves today are undeniably different from those of over a decade ago, even though its foremost aims have remained unchanged'.[7] Foremost aim was the stimulation of an 'imagination perhaps on the point of reclaiming its rights', as scouted when a 1924 *Manifesto of Surrealism* launched itself against the logics and socio-political rationalisms of European society:

> Under colour of civilisation, under pretext of progress, all that rightly or wrongly may be regarded as fantasy or superstition has been banished from the mind, all uncustomary searching after truth has been proscribed.[8]

Promoting 'everything that is opposed to the summary appearance of the real', and in favour of what André Breton called 'thought's dictation', Gascoyne quotes Breton's conviction that 'surrealism rests in the belief in the superior reality of certain forms of association neglected heretofore; in the omnipotence of the dream and in the disinterested play of thought' (pp. 61–2). Morgan has little time for superstition and seems congenitally suspicious of claims to omnipotence wherever they surface; but playing thought through speculative contexts is something he enjoys. He described 'CHANGE RULES' as the supreme graffito, and added: 'Gathering up the shards – "performances, assortments, résumés" – can hope perhaps to scatter values through a reticulation that surprises thought rather than traps it' (*Essays* p. vii). As slogan, 'change rules' assumes nothing static in nature and proposes nothing remaining the same in the human lifeworld; although some things need an imperative kick-start. Surrealists would have no difficulty with that, and Morgan shares their suspicion of representational fixity:

> I just like the idea of transformation. It's maybe a kind of dislike or fear of the stable state, and I suppose there must always be a tension in every society, in every age, between change and some kind of settled state or order, and it's just that I tend rather to like the idea of things changing than the idea of things being settled, though obviously there must be some kind of order in society, at every stage, at every period, that you can't avoid order. But I would tend to be more suspicious of the periods when there is a great deal of order and I would tend rather to like and to be attracted by the obvious hazards that there are in the periods of even quite violent change…. I think that any kind of revolution has got to face the central problem of how it is going to keep being revolutionary, and again if you believe the revolution is important, you must find some means of keeping it active. All these ideas certainly interest me a good deal. (NNGM p. 36)

Surrealism's assumption that logic invites dissolution might appeal technically, as might its restoration of desire in a demand for maximum liberty in every field. 'We have contended,' Breton argued in *The Second Manifesto of Surrealism* (1929), 'that the things which are and the things which might so well be should be fused, or thoroughly intercept each other, at the limits'.[9] Limits and interceptions continue to interest Morgan. 'I've rather liked the idea,' he said in 1971, 'that things are always upon a kind of knife edge, and always change, and are always in danger, if you like to use the word danger, of being transformed into something else' (NNGM p. 36). Gascoyne reminds us that surrealism neither offered a recipe nor specified a method: 'rather is it a starting point for works of the most striking diversity, capable of almost infinite variation and development' (p. 80). This might include poems 'composed from random newspaper cuttings', and we can see an outcrop in Morgan's *Newspoems* as well as in the cut-up effect he contrives for *Emergent Poems*. Tristan Tzara's 'shapes cut out of newspaper and incorporated in a design or picture [uniting] the commonplace, a piece of everyday reality, with another reality constructed by the mind' seems as relevant. Gascoyne's description of a game where a blank sheet of paper is passed around for participants to write in turn and improvise possible meaning, is redesigned and narrativised as playwrights developing scenes in 'Ingram Lake or, Five Acts on the House' (CP p. 50). Textual inventions of chance and hazard run through Morgan's work, as do dream worlds and a vein of nonsense: generic blurring, disruptive chronology and random collocations in *The New Divan* (1977) and elsewhere also owe something to surrealist precedent. Morgan's association has a long and flexible history; and if a Cold War nuclear balance of terror taxed even surrealism's pith, it was unwilling to lie down. May 1968 formed the kind of social pressure that cracked pure concrete principles for some of its French practitioners, and August of that year was to prove a testing ground for surrealism's continental survival. With Soviet tanks in the streets of the Czech capital, the *Platform of Prague* issued by surrealist groups in France and Czechoslovakia declared that any repressive system 'monopolises language, to return it to people only after it has been reduced to its utilitarian function or turned towards the ends of mere distraction':

> The role of surrealism is to tear language away from the repressive system and to make it the instrument of desire. Thus, what is called surrealist 'art' has no other goal than to liberate words, or more generally the signs, from the codes of utility or entertainment, in order to restore them as bearers of revelation of subjective reality and of the essential intersubjectivity of desire in the public mind.[10]

Subverting the exploitative utility of 'dark Satanic mills', a pluralising voice in 'The Mill' erodes traditional binaries by projecting a 'lovely devil' as liberator from angelic denial. As part of its assault on occult orderings for exploitative regimes, 'The Mill' sees Keats's sense of personal pleasure known by 'none save him whose strenuous tongue / Can burst Joy's grape against his palate fine' transformed into a religiously empowered expropriation:

> Like unripe grapes we were brushed
> In their mouths and rolled faintly,
> They bruised us without eating. (CP p. 248)

Otherworldly compensation for libidinal repression is nicely unsettled by the shifting ground of 'Then they hung us like fruit bats / tied to a desultory beam', before refusal makes itself felt as 'Hail hit[ting] the mill in handfuls'. In the poem's reversals a milling of experience stops when 'Hailstones bounding through a crack / baffled the grindstone', so that desire can celebrate being: 'We slipped our hooks. / The devil stroked us shrieking with fruit'. But if without contraries is no progression, with them is no promise of resolution: a coda conversationally cast as cliché

parodying prophecy, combines a resurgent repressed with an invitation
to embrace across difference:

> Tonight it's on the cards the mill
> blows outside in. Who'll fold who then? (CP p. 248)

As time passes in 'London', a drifting stream of consciousness folds
summer lovers into each other and across a mirage of locations and climates:
'orient wheat' blowing in St James's Park transforms first into snow then a
hot desert wind where Allah speaks in laughter. Broken messages received
by a stroller through Soho's red-light sex- and bookshops blur semiotics
into broken syntax, leaving future visitors with an analytic problem:

> Now bury this poem in one of the vaults
> of our civilisation, and let the Venusian
> computers come down, and searching for life
> crack our ghastly code. (CP p. 251)

The messages 'most heard' by 'The Post Office Tower' come from an
urban lifeworld that 'is its own telegrams':

> What mounts, what sighs,
> what says it is
> unaccountable
> as feelings moved
> by hair blown over
> an arm in the wind.
> In its acts
> it rests there. (CP p. 252)

For much of *From Glasgow to Saturn* Morgan is where he wants to
be and where he performs most successfully – re-centring attention by
reconfiguring from the edge of things; of political tolerance, of syntactic
transmission, of narrative space: and developing counter-identifications.
An elegy for Ernesto (Che) Guevara (1928–67), Bolivian theoretician
and tactician of guerrilla warfare, prominent figure in the Cuban revolution and later resistance leader in South America before being shot by
whoever shot him, superimposes on a bullet-riddled corpse the image of
'Che' seen on countless posters during the 1960s and after:

> a marble face,
> a broken body,
> the marble only
> broken by a smile. (CP p. 258)

A first-person narrative called 'The Fifth Gospel' redesigns biblical edict and Christian precept as a satire on New Testament parable and Gospel event. 'I have come to overthrow the law and the prophets', it begins; and shortly, 'I have not come to call sinners, but the virtuous and law-abiding, to repentance'. Rewriting Jesus's celebrated utterance (Matthew XXII, 21) as 'Give nothing to Caesar, for nothing is Caesar's', 'The Fifth Gospel' also varies the tale of the Gadarene swine (Matthew VIII, 28–34). 'Why,' Jesus asks the man possessed by demons, 'should I kill two thousand pigs?':

> Am I to bring these farmers and their families into destitution in order that you may sit clothed and in your right mind, sipping wine and paying your taxes? Go back to the tombs and cry in the darkness; and men shall learn from you, and you from the wilderness. (CP p. 260)

A last line seems both well earned and ironic: 'My yoke is not easy, and my burden is not light'.

'Not Playing the Game' (CP p. 277), plays with the idea of poem as game theory where construal depends on choices made by other parties or players, yet contrives to keep distance between achieved structure and free-fall relativising. And connection is the point when the buried voice of 'Last Message' aligns death-defiant pharaohs with post-nuclear fallout shelters:

> I wish you could hear the wings now
> scraping the pyramid, it must be
> an unspeakable anger to them
> that we few have saved our flesh
> and mean to live and think of them
> and of the world and of ourselves
> and the grey universe that rolls
> a thousand thousand thousand years. (CP p. 262)

Pushing semantic transmission into syntax where chaos and communication theory cross-fertilise, 'Frontier Story' tells a tall tale (also involving 'a bag of megatons [going] critical') to satirise Hollywood's dream factory through its once serviceable western genre; linking back to the 'dead dust' pyramid-dwellers of 'Last Message' and bringing saturating systems into issue:

> Meanwhile, back at the ranch factory
> they were turning out whole stampedes
> just for the hell of it, the mile-long door slid back

and they reverted to dust at the first touch of air.
But the music of the dust flowed back over the assembly-line
and that was the Christmas of a thousand million cowboys.

Hollywood fashioners of production-line aesthetics (of whom our speaker may be one), and its associated virtual realities routinely (and sometimes brutally) juggle geographical space and local histories for narrative convenience. Morgan's semiotic hinterland connects a Greek form with its Phoenician predecessor 'Baratanic' (country of tin) sometimes thought to be the derivation of Britain:

Or so we were told as we laid Los Angeles on Boston
and took a few states out, we were only playing,
pulled Mexico up over us and went to sleep,
woke up spitting out Phoenicians into the Cassiterides
and gave a yawn a wave as it flew out full of cowboys (CP p. 263).

Adapting surreal script to filmic mode generates a liminal syntax that disconcerts the tendency of language to naturalise and thereby fix the world it articulates. An urban nightmare in 'Rider' seems sometimes post-industrial: 'the nutcracker closed round Port Glasgow / it snapped with a burst / of docks and capstans downwind like collarstuds'; sometimes post-apocalyptic: 'a giant hedgehog [i.e. dredging machine] lifting the Necropolis [a Glasgow graveyard] / solid silver / to the moon / sang of the deluge'; or perhaps even post-global-warming:

butcher-boys tried to ward off sharks / the waters rose quickly /
    great drowned bankers
floated from bay-windows / two housemaids struggled on
    Grosvenor Terrace with a giant conger
the Broomielaw was awash with slime and torn-out claws and
    anchor-flakes (CP pp. 280–1)

Random figuration brings together Hungarian revolutionary Lajos Kossuth (1802–94), seen here drawing 'a mirage on electric air', Lanarkshire poet, dramatist and jazz musician Tom McGrath, Thelonius Monk, Charlie Parker and eighteenth-century balladeer Dougal Graham:

and far away the sound of hoofs / increased in moonlight / whole
    cities crouched in saddlebags
churches, dungeons, juntas dangled from reins / like grasses
    picked from the rank fields
and drops of halter sweat
    burned men to the bone, but the hare
like mad / played (CP pp. 280–1)

In a seemingly contrary direction 'Thoughts of a Module' manages interpretive possibility in unlikely context by producing fissured automated speech for an alternative take on the first moon landing: against the odds, the module can be made to deliver sense. 'It gets you into impossible situations now and again,' Morgan has commented, 'but people say that we can't go faster than the speed of light; well, that just sets me wondering [laughs]':

> Or to take another example: professional linguists are fond of putting forward what they call impossible sentences – 'you can't say that in English!' I would like to accept the challenge and devise a context whereby you *could* say that in English. I don't think there's anything you can't say, that wouldn't make sense if only you could devise a context for it.[11]

'To imagine a state of language,' Emil Benveniste suggested in ways that can seem inversely relevant to some of Morgan's procedures, 'in which certain objects would be *denominated* as being itself and, at the same time, something else, and where the relation *expressed* would be a relation of permanent contradiction, in which everything would be itself and not itself, and hence neither self or other, is to imagine a pure chimera'.[12] Chimeras and impossible sentences that work help to constitute Morgan's deliveries of alternative speech. A preliminary effect of constructing 'The Computer's First Dialect Poems' out of combined Northamptonshire and Lowland Scots usage is to startle received pronunciation into difference. An altercation between conceited male and sharp-tongued midwife in 'The Birkie and the Howdie' figures artificial intelligence devising a Scottish argument. But mutuality as a two-way requirement is discovered by 'The First Men on Mercury', a hilarious comedy of resistance to colonisation that identifies an assumption of primacy as the first mistake made by English-speaking space-travellers; of off-world submission to invasive hierarchies a second; the operational effectiveness of terrestrial perception and orientation a third; a presumption of intellectual superiority – 'is this clear?' – a fourth; the right to give orders a fifth. Since the first Mercurian word uttered is 'bawr', Scots for practical joke, other speech communities might take comfort from the Mercurians despatching their uninvited visitors with a flea in their ear (and another language learned): 'Go back in peace, take what you have gained / but quickly' (CP p. 268). It is then a matter for speculation that medieval line-breaks transmitting twentieth-century possibility in the moving tonal neutrality of 'Spacepoem 3: Off Course' (CP pp. 268–9) project astronauts spinning off into the cosmos and staying there singing their song. It does, at any rate, seem a matter of design after the riotous assembly of 'Rider', and before *From Glasgow to Saturn* returns to the urban realism of 'Glasgow Sonnets', that stream of consciousness presentation of a 'Guy Fawkes Moon' comes back to earth for 'Saturday Night' to confront us with the puke and debris of a night on the tiles. A sometimes feral city becomes differently affective when a heart attack claims one of its pedestrians: 'only the hungry ambulance / howls for him through the staring squares' (CP p. 283). The 'Stobhill' sequence of depositions about the temporary survival of a seven-month-old baby after the botched surgical termination of an unwanted pregnancy is set in the same urban environment. *Instamatic Poems* developed expressive detail as effective avoidance of explicit commentary: in 'Stobhill' personal statements by five people concerned in a mismanaged abortion indict individual and collective irresponsibility in a powerful plea for the reconstruction of personal and social practices.

In December 1973 Morgan wrote the first poem (which became the sixth) of an ambitious, sometimes autobiographical, sometimes historical and pre-historical, sometimes futuristic sequence centring on his time with the Royal Army Medical Corps in the Middle East. Appearing in portions over the next couple of years, it was completed in 1975 and provided the title for a collection called *The New Divan* in 1977. 'Though we were there in wartime', Morgan has commented, 'the sequence goes right back to history and pre-history:

> It also goes forward beyond the war to include the kind of violent incident you would have in more recent times, perhaps in the late sixties. Parts of the sequence come from my own experiences over there, other parts are invented characters, not me at all. Probably all of them are based on something I saw or heard, but much of it fictionalised into bits of story telling. I don't think there's a continuous story; I didn't see is as that, certainly. There are bits of narrative here and there, and maybe they do impinge on one another. But the poems are based upon people I met or knew and just slightly built up into fictional characters.[13]

By addressing in its first and last lines the fourteenth-century Persian poet Hafiz, whose *Divan* is one of the classics of that country, and maintaining a periodic dialogue with him, 'The New Divan' extends a flexible time-frame to contrast wealth and poverty across age-old and continuing subjection of the many by the few:

> Thousands
> are in hunger, see no glory, and
> all are in desire so great and ancient
> nothing heaven brings round, nothing behind
> or present or to come can fill their house
> with what they feel they need, or quieten them. (CP p. 297)

Repressive violence figured on antique stonework read as 'a grand inverse foreboding / of running feet under redder skies' (CP p. 302) connects with desert ruins seen in a snow-storm: a 'dangerous / place without hope / that anyone millennium-old in the sleet who / glistened there was glazed with / the peace of the grave or any human trust' (CP p. 305); and forward to living memory of 'people / … running down the world's roads among / columns of smoke, with no more belongings than / a back can take'. Charred bodies now compose a seemingly endless 'braille conducting / us silently from country to country / to country to country' (CP p. 316). Archaeological discovery of a king whose 'whole retinue has been burnt like coal / to warm his afterlife' prompts thoughts about the investment of earthly submission in blissful eternity – and the need for a proper burial:

> When the world is old
> and nodding in its shawl of science,
> and Prometheus's ray grows dim, and you and I,
> Hafiz, are cold particles unknown, a
> gem is to be made, they say, of suffering, to
> glow and harden God knows where. Electric
> sparks arc faintly. The damp
> sizzles, the prophets sleep. The
> story of the gem is what we tell our cat
> at a drowsy firefall, disbelieving. Those were
> the murdered. Pick and
> spade are the best incantations. (CP pp. 305–6)

A shifting 'I' speaks sometimes in a remembering present, sometimes a remembered past, sometimes in speculative temporalities; now mourns the death of a child, now recalls a son's behaviour; celebrates now a marriage, now homoerotic desire in a monastery. Dissolving conventions of character and narrative time, and so reading more like a postmodern fantasia on traditional form, the sequence tangentially preserves classic dimension and epic scope in a clearly marked beginning, middle and end; in its extended memory and vision; its warfare, journeyings, feastings, arrivals and departures; its ironised gestures to transcendent belief systems, and its inclusions of future event as speculative (and sometimes radioactive) possibility: 'ships like peacocks / spread vanes near Mars, wear out, are souvenirs. / Their very scrap's too active yet by half' (CP p. 304). A machinery of gods is figured subversively, as sages smoking hashish 'in full divan / in the anteroom of heaven' (CP p. 322); or when 'angels with abacuses called their calculations / once, in an ancient scene of souls' (CP p. 327). And in the ancient scene of Hades constructed here with echoes from Milton and Dante, the last surviving pain is dry-eyed memory of earth for figures 'Writhing like grasses, gasping clasping, / flaking out in beds of lava':

> we were speadeagled over gulfs
> so far below us we heard sighs
> where nothing else could be exhaled
> and even suffering was not seen.
> Sultans who had dungeons once
> – they say – stood there impaled.
> We never thought we'd never weep
> but that was so, oh that was so.
> We never knew we'd have no more
> to feel except one pain, one glow
> memory blows us to, like coal. (CP p. 323)

In a lecture about extended verse narrative Morgan suggested that Pound's *Cantos* and Olson's *Maximus* poems invite us to consider how 'a man's life has its own mysterious forms and patterns' that 'may be transferred to the poem in subtle and elusive ways'. He thought of Wolfgang Iser's inclusion of narrative indeterminacies as enabling condition for the 'constitution of an imaginary object during the act of reading':

> Iser is not saying that the reader can fill in the blanks with anything
> he likes, in jumping from one section to another, but that the
> author should ... be tempting the reader to sniff the air between
> the sections and relate this to the atmosphere of other sections or
> of the whole work.[14]

A 'ruffian sage' in poem 68 of 'The New Divan', continuing his tale over a long night's drinking begun in the 67th, embeds and connects storytelling in self-reflexive ways: '"space arches, / I call them, the continuum's different, / thinner"'; and the sequence grew as it was written:

> I spent almost the whole of the war in the Middle East and got to
> know something about their arts, and this word Divan is used by

them in ways not common with us. From its meaning as couch or
sofa, the same word is also used for a council chamber. And the
other meaning is a collection of poems. It's the same word and
comes from the same meaning in that the poems are all sitting talking together, as it were, in these collections. They can sit where they
like on these sofas, these divans, but there's something going on
between each of these poems, there's some kind of mysterious conversation going on between them.

'The New Divan' frames individual spaces within freely associating relationship partly because 'in Middle Eastern Divan poetry they like this
idea':

> They are not driven quite so hard as we in the West drive our read-
> ers.... In Divan poetry they say no; let people wander among the
> groves, play a flute, watch a fountain, meet someone and not see
> them again, that kind of thing. And yet they maintain that this kind
> of poetry is not so chaotic as you may think.... This appealed to me,
> perhaps because of what we were saying about the libertarian ele-
> ment in my writing. But I make a slight compromise, because I do
> give it some structure. It's slightly Westernised, it's not entirely of
> the East.[15]

'I think my attitude,' he said on another occasion, 'is not one of
theory ... so much as one of practice' (NNGM p. 116). One of the theories assumed into the structural practices of the divan poems connects
Iser with textual elements that Salman Rushdie over a decade after the
publication of Morgan's sequence would be describing as constitutive of
narrative itself in the new dispensations of post-modernity: 'hybridity,
impurity, intermingling, the transformation that comes of new and unex-
pected combinations of human beings, cultures, ideas, politics, movies,
songs'.[16] Nearly twenty years on, Andrew Gibson is citing Paul Virilio on
what was now being called the 'current crisis of "whole" dimensions ...
in which our traditional notions of surface, of limit and separation, have
decayed, and given way to those of interface, commutation, intermit-
tence and interruption':

> Visual culture, for instance, has long been insistently displacing the
> spaces, dimensions and regularities of what we think we see.... Film
> can double or multiply visual spaces, constitute, dissolve and recon-
> stitute different visual spaces or make them exist simultaneously ...
> both maintaining the representational image and blurring it and
> causing it to disintegrate. It therefore offers the space of the real as
> a multiple or radically indeterminate space.[17]

A cinema buff from childhood, Morgan's senses of the real include long-term familiarity with what he called the 'totally new effects' film narrative can produce: 'effects ... you wouldn't see anywhere else ... which came from the purely technical aspects of how you use a camera'. If we accept the invitation to 'dance [ourselves] into the masks' (CP p. 295) and wander through these interactive poems, we see and hear the sights and sounds of the desert, its towns and villages; meet an old man under a date-palm, attend a banquet or night club strip-tease, witness a funeral or visit a bazaar where biblical icons are standard market fare:

> The power and the glory walked
> here? Buy some statuettes,
> blue and white, nothing looking blander
> ever shot from the mould. (CP p. 316)

Archaeological imagery and futuristic vision assemble meditations on time and change to persuade us among other things that 'many and great delusions is the history / of the desert' (CP p. 306). To exercise a narrative determination that 'nothing that was not past could ever be dull' (CP p. 303), in an environment where any 'pattern / a swirling moment gave went quickly' (CP p. 319), and where 'the way of the thing was all prodigal' (CP p. 326), Wittgenstein is brought ironically back into play as a gardener tending fish: 'He lived like them in that great theatre / where the world is everything that is the case' (CP p. 312). Where a-temporal relationships and associations are the order of the day, a mirage can appear for 'sweaty ancient pilgrims' who are 'hungry / for vision yet thirsty for water':

> With
> thoughts withdrawn from emptiness
> a while, we watch the flickering meadows.
> Hedges of air that never flowered
> flower, bands of dust that never moved
> move now. Jinn's villages, different
> from ours, the springs in their meadows
> beckon dry as light. But we've come to
> the casting place, the arena we're in
> shimmers with the real life still unseen. (CP pp. 328–9)

As the emotional infrastructure of an autobiography is elliptically plotted and partially pieced, free-flowing patterns of relationship and connectedness incorporate war – 'the night is Rommel's tree: / searchlights cut it, history the secretion' (CP p. 328) – guerrilla activity closer to the writing present (as in poem 77), and a range of remembered excitements:

'Domes, shoeshines, jeeps, glaucomas, beads – / Wartime Cairo gave the flesh a buzz, / Pegged the young soul out full length' (CP p. 328). Reconstructing that soul in ways not religious in any accepted sense: 'For you / and me, the life beyond that sages mention / is this life on a crag above / a line of breakers' (CP p. 330), Morgan agrees that the sequence stretches context:

> I was in the desert for a large part of the war and in times like that it can be a dangerous and unpleasant place. But desert landscapes do give you long thoughts, you know. I felt very strongly the appeal which so many others have felt before me. There's no doubt, it lingers in the mind. If it's peaceful and you're out in the desert at night you certainly are aware of the vast extent of stars which in our islands you can hardly ever see. But the skies there are so clear, and so black; you can see all these constellations, and you have thoughts that are on the verge of being religious. And while they're not exactly that, you can begin to understand why monotheism – Islam after all means submission – did arise in those parts.[18]

The vast extent of stars, often associated with time-travelling speakers, is another long-term fascination. In 1964 Morgan wrote 'In Sobieski's Shield' to get inside the responses of a deep-space survivor of dematerialisation and subsequent molecular reassembly set in train on an earth at the entropic extreme of 'the day before solar withdrawal' (CP p. 196). The poem uses the fluid uncertainty of deleted punctuation to register its speaker's anxiety at anatomical alteration in himself, in his son's single reconstituted nipple and in the mutation of his partner's 'strange and beautiful crown of bright red hair'. With human memory the inner space where trans-individual continuities are inscribed, specific detail gives 'In Sobieski's Shield' an uncanny verisimilitude. The 'most curious / I almost said birthmark and so it is in a sense / light brown shaped like a crazy heart spreading / across my right forearm', prompts something our speaker in the present limbo he shares with his wife and son has only read about (possibly ironising the most popular poem of the First World War, the Canadian John McCrae's 'In Flanders Fields'); 'was it called France Flanders fields':

> I can see a stark hand brandishing nothing through placid scum
> in a lull of the guns what horror that the livid water
> is not shaken by the pity of the tattoo on the dead arm
> my god the heart on my arm my second birth mark
> the rematerialization has picked up these fragments I have
> a graft of war and ancient agony forgive
> me my dead helper. (CP p. 197)[19]

Mediating his rematerialisation as an act of historical memory, and choosing to believe that 'we are bound to all that lived', this survivor determines to 'take our second / like our first life out from the dome are the suits / ready the mineral storm is quieter it's hard / to go let's go' (CP p. 198). Alterity configures differently when a 1965 poem takes off from Edgar Allan Poe to locate space-visitors in a primitive human settlement where 'of course / they could see nothing, on their time-scale'. These humans can, though, sense the presence of Other and their reactions test the strength of secular conviction:

> A sweating trumpeter took
> a brand from the fire with a shout and threw it
> where our bodies would have been –
> we felt nothing but his courage.
> And so they would deal with every imagined power
> seen or unseen.
> There are no gods in the domain of Arnheim. (CP p. 199)

Tuning into 1960s ecstatic politics, 'For the International Poetry Incarnation' re-sites myth as space travel and rewrites inherited narrative as paradigm of renewal: 'Prometheus / embraces Icarus and in a gold shell with wings / he launches him up through the ghostly detritus / of gods and dirty empires and dying laws ... and he shall be the unburned burning one' (CP p. 199).

'From the Domain of Arnheim' ends with an inter-galactic voyager reflecting that 'from time the souvenirs are deeds' (CP p. 199). For tape-recording time-travellers in 'Memories of Earth' it might read 'within time souvenirs are emotional responses to experiential witness'. Morgan's epigraph spoken by Oothoon, ideal of physical freedom and figure of thwarted love, after her rape by Bromion (incarnation of instrumental reason), while on her way to Theotormon (realm of love), relates 'Memories of Earth' to William Blake's myth-figures in 'Visions of the Daughters of Albion':

> They told me that the night and day were all that I could see;
> They told me that I had five senses to enclose me up,
> And they enclosed my infinite brain into a narrow circle
> And sunk my heart into the abyss, a red round globe hot-burning,
> Till all from life I was obliterated and erased.[20]

Blake's poem binds Bromion and Oothoon 'back to back' in mutual hostility and Oothoon thus becomes a figurative voice caught between desire (Theotormon) and legislative rationalism (Bromion); a network

'Memories of Earth' modernises. Bromion is the transgressor who pursues knowledge 'spread in the infinite microscope, / In places yet unvisited by the voyager, and in worlds / Over other kinds of seas, and in atmospheres unknown', from where 'Memories of Earth' is spoken.[21] Developing his precursor text's concern with ideological tyranny and existential slavery, Morgan's exercise of memory across space composes a futuristic meditation on the republic of desire and its discontents. It constitutes in the process a postmodern report on the fate of narrative strategies associated with European realism and the outward colonisation of territorial space its canonical avatars proposed. Fascinated like some of his contemporaries by the difficulty of bringing together 'the idea of a lengthy work and the idea of quickness or simultaneity' (NNGM p. 56), Morgan deploys a continuous blank verse medium to problematise the progressive expansion in time and consequent specific ordering implied by linear narration. The poem exploits a sense that memory's normative synthesis of past and present as simultaneous contradicts the logic of linear progression through time: but Morgan also knows that narrativisation conventionally encodes both the linear construction of event synchronically and the reconstruction of historical sequence diachronically. To set a verbal stage for linkage and differentiation by fulfilling a movement sought in MacDiarmid's 'On a Raised Beach' ('I must get into this stone world now'),[22] the cosmically expansive journey these off-world time-trippers take is simultaneously miniaturising, into a fist-sized stone on 'the north shore' of an inland sea: 'The stone we are to enter is well marked, / lies in a hollow and is as big as my fist. / Indeed the temptation to cup it, lift it, throw it / is strong. / We resist' (CP p. 331).

Paradigmatic of entry into the symbolic order of language, 'Memories of Earth' dramatises by internalising a narratorial conflict between duty to rational sequence and emerging dissident sensibility. While suspension between simultaneity, linear narrativity and reconstructive recall further complicates our time-travellers' encounters, their experience of sensation beyond approved discourse alienates them from a prescriptive home environment and reduces them, as Erlkon's closing monologue puts it, to presenting their report 'in a troubled confusion', because 'memories flashing between sentences / … make us falter' (CP p. 339). They were ordered to earth to decode its signs, and textual signs are compounds of signifiers and signifieds. The poem pre-scribes Baudrillard's conviction that the methodology of the separation of the signifier and signified holds no better than the methodology of the separation of the mind and the body: 'the same imaginary in both cases. In one case, psychoanalysis came to say what this was, as, in the other, did poetics'.[23] Dematerialisation in 'In Sobieski's Shield' is here replaced by micro-miniaturisation of characters for whom the landscape plays different variations on Poe's 'Domain' by seeming to explode: 'upwards, outwards, the waves rise up / and loom like waterfalls, and where we stand / our stone blots out the light above us' (CP p. 331). 'Have we moved at all?' wonders Erlkon, and then: 'I am not to speculate, only to explore / as commanded', which is the contradictory nub of his situation. As part of the poem's problematic co-ordination of narrative progress, simultaneity and recall, the visitors' time-scale and earth's 'can never be in phase, / its images, its messages, its life / must come to us like an eternal present' (CP p. 333); and so they do. With the thought that Tromro the team's systems analyst and code-breaker will have his work cut out, the first tape does the same. The second fragment opens with confused questioning and a mobilising acknowledgement that 'nothing / can quite put down susceptibility', and 'Memories of Earth' valorises Erlkon's capacity to receive and be affected by hitherto proscribed and unfamiliar sensation. What is 'put down' in the first time-phase they witness is György Dózsa, leader of a Hungarian peasant revolt in 1514 (remembered by our narrator as belonging to distant but politically resonant 'red days of action'). For which, as here described, Dózsa wearing a crown of fire was burned on a mock-throne. Not here supplied (but later, 'Tromro has taught us much' about the value of decoding messages), is the information that the Hungarian Council (Diet) of the day entrenched their hold on power by imposing like Bromion 'one law for the lion and the ox', condemning the entire peasant class to 'real and perpetual servitude', binding it permanently to the soil by increasing the number of days peasants had to work for their lords, and imposing heavy taxes to pay for their rebellion. In a finely executed transition we next see Wordsworth, 'one gaunt man', separated from his companions on the summit of Snowdon; then American teenagers at a drive-in movie where a Tom and Jerry cartoon 'howls distorted sound at love-bites' in 'erotic jalopies'; then a Nazi death-camp presented in such telling yet apparently disengaged detail that one of the astronauts, Baltaz, weeps 'as if she was a woman of the earth'. After Baltaz looks at a butterfly 'as if she would cup its frailty for ever / against the eerie furnaces', an effectively rendered sunset ('shapes we'd never give a name to in / a hundred days of watching them dissolve' impacting on a speaker from a place where clouds don't move) gives way to a screen-image of what might be famine or post-nuclear survivors: 'all in such a case / we can but take as last or next to last / in desperation, and the time unknown / past, future, or the

myriad-to-one / unthinkable and terrible present'. At which a speaker
who earlier insists 'we have no pain, we cannot suffer pain', now says
'what we feel must surely be pain'.

Setting an alien narrator from a planet where questions are forbidden and thought-control internalised, 'even to think of those days is a
reproach' (CP p. 334); a narrator ideologically programmed to resist the
impact of alterity and required to report back from a human lifeworld of
flux and difference on an earth 'labouring in memories', does more than
satirise the sterilised discourse of administrative control: at issue is offi-
cially valorised discourse. The injunction laid upon Erlkon to compile
value-free reports from fragmentary tapes or voice-prints places him in a
postmodern predicament here turned to constructive resistance by
memory: 'since we came back from earth, nothing's the same' (CP p.
330). Narrative here is voyage, where metaphors of clouds, flows and tur-
bulences help to destabilise the schematising rationality of mastery it is
the travellers' duty to replicate. The activity of remembering earthly cultures introduces different forms of thinking and feeling into the ordered
space of their distant present: for these now returned and erstwhile obe-
dient subjects the 'other' is internalised as memory itself which 'spatialises' time by seeing the past as aspect of the present, and so disrupts
the logic of their inherited proceduralism. Decoding is a form of analysis, and analysis a form of involved participation: rather than distance
themselves from the object of their study, these visitors become active in
it.[24] So must the reader. 'Memories of Earth' adapts Heisenberg's uncertainty principle to undermine realism's assumed equation of epistemology with the representation of external facticity for experiencing subjects:
'by our very meagrest interfering / we trigger fragments of the vanished
prints / but have no key to make the sequence clear' (CP p. 333):

> It seems this is a world of change, where we,
> observing, can scarcely fix the observed
> and are unfixed ourselves. (CP p. 337)

As the narrative ruptures linear sequence but preserves ontological
development, prior lack in space-visitors issues in a self-motivating
expansion of thought and feeling, and consequent desire to negate the
frozen hierarchy of their world. Sympathetic identification with some of
his earthly perceptions, most strikingly with early Polynesian voyagers
out into the 'dangerous immensity' of the Pacific (CP p. 338), and antag-
onism to the passionless imperative – the 'plain figure of promised order'
– issued by his governing Council, leads Erlkon (together with his five
companions) to recognise (in the poem's recursive structure he has

already recognised) value in change. Wordsworth on Snowdon is heard contemplating:

> The emblem of a mind that feeds upon
> Infinity, that broods over the dark abyss,
> Intent to hear its voices issuing forth
> To silent light in one continuous stream (CP p. 335).[25]

This is not how their flickering impressions impact on Erlkon and his team, for whom the journey is also more formatively an inner than an outer one. Memories of the deaths, exploitation and control they witness produce hitherto prohibited self-reflections that evolve as an oppositional strategy. For characters thus intent to hear, the silent light of one continuous stream is too much like their home condition. 'Mine have voice', says Erlkon of his tapes, and the dissident cadre the returned six now compose work together to transform their governing Council's continuing priorities. So in necessarily partial ways, because here politicised in the sense of actively participating in social systems of interpersonal communication, 'Tintern Abbey' becomes more relevant than Book XIV of 'The Prelude', both for its imbrication of returning memory with what Erlkon terms 'the sheer presence' of 'here, here, here', and for its existential engagement with 'all the mighty of world / Of eye, and ear, – both what they half create, / And what perceive'.[26] 'Dialectic', says Roy Bhaskar in different discursive mode but also in terms that seem applicable to Erlkon and his friends, 'is the yearning for freedom and the transformative negation of constraints on it.... The strength of its presence is the measure of the pulse of freedom – of its health, or transforming power'.[27] In the structure of Morgan's poem the ineluctable modality of the visible is held in tension between event of record and recording sensibility and, mindful of the imagined communities being remembered and formed, it then seems intertextually and transhistorically appropriate that 'Memories of Earth' sings of aliens' 'first disobedience, and the fruit / Of that forbidden tree, whose mortal taste / Brought pain into their world, and all their woe' – a transgression that expands the subject towards political freedoms.

After their verdict that 'feeling and action had besotted' the time-travellers who record their memories of earth, Erlkon's ruling Council is already 'training non-susceptibles / for a further expedition', reinforcing his sense that 'susceptibility's a pearl of price' (CP p. 339). It was a price Plato did not want republican citizens to pay; to guard against which he devised his educational training programme and schema for public performance. One of his main worries was a practice of mimesis that produced visual and auditory likenesses to give a sense of presence to the spoken other. Rhythm and metaphor are dangerous because they can make imitated characters real to our senses in ways that bypass the rational mind's normal processes of judgement. It is as if for Plato, M. F. Burnyeat comments, 'eyes and ears offer painter and poet entry into a relatively independent cognitive apparatus, associated with the senses, through which mimetic images can bypass our knowledge and infiltrate the soul':

> By encouraging us to enter into the perspective of strong emotions, [poetry] will gradually erode the ideals we grew up with, even if they go on being what our better judgement tries to live up to.... It is dangerous to enter feelingly and uncritically into viewpoints that our better judgement, if it were active, would not approve.[28]

As well as musical poetry, Plato is concerned with epic performance and with the staging of tragedy and comedy. These things are grist to Morgan's mill, and his dramatising of alterity across a spectrum of emotional circumstance – from computer-speak to a cracked windscreen or Mao's cat – sets him as radically at variance with Plato's priorities as Erlkon and his group become with their ordered world. Setting mundane disarray against Plato's purged polis, a speaker in 'The World' begs to differ:

> I don't see the nothing some say anything
> That's not in order comes to be found.
> It may be nothing to be armour-plated. (CP p. 346)

'The ideal city,' Burnyeat continues, 'is like a symphony orchestra, in which each member plays just one instrument, so that together they create a beautiful whole called "Kallipolis" [city of beauty]. The dramatist is a walking-talking-singing-trumpeting-thundering subversion of the "one man – one job" principle responsible for this happy result' (p. 6). Morgan subverts the subversion as he caps Socrates outlining 'the other kind of speaker' to Adeimantus, 'the more debased he is the less will he shrink from imitating anything and everything':

> He will think nothing unworthy of himself, so that he will attempt, seriously and in the presence of many, to imitate all things, including ... claps of thunder and the noise of wind and hail and axles and pulleys, and the notes of trumpets and flutes and pan-pipes, and the sounds of all instruments, and the cries of dogs, sheep and birds; and so his style will depend wholly on imitation in voice and gesture, or will contain but a little of pure narration.[29]

Alternative republics where repressed modes thrive are mooted when 'Shaker Shaken' teases sense out of mid-nineteenth-century dissenters; and the opening drum of 'Ten Theatre Poems' plays havoc with prescriptive metaphysics by insisting on readers imitating an instrument. In open defiance of *The Republic*'s requirement for performing arts to articulate and reinforce an actually existing politics, 'The Chorus' suspects the set-up: 'Once the oracle / has spoken, we shall be more doubtful'; and the poem makes mischief out of a deleted definite article: 'We wonder what the gods are doing / We never understood gods' (CP pp. 356–7). Speaking the mimetic variety Plato explicitly deprecates, 'The Mask' declares its duty to 'make you uneasy'. The speaking fan of a strip-tease dancer brings reification into responsive discourse and extends 'the metaphor of the return of the inanimate' which Lacan describes as 'that margin beyond life that language gives to the human being by virtue of the fact that he speaks':[30]

> Out there, you'll never come so close,
> nipples and belly in a dream
> and only as sweet as a dream thrown
> on cigarette smoke and waves of heat and sound
> like a screen. I am the screen
> of what standing still would cheapen,
> a beauty that moves and is never seen. (CP p. 358)

Interactive movement is valued by 'The Skomorokh' (medieval Russian wandering player), who ironises oppression: 'Rich and poor are born, / not made, yes yes, amen', and with a well-placed Scots word changes his terms of repetition to challenge land-owning power: 'We'll jouk the rope and boiling tar / and let the bear eat the boyar' (CP p. 358). In 'The Shadow' imagined communities of Hindu mythology stalk *The Republic* with otherness: 'Plato never saw / Rama kill Ravana' (CP p. 359); and when 'The Soliloquy' speaks of the controlled individuation Plato favours, it projects a terminal post-Freudian nightmare:

> Before I die they want my voice, in dreams,
> in pain, in sweat, the last capitulation
> of the body, they're waiting for it, but
> I am going to be awake to the end,
> As something cool visits my brow (CP p. 360)

When 'The Codpiece' says 'I die facing the enemy', we know plurality of interpretative option; and when a Japanese theatre platform speaks in 'The Hanamichi', we hear that 'only players cross'. 'Five Poems on Film

Directors', mimetic of their subjects' techniques, modernise as they
explode Plato's regulations for representation in the city. Four poems
tracing different pedagogies in 'School's Out' mingle narrative and
mimesis to vary a social commonwealth by opening with the doubts of
one of Plato's young guards (or a modern public school descendant):

> A colonnade, binding light in fasces
> of striped stone and shadow, suited Plato.
> 'Tight reins,' he used to say, 'all training
> is restraint.' Are boys like horses then?
> Stupid questions got no answer, but
> a thin smile came and went, left no trace.
> We were born into Utopia:
> cold baths, porridge and Pythagoras,
> Pythagoras, porridge and cold baths.
> We never exactly hated the routine
> but felt there must be something else. (CP p. 365)

After which one of Milton's students recalls wondering 'what it was all
for – / and then I remember that sardonic voice / pausing in its anatomy
lesson to say / why heads of kings come / off so easily' (CP p. 366).

Morgan recurrently constructs experimental science as imaginative
writing and he spins work out of recent discovery. 'Adventures of the Anti-
sage' are adventures in resistance and escape sometimes in elusive syntax,
and include an early example of cybernetic incorporation ('Electronic').
Six 'Particle Poems' were written and published in 1977 when hunting the
quark, thought to be a more fundamental building block of matter than
any then known, was a major effort in particle physics. The poems
appeared in March: four months later *Nature* was advising its readers that
quarks had not been found free in nature because they were thought to be
permanently confined to the interior of the particles they compose. But
Nature soon reports the discovery of a new, heavier quark: 'The old quarks
are much lighter', some of them even massless (OED). The 'old old old
old' camp and semi-rhyming particle who speaks first in Morgan's
sequence has four of these things orbiting inside him; the charm he claims
has 'led me where I am' doubling as a term in physics denoting the quan-
tum properties that distinguish different quarks. His reference to nanosec-
onds – one-thousandth-millionths of a second – helps to make an exercise
in relativity out of a poem that finds existential truth in the invisible world:
'would you not say I'm easily // the nearest thing to doom and centre-
hood / you've ever been unable to preclude?' (CP p. 384). But the interior space of material being is still material being, and a young

motorcycling particle who 'screamed round the bend / braked hard, broke' personalises the metempsychosis that particle physics discloses as universal movement. Christian myth re-codes as 'Three particles lived in mystical union', and the visibility of invisible matter in motion is topic in poem four. Particle physics reconfigures earlier language forms, and since we do nothing without those particles they constitute an efficient transmission system for the delivery of story:

> Better than ogam
> or cuneiform the tracer
> of telling particles
> fans out angrily
> itself, itself, itself –
> who we were
> were here, here,
> we died at the crossroads
> or we defected
> or we raced ahead
> to be burnt out. (CP p. 386)

'Particle Poems' were included in the science fiction collection *Star Gate* (1979) which opens with a Russian moon-buggy discovering a lunar plinth partially inscribed with Stanley Kubrick's name, and registers, in 'The Worlds', an excitement of the time: 'Time has entered space. / Earth is again the centre and the favoured place'. 'Foundation' makes entertainingly clear that language articulates these discoveries and that a clarifying arena for language is the poem. A later one thinks of imagination as 'the nose-cone of the race' (VR p. 75). 'We are here,' says a speaker on 'Ganymede' in the 'Moons of Jupiter' sequence: 'and our sons or our sons' sons / will be on Jupiter, and their sons' sons at the star gate, leaving the fold of the sun' (CP p. 393). Open-ended continuities at the frontier of otherness are suggested when a 'band of tranquil defiers' somewhere in orbit finally cut the cord with earth and set out to find 'A Home in Space'.

In his British Academy lecture on the sublime, Morgan traced its survival in nineteenth century texts where technology and change were re-ordering everyday perception and practice, and where he finds 'vastness and obscurity, darkness and terror, power and astonishment, all discover[ing] a new lease of life'. He also notes 'a heightening, often an alienated heightening, of human experience' associated with the growth of industrial cities.[31] Morgan's attention to his city's historic mobilisations and its political and social values connects with a fascination for locating speech in speculative futures. Finding ways of thinking and feeling about scientific possibility by re-contextualising cognitive practice in speculative relationships, he includes futuristic memory to internalise responses for speaking subjects. In specific ways, writer's block on 'Amalthea', industrial unrest on 'Io', explorers on 'Europa', each engage alterity in unfamiliar spaces, including loss and regret for a voice not singing on Callisto's inhospitable terrain because:

> the grave-like mounds and pits
> reminded me of one grave long ago
> on earth, when a high Lanarkshire wind
> whipped out the tears men might be loath to show,
> as if the autumn had a mercy I
> could not give to myself, listening in shame
> to the perfunctory priest and to my thoughts
> that left us parted on a quarrel. These
> memories, and love, go with the planetman
> in duty and in hope from moon to moon. (CP p. 394)

Moons and planets were named for gods and goddesses. Making an art of the real out of canonical fictions, studies of the feminine in 'An Alphabet of Goddesses', which came together as completed sequence in the 1985 *Selected Poems*, appropriate a classical pantheon with honed, Glaswegian nous. In a catalogue note for the Pat Douthwaite exhibition that set Morgan to work, Robert Graves reminds us that for a subscribing community where goddesses were all known by name, they once had 'a recognisable existence' in the cognition of those who named them: 'in the sense that one talks of "melancholy" or "love at first sight" or any such emotion as "irrestrainable anger"'. Graves didn't warm to Douthewaite's pictures, but claimed that their subjects derived from an originating matriarchy anciently usurped by the male; adding that the position of women further worsened 'when the religion of the Greeks, adopted by their Roman conquerors, was superseded by Christianity'. He hoped that if Pat Douthwaite 'cares to identify herself with the divine images she has drawn, they may pass into literature'; and Morgan's responsive lexicon exploits a mythical bricolage of multiple and cross-pollinating genealogies to escape from traditional hierarchies in inherited narrative by reconfiguring customary identifications and transforming access to the power of definition.[32] Since males exercise continuing and often decisive dominion over the progress of sex and gender conflicts, 'An Alphabet of Goddesses' makes use of multi-layered, cross-gendered Greek myths of originating practice to modernise classic figuration as esoteric site for subversive impulse. Aware that any attempt to record gender difference is a matter of inscribing gendered subjects within fictions of one kind or another, Morgan's different take on the discourses of sexuality and gendered behaviour breaches the order of heterosexual relationship: his mothers and daughters of invention rooted in antique text are routed into contemporary resonance where gender and genealogy relationships within and across context compose a fantasia on modernity's ego-psychologies. The butch 'Aphrodite' who 'tramps in long tight boots like a hussar' into the opening line of 'An Alphabet' is goddess of desire and figure of the feminine 'chockful of longing but not forlorn', who 'cannot know who follows her, kingfisher, queenfisher' (CP p. 464). Given the history of her textual transmission and its evolving signification, her uncertainty shouldn't surprise.

When young Cronos tossed his father's gonads into the waves the resultant foam launched Aphrodite into an originary aporia – as woman either created by the sea, or born of the god's seed. Adaptable to preference in Morgan's version, she can slide out of 'crimson velvet and smoky mink' to become a 'Red captain wrinkling on her gloves' as occasion requires. She also 'shakes like a tumbrel,' so must be handled with care. In one of the cross-fertilising cosmogonies we look back to, Gaea, primordial being and source for both Titans and Olympians, is the mother (and father) of all mothers and fathers. First to exit chaos into being, and without male intervention giving birth to heaven (Uranus), land and ocean; when Gaea coupled with her son, they produced the six males and six females endowed with will, choice and capacity who constituted the original rule of the Titans. She continued to be a prolific birth-giver, while, by forcing his children to remain in their mother's womb, Uranus came to figure repression: but when Gaea gave her youngest son Cronos a sickle to castrate his father, blood from the wound in one version of the tale fertilised the mother again. 'Gaea' catches this matriarch at home, whistling in a fire cave, grinding 'the sea in a pot', and feeling less than maternal about the fruits of her womb; some divine, some now monstrous and the difference difficult to discern. The poem charts a separating agency of masculine violence, and wonders what was Gaea 'feeling for in her gross, careless prime?': 'Not giant times, / not beauty then, / not goodness yet, / but women, men' (CP p. 467). One of Gaea's daughters, Rhea married Cronos her brother and gave birth to Zeus, last Titan and first Olympian, who came in turn to displace an originating matriarch by assuming the title of father of gods and men, and whose coupling with his mother brings us further into genetically uncertain engendering by setting Rhea's memory of serpentine embrace against subsequently evolved practice:

I thought I would never go back to crude hugs
the first time I felt the slow travelling ripple:
it catches every inch of you in its squeeze
but in succession, severally, subtly, not
with one blunt anthropomorphic gasp
as four limbs fall on you dumped on a bed.

Two women sharing confidences set the scene for primal encounter –
'Zeus was a snake / and I was a snake. *That* never came / out of my
womb. / Use your imagination', and Rhea's spirits revive (CP p. 473).

This kind of strategic 're-vision', says Adrienne Rich, 'of seeing with
fresh eyes': 'of entering an old text from a new critical direction, is for us
more than a chapter in cultural history; it is an act of survival.... We need
to know the writing of the past, and know it differently than we have ever
known it; not to pass on a tradition but to break its hold over us'.[33] Fear
of patriarchy suppresses redefinition in one of the women made an offer
by Zeus she couldn't refuse; that of raising his twice-born son Dionysus.
'Bacche' has to cope with an unusually engineered subject. Six months
into her pregnancy something about Zeus struck Dionysus' mother
dead, whereupon his father moved him from her womb into his own
thigh until the infant Bacchus came to perfectly formed term: 'her skit-
tish changeling' in the poem. Turning him into a kid to conceal his existence from Hera his sometime partner, Zeus leaves 'a half-horned
stinking growing / goat-thing' for women to look after. Fuming at this,
Bacche wishes the whole empowering and subjecting set-up in hell:

She raged down into Africa
for a child to give honey to,
and gave all the gods to Gehenna,
and the goat-god to the pits below Gehenna
even as she fed him
from her commanded hand. (CP p. 465)

Deriving real world dissonance from cultural mytheme, 'Demeter', sister
and consort of Zeus and sometime great mother of the gods, rages
around recognisable topography with paraquat and chainsaw looking for
a violated daughter. But her mood changes when she remembers being
mounted by Poseidon metamorphosed into a horse: '"It is not every
day" – she mused / and nicely showed her teeth' (CP p. 466). If that
reconstructs a present sense for fabled experience, 'Eileithyia', goddess
of childbed and mother of gods and men, is seen about to give birth
'crouching / in the foul rubble of a shelled / city with shudders too early,
/ caught without a telephone in a rush of blood' (CP p. 466). Sensitive

both to narrative codings of ideas and feelings, and to myth-signifiers as effects in language, Morgan brings classic figuration into contexts where 'Hecate' is 'only your shadow, maybe', and present contexts are voiced in different mobilisations of story. 'I shall not cry out or faint,' says 'Ismene' to Antigone, 'but put / my head on your shoulder, sister, if I may, / in that tomb' (CP p. 468). A suicidal 'Jocasta' is comfortless in the assonance and alliteration across carefully broken lines which tell her ending; while 'Kore' justifies direct sympathy with Demeter's raped daughter, here 'bound for the underworld' of continuing subjection:

> and the creaking bed
> of grim, strong, aged
> pitiless Hades.
> Through his cold thrust
> Wish her well. (CP p. 469)

A prayer for women dead at the hands of men taps the resources of a pagan underworld to re-direct a grounding locution in western belief. Because Morgan's 'Lethe' is bent on remembering a catalogue of destruction:

> There is nothing you can pay her for the waters
> of oblivion. High in a glittering sieve
> she holds them, pans for grains of mercy.
> There is no ferry, no other life.
> Hunger and thirst after righteousness. (CP p. 470)

Continuities resonate when Creusa, the woman for whom Jason left 'Medea', wears a wedding-dress designed by the deserted partner: 'up she went / in flames, and it stuck to her like napalm / as she ran through the palace, setting fire to others / in a chain of charred vengeance'. A multiple murderess adds linkage of her own by claiming not to be accountable for her actions (CP p. 470). The following poem updates willed optimism and intelligent pessimism as existential 'Nemesis':

> She controls the roulette-wheel – but don't bet on it.
> She holds the ladder for you, and kicks it away.
> Don't cry, How tragic! She loves comedy.
> Don't laugh your head off; she might keep it.
> One thing, though; never try to deceive her.
> Propitiation is her *bête noire*.
> But you must hold yourself in readiness,
> And put your advisers on a slow train. (CP pp. 470–1)

Where an effective circulation of deception and double-speak exhausts a riddling 'Sphinx' which none the less continues to ask 'pedestrians / endless questions and when they cannot answer / swings round its huge hungry lion-haunches and / strangles them with its sphincter' (CP p. 473), the sequence looks for possibility where it can. When a 'swelling, gorgeous, bloody' universe 'kicks / itself out' of Oreithyia's womb, her rape by Boreas is displaced by the creative feminine in implicit plea for the non-sexist future that is the sequence's keel. Replicating on video a transsexual and multi-media rave, 'Terpsichore' – 'In the twenty-first century AD/BC AC/DC she / is a body-stocking of poetry and pleasure' – will 'dance heaven into your arms' whatever your inclination, destabilising Roman dispositions of marriage property as she moves:

> The paraphernalia roll off like tumbleweed.
> Cameramen hold their ground. She looks at them.
> They make her most beautiful video
> of dawn, and the dying dance. (CP p. 474)

'Urania', goddess of astronomy and so favoured figure in Morgan's conspectus, wears a comet for headdress, 'and the sands / of Mars were sown into her streaming robes' in a poem which centres her as stellar map-maker:

> Her signals travelled on a million bands,
> and when she launched her own Olympian probes
> it was to star and brim the starless charts. (CP p. 475)

Urania was sometimes a byname for Aphrodite, and conflict between the latter and a 'Pasiphae' struggling with unusual passions produces a 'desperate lament' in a poem which leaves her 'sawing the impotent air' (CP p. 472). In a complicating spin of the double helix, Zeus ate his first wife and the daughter she was carrying (subsequently to emerge from his troubled brow as fully armed Athena). Existentially subjected to consuming male force, the 'Wisdom' of this first wife consists in awareness that 'gross bold Jove waits at her side':

> to cut her exponential empire,
> to divorce her troubling wisdom,
> to devour her threatening knowledge,
> but she does not know when.
> She spreads her arms along the back of her throne.
>   (CP p. 476)

As it re-fictionalises remembered fictions, 'An Alphabet' scrutinises its own procedures. To make the point that Hebe's 'merry heart is only memory', a penultimate poem deftly engineers a present tense for a daughter of Zeus and Hera, then kills off the fabulously unageing cup-filler to the gods in the second stanza. Without writing, memory does not long survive death; with it, fable can be redesigned at will. And since 'Youth' must die the poem reassigns to the phenomenal world a power to compel language that constructs the belief it enacts:

> Her merry heart will be the memory
> of youth that passes, and if it could last
> would lose its happiness. Pitchers pour
> without stint when they make us say they do,
>
> in glasses on the changing changeless table. (CP p. 477)

Finally, Zeuxippe leaves her voice to the wind when she relinquishes god-head to run free 'with her horses along the broken strand, / the wild gusts blowing off to the horizon / her "Hey!" and "whoa!" and "Holaho!"'.

'An Alphabet of Goddesses' pluralises temporalities for erstwhile deities; and Morgan exercises syntactic invention against engrossing definition wherever he looks at real world affect in practices sustained or validated by otherworldly reference; whether Islamic retribution in 'Iran' (CP p. 420), or the subjection 'Dom Raja' commands on the banks of the Ganges (CP pp. 534–5). 'Twilight of a Tyranny' sets polyphony at large: 'Your thrones are death. Ours is the reign of speech' (CP p. 346), and that collective self-rule enacts a determining energy in which for Morgan as for Bakhtin, active and oppositional modes of cognition develop a 'carnivalesque dispersal of the hegemonic order of a dominant culture'.[34] Often using what Bakhtin calls 'the permanent corrective of laughter', Morgan reaches through conventional categories for 'a different and contradictory reality that is otherwise not captured in them'.[35] Repeatedly using prior text (including extensive translation) to negotiate otherness, test relationship and look for the angle that will suitably refract the utterance at hand, Morgan plunders the archive. A recasting of Shelley's 'Ozymandias' as gagged and cursing 'Mummy' (CP p. 397) vivifies a precursor republican text by pricking immortal power and French state theatre at Orly airport in 1976; and 'Byron at Sixty-Five', unsettled by *Moby Dick* (1851), is left wondering what kind of society Babbage and Marx might bring. This ageing Byron remembers sending *The Communist Manifesto* '(in German of course)':

To Wordsworth, with a pleasing dedication
'To our oldest living renegade'. The force
Of this last-minute well-meant operation
To save his soul proved to be over-coarse,
Or else the man was well beyond salvation.
Soon afterwards, he went to meet his Maker,
An unrepentant stupid Tory Laker. (CP p. 525)

If imagining subjects are not to be idolised, imagined objects are to be brought into dialogic use. A series of 'Reconstructions' written during 1986–87 re-design earlier text to have fun with the idea of poem as verbal icon. Matthew Arnold awe-struck by (and envious of) Shakespeare's emotional rapacity; Tennyson's 'To the Queen' reformulated as a hymn to Liberace; Pope snatching a grace beyond the reach of art considered sympathetically, 'even when classic numbers mow the ground / flat'; Milton's reflections 'On Time' put into different perspective when a speaker booked for a cruise on the 1992 space shuttle sees his hopes explode; Shakespeare's sonnet 55 beginning as Wallace Stevens placing in Tennessee not a jar but a profitably marketed 'Sqezy bottle' ('misspelt, unpronounceably / itself'). Perhaps because the materialist edges of Scottish empiricism are also part of Morgan's inheritance, ideal spaces in Byron's 'Sonnet on Chillon' are brought into real-time dissonance by reference to the South African activist Steve Biko's murder:

My God we must repel a plea for dungeons
even by the back door of mind over matter.
Anyone who says Biko's mind
was chainless underwrites tyranny. (CP p. 529)

There is, in all of this, another and difficult boundary that Morgan repeatedly scouts, between art and answerability, which in the early years of the soviet state exercised Bakhtin as a struggle for the centring of the personal in matters social and political; not a favoured emphasis at the time, and a theoretical openness for which Bakhtin suffered. 'This is not,' he maintained, 'simply an affirmation of myself or simply an affirmation of actual Being, but a non-fused yet undivided affirmation of myself in Being: I participate in Being as its sole actor. Nothing in Being, apart from myself, is an I for me. In all of Being I experience only myself – my unique self – as an I.[36] At which point Morgan takes off on his pluralising mission, dissolving the subject/object binary into a carnival of variegated speech.

Notes

1 Jameson, *The Political Unconscious*, p. 35.
2 Morgan, *Hold Hands Among the Atoms*, p. 67.
3 Morgan, *Fifty Renaissance Love-Poems*, included in CT, pp. 159–82.
4 Morgan, *Virtual and Other Realities*, pp. 64, 65, 78, 84, 88, 90, 94.
5 For a critical reading of Morgan's sometime reticence see Christopher Whyte, 'Now You See It, Now You Don't: Revelation and Concealment in the Love Poetry of Edwin Morgan', *Glasgow Review*, 2, 1993, pp. 82–93.
6 Morgan, 'Books I Have Read (1927–1940)', p. 270.
7 David Gascoyne, *A Short Survey of Surrealism* [1935], London, 1970, p. 57.
8 Cited in Gascoyne, *A Short Survey of Surrealism* p. 60.
9 Gascoyne, *A Short Survey of Surrealism* p. 88.
10 Cited in Franklin Rosemont, *André Breton and the First Principles of Surrealism*, London, 1978, p. 74.
11 Interview in Nicholson, *Poem, Purpose and Place*, p. 65.
12 Emil Benveniste, *Problems in General Linguistics*, trans. M. E. Meek, Miami, 1971, pp. 71–2.
13 Nicholson, *Poem, Purpose and Place*, p. 70.
14 Edwin Morgan, 'Long Poems – But How Long?', W. D. Thomas Memorial Lecture, University of Wales Swansea, 1995, pp. 9, 14.
15 Nicholson, *Poem, Purpose and Place*, pp. 70–1.
16 Salman Rushdie, *In Good Faith*, London, 1990, p. 14.
17 Paul Virilio, *The Lost Dimension*, New York, 1991, p. 110, cited in Andrew Gibson, *Towards a Postmodern Theory of Narrative*, Edinburgh, 1996, pp. 8–9.
18 Nicholson, *Poem, Purpose and Place*, p. 72.
19 Paul Fussell, *The Great War and Modern Memory* [1975], Oxford, 2000, pp. 248–9.
20 William Blake, *The Complete Poetry and Prose*, ed. D. V. Erdman, New York, 1988, p. 47.
21 *Ibid.*, p. 48.
22 MacDiarmid, *Complete Poems*, p. 426.
23 Jean Baudrillard, *Symbolic Exchange and Death*, trans. I. H. Grant, London, 1993, p. 222.
24 I adapt these sentences from Claire Colebrook's discussion of Michel de Certeau in *New Literary Histories: New Historicism and Contemporary Criticism*, Manchester, 1997, pp. 125–6.
25 William Wordsworth, *The Prelude: or Growth of a Poet's Mind*, ed. E. de Selincourt, rev. ed. Helen Darbishire, Oxford, 1959, pp. 483–5.
26 William Wordsworth, *The Poetical Works*, ed. E. de Selincourt, Oxford, 1944, vol. 2, p. 262.
27 Roy Bhaskar, *Dialectic: The Pulse of Freedom*, London, 1993, p. 378.
28 M. F. Burnyeat, 'Art and Mimesis in Plato's "Republic"', *London Review of Books*. 20, 10, 21 May 1998, pp. 8–9. I adapt sentences from Burnyeat in this paragraph.
29 Plato, *The Republic*, trans. Paul Shorey, Loeb edition, London 1937, vol. 1, Bk. III, p. 241.

30 Jacques Lacan, *Écrits: A Selection*, trans. A. Sheridan, London, 1977, p. 301.
31 Morgan, 'Provenance and Problematics, p. 301.
32 Jan Montefiore, *Feminism and Poetry*, London, 1987, p. 56.
33 Adrienne Rich, 'When We Dead Awaken: Writing as Re-Vision', in B. C. Gelpi and A. Gelpi (eds), *Adrienne Rich's Poetry*, New York, 1975, pp. 90–1.
34 M. M. Bakhtin, *Art and Answerability: Early Philosophical Essays*, eds M. Holquist and V. Liapunov, trans. C. Emerson and M. Holquist, Austin, 1990, p. 22.
35 M. M. Bakhtin, *The Dialogic Imagination: Four Essays*, trans. C. Emerson and M. Holquist, ed. M. Holquist, Austin, 1981, p. 59.
36 M. M. Bakhtin, *Towards a Philosophy of the Act*, eds. V. Liapunov and M. Holquist, trans. V. Liapunov, Austin, 1993, p. 41.

6 Reconfiguring subjectivity

Democracy is daily dialogue, and true democracy lies in the equality and equal power of all parties to that dialogue. (Tom Leonard)[1]

Whatever you have of imagination/ you must use. (Edwin Morgan)[2]

In 'Glasgow Sonnets' Petrarch's rhyme scheme carries a world whose twentieth-century deprivations weigh its renaissance rhythms like a judge. In *Sonnets from Scotland* (1984) Morgan reinvents the form, devising an *abbacddcefgefg* pattern to frame expeditions into strange places, where free-floating, time-travelling speakers construct a space-time continuum for alternative takes on Scotland's imaginable pasts, presents and futures. The first of its fifty-one poems to be written, 'The Solway Canal' identifies an engineering possibility that would put clear blue water as the border with England and is, Morgan comments: 'obviously, connected with Scotland's identity and place, its reality or non-reality as a nation'. The series grew out of that and a need to address more fully the impulse to self-government that seemingly crashed in the Referendum of 1979, when a Scottish majority in favour of change failed to meet the numerical threshold set by Westminster:

> There was a sense of political numbness after that. I had been hoping that there would be an Assembly, and the sense of let down was very strong. But despite that, or maybe even because of it, the 1980s have been a very prolific period for Scottish writing, both in the novel and in poetry. I felt impelled to write a lot in the eighties and this sequence was the first fruits of that.[3]

As it organises its themes and variations, from first formation on the earth's crust to future political republic, *Sonnets from Scotland* constitutes a performative assembly across time, and an interactive force field of imagined becomings since described as a key work of the post-Referendum period.[4]

Spoken from the endless perspective of what might be Time Lords, a strong sense of let down measures the first poem's earth science activation of the effort at renewal: 'Immensities / are mind, not ice, as the bright straths unfreeze'; and post-Referendum disappointment finds geological expression: 'Drumlins [long whaleback mounds of glacial deposit] blue as / bruises were grated off like nutmegs'.[5] That is a large hurt and Morgan is anxious to put it to use: 'Slate' exits on an emergent, surreal landscape impatiently kicking its heels (CP p. 437). Later on the evolutionary scale, when what might be a dolphin speaks 'Carboniferous', what would become one of Glasgow's middle-class residential districts, Bearsden, is still ocean; and fear of difference – '*Et in Arcadia*, said the shark, / *ego*' – is reconfigured to measure the self-doubt signalled in the recent vote:

> We feared instead the force that could inter
> such life and joy, in fossil clays, for apes
> and men to haul into their teeming heads. (CP p. 437)

To disinter that promise, 'Post-Glacial' melts into renewal:

> when mild rains
> drive back the blizzards, a new world it is
> of grain that thrusts its frenzied spikes, and trees
> whose roots race under the stamped-out remains
> of nomad Grampian fires. (CP p. 438)

Scotland's linguistic cultures identify Argyle as the region where Ireland's mission to spread Celtic religion and language took root around the middle of the sixth century. Columba had a biblically scripted Jesus (and an enchanted world) for his empowering text: in a window-opening association, 'In Argyle' finds on a beach there the skull of a Sumerian poet, and elegises instead the maker of the cuneiform *Gilgamesh* epic inscribed at the dawn of writing on Mesopotamian clay about powerful Middle Eastern passions and a quest for immortality: 'Now he needs neither claws nor tongue to tell / of things undying. Hebridean light / fills the translucent bone-domes' (CP p. 438). Morgan was sufficiently intrigued by this inaugurating narrative of male bonding in urban contexts to write a version for the stage, and his poem delivers its sense of scripted transmission of origin and early record as an irreducible combination of narrative invention and memory, which constructs the truths it discovers, and encrypts into myth (like the text and stories Columba came to read and tell) when used to fix criteria of verification and validity for evolving life-worlds.[6] To open up that ideological closure, 'In Argyle' includes immortality signifiers as a function of speech that dies with the speaker:

> Nothing brings
> the savage brain back to its empty shell,
> distracted by the shouts, the reefs, the night,
> fighting sleet to fix the tilt of his wings. (CP p. 438)

In Morgan's text, the poet's skull 'watches westward still'. Pluralising Hugh MacDiarmid's 'Perfect' by rewriting its first line, 'I found a pigeon's skull on the machair' as 'We found the poet's skull on the machair' (CP p. 438), the sonnet mobilises other fables of invention. MacDiarmid was accused of plagiarising 'Perfect': 'In Argyle' mimics the act as one of the ways writing enters other writing; slippage embedded in crafted form, and an example of the legendary (what is read) speaking prior text.[7] Since myths of identity transform in time and space, the skull-discoverer who speaks 'In Argyll' stretches locally scripted occasion by an infinitive rewriting – 'to fix the tilt of its wings' – of MacDiarmid's 'Perfect' closure.

Columba and Kentigern (traditionally Glasgow's first bishop), break off their 'Colloquy in Glaschu' in surprise at hearing a Highland fighter appropriating Latin song: their story is already developing in ways then unforeseen. The poem (and the series) explores tangential and speculative relationships to scripted and imagined event; and speculative relationships instantiated in sonnet structure bring into play some of the ways in which the measuring of recorded event becomes a reality on account of the emergence of measurement itself – story becoming history as conventionally written and received. Energising the making of story in its own right (and activating the political impetus of the collection's epigraph about changing times being the hope of the people), 'Memento' includes the chalk circles that Brecht made famous, and postpones its verb until the penultimate line of a mission 'over the hills and far away to bring / over the hills and far away to mind' (CP p. 441). With transformation at the heart of the sequence, reality as the clock ticks is radically adjusted when 'The Ring of Brodgar' viewed through a 'timeprint' unearthed in the distant future brings into focus the largest megalithic circle in Scotland; originally sixty stones (the tallest 4.5 metres high) chopped by pre-Bronze-Age people out of Orkney rock, carefully placed in possible relation to lunar or astral observation and evidently arranged according to specific measurement. The standing stones of the Picts take us back to a vanished precursor society and to early stirrings in a complex process of nation-making by which 'a cluster of different peoples – Britons and even some Scandinavians as well as Picts and Scots – came in the ninth and tenth centuries to owe common allegiance to a

single king, "of Scots"'.[8] 'If those stones could speak' is all an interlocutor has time to utter when Morgan projects this initiating bricolage; the
timeprint 'with truths to bring / into the freer ages' delivers to a construing audience grim senses of living and dying in a harsh time – and
ends echoing painful memory:

> A thin groan fought the wind that tugged the stones.
> It filled an auditorium with pain.
> Long was the sacrifice. Pity ran, hid.
> Once they heard the splintering of the bones
> they switched the playback off, in vain, in vain. (CP pp. 438–9)

Moving in and out of dateable event and imaginative fiction, as successful ideologies customarily do, *Sonnets From Scotland* weaves a vari-
ously connecting record in its own account. Around a 2,000-year-old
yew tree in a graveyard at Fortingall in Fife, and a nearby rectangle
defended by ditches, a legend developed identifying the site as Pontius
Pilate's birthplace: 'They told us he sat here beneath the yew / even in
downpours; ate dog-scraps. Crows flew / from prehistoric stone to stone
all day'. This apocryphal tale shifts orality into print to dramatise linguistic cross-pollination – here figured as a 'Latin harsh with
Aramaicisms' – shaping Scottish utterance and satirising trauma:

> He crawled to the cattle-trough
> at dusk, jumbled the water till it sloshed
> and spilled into the hoof-mush in blue strands,
> slapped with useless despair each sodden cuff,
> and washed his hands, and watched his hands, and washed
> his hands, and watched his hands, and washed his hands. (CP p. 439)

As Morgan generates alternative political sensibility, inherited belief-
systems and genealogies fabled or otherwise are up for appropriation;
and he continues to scrutinise his own procedures. Time Lords recording earthly event from deep space thematise codes of representation as
preferred productions of meaning when 'The Mirror' refracts lived experience through speaking and scripting systems, and where slippage is the
order of the day: 'The multitudes of the world cannot know / they are
reflected there; like glass they lie / in glass, shadows in shade' (CP
p. 440). Shadows in shade vanish, but lying in glass is nicely ambiguous
for breath that fades and language that mirrors its own production;
evanescent and renewable, delusive and of determining power. Witness
Tacitus in *Agricola* – part biography, part eulogy, part history of his

father-in-law's conquests – translating into his own tongue the Pictish King Calgacus: 'Do you imagine that the Romans' bravery in war matches their dissoluteness in time of peace? No! It is our quarrels and disunion that have given them fame'. Scripted utterance becomes differently extensible when 'they create a desolation and call it peace' resonates a continuing determination.[9] In answerable gesture, 'names as from outer space, names without roots' are written out in 'The Picts', where origin myths associated with a culture that has vanished more effectively than the blue dye with which its warriors painted their bodies, retain appeal as imaginative systems of self-identification: 'writers / like us regain mere pain on that blue road, / they think honour comes with the endurance' (CP p. 440). In Morgan's scriptorium the record shows endurance as a tested attribute. It needs to be: on the distant threshold of the Gutenberg galaxy, 'Matthew Paris' (c. 1200–1259), in quotation marks to include his putative utterance as Scottish verse, shows early versions of Scotland's story developing within perspectives and parameters centred elsewhere. Paris, whose *Historia Anglorum* included Scottish territory, and for whom the north 'is great and strange, a mouth / of baleen [whale] filtering the unknown', is left bemused if curious – and waiting to colonise textual space: 'their element, my margin, waits' (CP p. 441). He in turn forms a thread in Morgan's firmly tethered, sometimes surreal and open-ended design; as does the Italian optimist who survived flying off the battlements 'At Stirling Castle, 1507'. Elliptical and cross-fertilising connections in *Sonnets from Scotland* are implicatory and provocative as they accumulate a ringing clarity of attitude; with Morgan writing a permissive constitution of subjectivity as traceable histories unfold. Milton politicised the English sonnet in helpful ways and Morgan acknowledges the debt; but Puritan ethics are another matter. Reversing an assumed flow of influence, inverted commas insert the testimony of a Scottish theologian from the generation after Knox, an impeccable Calvinist, anti-Episcopalian propagandist and a 'strong sound sergeant of the creed', one 'Thomas Young, M.A. (St Andrews)', tutor to a youthful Milton who 'never understood predestination, / but then who does, within the English nation?'. Young connects republican phrasing with continuing struggle: 'John could only ask how God was served / by those who neither stand nor wait, their ardour / rabid (he said) to expunge virtue's seed' (CP p. 442).

A religious history is also a political history that sometimes broke out in civil war entailing brutal domestic effect. Aristocratic ruthlessness and the abuse of women are personalised when 'Lady Grange on St Kilda' implicates monarchist politics in negative ways, and speaks its refusal of

masculine practice by memorialising a woman whose death was
announced in Edinburgh in 1731, and a mock funeral staged by her hus-
band, then Lord Justice Clerk of Scotland and brother of the 6th Earl of
Mar, a leading figure in the 1715 rising. After threatening to expose continuing Jacobite activity, Rachel Chiesley was spirited away to offshore
islands and kept there for the rest of her life: 'so strong / they thought
I was and so I am' (CP p. 442). The textual body politic assembling here
is as gapped and fissured as any other on offer, but its prospective inclu-
siveness asserts interaction rather than opposition across Scotland's linguistic inheritance. Morgan assembles Scottish elements 'as a *totality*
rather than as a series of fragments, as an inner dialectic (and a dialogue
of dialects)'.

The Edinburgh geologist James Hutton recognised the igneous
nature of rock formation and, in *A Theory of the Earth* (1785), helped
lay the basis for modern geology. By bringing him into conversation with
his contemporary Robert Burns, Morgan coordinates poetic Scots and
rational English, sometimes held to be an operative division in Scottish
culture since the eighteenth century.[10] 'Theory of the Earth' represents
geologist as man of imagination and, in closing lines that catch the vanishing of earth's detail, reconstructs Burns's 'A Red, Red Rose' in the
light of scientific discovery. Inclusion of Hutton's 'We find no vestige of
a beginning, / no prospect of an end' stretches temporality for them
both; linking internally with the sequence's opening phrase 'There is no
beginning', and perhaps sub-textually with De Quincey.[11] As part of a
complex, evolving rootedness, real-time visitors to Morgan's home city
bring into issue mobility, invention and adaptation; figured now as a
Glasgow lad with several worlds before him enlisting as cabin-boy to 'Poe
in Glasgow' and setting off for Arnheim; now as a radically stoned 'De
Quincey in Glasgow' (but at the time semi-permanently in another country of the mind), conjuring vengeful visions of the city graveyard known
locally as the Necropolis:

> Its crowded tombs rise jostling, living, thronged
> with shadows, and the granite-bloodying glow
> flares on the dripping bronze of a used kris. (CP p. 444)

Different aspects of that shadow world strike Gerard Manley
Hopkins, 'melted / by bulk and warmth and unimposed rough grace',
as he moved through 'Irish Glasgow' slums and who, after witnessing
the human effects of a nineteenth-century's jealous god, troubled his
Jesuit superiors by flirting with radical politics: 'Industry's pauperism
singed his creed' (p. 445). Together with de Quincey's melodrama (and

each of the sonnets), a sensitive and repressed Englishman moving through complex sound-worlds he finds non-threatening is both dialectally and dialogically engaged in Morgan's project. As, differently, is George Seferis gaily sniffing Greek air on a Scottish island: 'he thought the dancing sea, the larks, the boats / spoke out as clear as from Aegean throats'. Freely associating on Eigg, Seferis remembers reading about Walter Scott 'purloin[ing] a suffocated clansman's skull', thinks of him as a 'tawdry Ulysses', recalls that 'crowns of Scottish kings were sacred', and by refusing the hierarchies they symbolise enlists in the civil society of the sequence (CP p. 448). Morgan remains a real-world analyst: Seferis would not survive to speak on his island if the West of Scotland were targeted by nuclear weapons. Bringing home the possible consequences of so much annihilating potential packed into small geographical space, and implicitly returning self-government as an urgent priority, a serial apocalypse projects Jehovah the Destroyer as nuclear-armed male locating the region as 'The Target'; and life persisting in a distant future 'After Fallout'. The closing lines of 'A Golden Age' counsel resilience: 'in thistle days / a strengthened seed outlives the hardest blasts (CP p. 457), thereby individuating the 'millions of seeds' blown through a devastated Edinburgh in 'The Age of Heracleum' (CP p. 453). As apocalyptically, 'Computer Error: Neutron Strike' transforms the horn that stirred Columba and Kentigern into 'an automatic foghorn' in a world of absence, whose light 'warned out to none below, and none above' (CP p. 453).

'Theory of the Earth' dramatises an operative conjunction between the English of the Enlightenment intellectual and the Scots of the ploughman poet.[12] When a slowly mobilising Glaswegian realises that his street-fighting friends are drunkenly incapable, the poem called 'Gangs' shifts from threatening group to the sense of movement Burns knew, to deliver a clear understanding and bristling, street-wise refusal of contemporary governing priorities and their anodyne (and repressive) formulations, here figured as words and slogans displacing local graffiti: '*YY Zero Wage Increase*'. Given that disruptive lexical environment, the terms of this speaker's refusal – 'Ah'm oan ma tod. But they'll no take a len / a me, Ah'm no deid yet, or deif, or dumb!' (CP p. 449) – make his urgent demotic an energising core for the sequence. In concert with a range of remembered voices; a 'Colloquy in Glaschu', the 'hoarse voice singing *come love watch with me*' (CP p. 448) of folk-singer and song writer Matt McGinn who died two years before the referendum, and a broken-winged angel in 'Post-Referendum' who stirs to 'hear a meeting sing'; 'Gangs' dramatises a combative vitality for self-identifying

sound-worlds threatened by invasive and subordinating practices. In the
public address of the sequence motivating speech opens 'The Ring of
Brodgar', and space visitors lost in the forests of 'Silva Caledonia',
hoping to hear voices they have heard before, present a parable of
impending movement:

> Marsh-lights, yes, mushroom-banks, leaf-mould, rank ferns,
> and up above, a sense of wings, of flight,
> of clattering, of calls through fog. Yet men,
> going about invisible concerns,
> are here, and our immoderate delight
> waits to see them, and hear them speak, again. (CP p. 439)

When 'Caledonian Antisyzygy' pushes sonnet to ludic limit, the divisions and self-divisions a complicating linguistic and cultural inheritance
has bequeathed as cultural mytheme for Scottish self-scrutiny are abolished in a series of idiomatic jokes that transforms local reference to
grave-robbers and their medical customer into tabloid cant and television trash – 'Doctor knocks box talks. / Claims T.V. favours Grim Duo,
Burke, Hare'. The poem listens instead for responsive sign:

> – Right, join hands. Make sure the door is locked, or
> nothing will happen. – Dark yet? – Cover clocks.
> – Knock. – Listen! – Is there anybody there? (CP p. 447)

Deriving playful possibility from prior text, '1983' includes limerick
to rewrite a newspaper report that 'a parrot Edward Lear drew has just
died' as the parrot's testimony to Lear's exuberance. Diversifying this
strategy by listening to the 'infinitely various waters' of Scotland's coast-
line, 'A Place of Many Waters' bubbles a plenitude 'true / as change is
true' (CP p. 450). In refusal of pre-constituted fixity, and making story
out of 'The Solway Canal' trope that separates Scotland at its English
border, 'Outward Bound' (and *Sonnets From Scotland* generally) reverses
the political implosion of 'Inward Bound' by moving 'on pure sound' to
stimulate recognition in a responsive geography:

> Greenland twisted round to hear it, Key West
> whistled, waved, Lanzarote's ashy face
> cracked open with laughter. There was no ground
> of being, only being, sweetest and best. (CP p. 456)

Meanwhile, structures of feeling including the 'unforeseen reluctance'
of departing visitors in the last poem, inscribe certifying presence in

uncertain medium: 'like a slate we could not clean / of characters, yet could not read, or write / our answers on, or smash, or take with us' (CP p. 457).

Stockades, schiltrons (a defensive formation of three rows of Scottish spearmen in close formation whose ranks cavalry were unable to break, and whose invention is accredited to William Wallace) and 'forced ranks' help to justify 'The Poet in the City' among scavenging gulls dreaming of a decidedly non-Presbyterian existentialism without angst: 'of freedom with all guilts and fears unfelt' (CP p. 451); and realism turns again when 'After a Death' personalises love and loss and memory of both:

> A writer needs nothing but a table.
> His pencil races, pauses, crosses out.
> Five years ago he lost his friend, without
> him he struggles through a different fable. (CP p. 449)

Further on in time 'The Coin' redeems the one that 'clattered at the end of its spin' to close 'Post-Referendum' by producing a science-fantasy fable of self-defining statehood out of politically authorised numismatic inscription: 'Respublica Scotorum'. Read by departing space visitors as sign of a temporary soundlessness, the date has been worn away because, our speaker realises as he climbs into his machine:

> as many fingers had gripped hard
> as hopes their silent race had lost or gained.
> The marshy scurf crept up to our machine,
> sucked at our boots. Yet nothing seemed ill-starred.
> And least of all the realm the coin contained. (CP p. 455)

Contriving past futures and future pasts, *Sonnets From Scotland* achieves much of its transhistorical and intertextual objective by engineering syntax through conversational rhythm to keep the logically formal and the dynamically transfigurative in operational conjunction; constituting an open society of individually self-identifying and cross-referential structures, and a collective expectation. Morgan's interplay of subjectivity, agency and time includes a series of powerful imaginers, and Douglas Dunn's reminder is well taken: the power of imagination is 'close to the core of Morgan's meaning'.[13] Perhaps that is why, when time-travellers register their reluctance to leave, a final horn issues its 'Summons' by echoing others in the collection:

> If it was love we felt, would it not keep,
> and travel where we travelled? Without fuss
> we lifted off, but as we checked and talked
> a far horn grew to break that people's sleep. (CP p. 457)

Back in conventional time frames, the power of what was being called the 'whole flow' of continuous television production was a widely shared social experience long before the 1979 Referendum campaign.[14] Two years after Morgan's book of sonnets, *From the Video Box* (1986) reworks strategies of transmission to put everyday practices of epistemology, subjectivity and representation under scrutiny. It was the idea of random individual access to public screening suggested by the 'Right to Reply' programme on television's Channel Four that first provoked Morgan to try embedding screens of talk:

> Eventually I came to the conclusion that I would like to write something that would be a kind of equivalent in words but would be different in the sense that it opens the whole thing out imaginatively. I wouldn't write about actual programmes: my people would go into the box to talk about unreal or impossible programmes, or something that isn't a programme at all. This actually happens; television people would confirm that individuals go into the video box in Glasgow just to get something off their chest. This, too, appealed to me.... I like to dramatise everything, I do feel that. And in presenting characters I try to make them as distinctive and real as I can in short space, to give them all the life I can. So you've twenty-seven people going into the box, and each one is meant to be alive, so that you can actually see that person.[15]

Yet if we discount the erect penis displayed for a wager in poem 14 there is no physical description of Morgan's speaking subjects. The closest we get is poem 24's hamster-loving psychopath who threatens viewers with a Stanley knife (and who redirects the sequence's epitaph from *Letters to Atticus*, Cicero's friend and a patron of art and literature – 'he came up close to you, as I see'): 'you can see from the look of me I mean that' (CP p. 497). Visual imaging derives from turn of phrase or trick of speech delivering sense of personality, and a sometimes freaky gallery of voices focalises the performing and interactive reader by dramatising speech acts that presuppose a responsive addressee.

To ground the video fantasies he constructs, Morgan operates a fundamental narrative assumption that by the very act of narrating the subject of narration addresses an other and structures the narration in relation to this other. As Kristeva puts it: "'I speak and you hear me, therefore we are'".[16] But in contexts that problematise notions of subjectivity as coherent and at the centre of a perceptual world significantly constructed by saturating powers of representation centred elsewhere, narration produces unusual challenges. An astrologically inclined hedonist who succumbs to the whole flow in poem 23 thinks of his satellite dish as poetry and of *Agamemnon* as a precursor mode of television soap. Although he reads the social transmission of *Genesis* as a continuing representational displacement of real world space 'where Adam covers half Iraq / and Eve in clouds bends over him', his wish to 'climb into my dish / and curl up like an oyster there, / swept by tides from everywhere' individuates reception as personal closure. From the same domain virtual reality assembles as technological nirvana when the speaker of poem 20, lost to any sense of quality control, substitutes for Shelley's image-making 'a total mobile wraparound':

> a dome of many coloured glass, in fact,
> that will not only stain the white radiance
> of any eternity there may be but
> oh, oh,
> positively dance round the
> threescore, fivescore wedded embedded
> screens of talk, tale, trail, and trial. (CP p. 494)[17]

Morgan figures unusual representations for everyday practices that have been theorised in ways relevant to his technique. Guy Debord's perception that 1960s audiences in thrall to image-management and spectacular projection were participating in a structured intention 'to promote reconciliation with a dominant state of things from which all communication has been triumphantly declared absent' is one to which the video poems respond. 'Wherever one looks', Debord wrote, 'one encounters this same intent: to restructure society without community'.[18] He also realised that examining the spectacle meant 'talking its language to some degree – to the degree, in fact, that we are obliged to engage the methodology of the society to which the spectacle gives expression' (p. 15). His notion that 'the spectacle is by definition immune from activity' invites the radical inspection that *From the Video Box* activates through a distinction that would later be made between a reading of the world that 'invites us to think difference from the standpoint of a previous similitude or identity', and one which 'invites us to think similitude and even identity as the product of a deep disparity':

The first reading precisely defines the world of copies and representations; it posits the world as icon. The second, contrary to the
first, defines the world of simulacra; it posits the world itself as
phantasm ... So 'to reverse Platonism' means to make the simulacra
rise and to affirm their rights among icons and copies.[19]

Morgan filters a complex and volatile critique (and an entertaining
fascination) into forms of utterance addressed to a recording lens about
a recording lens, personalising oral encounters with the centring instrument of television in a globalising order of multi-media transmission. He
thereby individuates Jean Baudrillard's recognition that by virtue of its
omnipresence television has become the social medium in itself, making
obsolete Orwell's projection of univocal state control through the silver
screen:

There is no need to imagine it as a state periscope spying on everyone else's private life – the situation as it stands is more efficient
than that: it is the *certainty that people are no longer speaking to each
other*, that they are definitively isolated in the face of a speech without response.[20]

The video box makes space for responsive speech by deferring orality's
immediacy of address, and its participating speakers contextualise relationship between invented performer and inventive scriptwriter. And as
far as writing is concerned, Walter Ong reminds us, audiences are always
part of a fiction-making process: 'For a writer any real recipient is nor-
mally absent ... the fictionalising of readers is what makes writing so difficult'.[21] The continuous flow of broadcasting routinises that too, and in
the year that Hans Magnus Enzensberger described television as pre-
venting rather than serving communication because it allows no reciprocal action between transmission and receiving subject – 'technically
speaking, it reduces feedback to the lowest point compatible with the
system' – Raymond Williams was wondering 'what would have happened
if there had been, for example, outside broadcasting facilities at the
Globe?'[22] Assuming the ease of camcorder access, *From the Video Box*
adapts classic performance text to video representation through the
medium of scripted language designed to simulate an immediacy of
speech.

When poem 10 details the circumstance of Ragozine's death to
which *Measure for Measure* briefly refers (IV, iii, ll. 67–74), vivid imaging at the interstices of canonical text narrativises a Shakespearean
moment as recent memory. But technologically transmitted commodifi-
cation – 'that extract of the death / of Ragozine' – leaves a speaking

viewer with no idea of context: 'we were not told / what play it was' (CP
pp. 486–7). Further scrambling the organised time of cultural programming in relation to Shakespeare, a misogynist devoted to his hate-object
Sycorax pops into the video box to say:

> I love it when
> there's no morality left, not a chink or a cheep
> from damned good or damned evil we keep
> hearing about, nothing but a screen
> brimmed up with pure force and nothing lagging
> in the energy not a stint in the energy
> it pushes into our veins like acid.

This voice comes to praise a screening of Caliban's birth, an event that
precedes *The Tempest* but is implicit in it, leaving the virtual space of writing to set the scene for Sycorax 'straining at last / like a wombed Samson
between two pines':

> She never brought the sky down but she brought
> thunder down without a groan as she straddled
> her slippery man-child brought down
> wawling in a squall and squelch
> of monsoon rain. She reigns,
> bitch-queen, batch-quern, grinds out
> pure nature, calves icebergs, makes archipelagos,
> and I saw her suddenly in a final shot
> solid with her thighs about the world,
> frowning at a thousand twangling instruments
> that to her were neither here nor there.
> How good it is to have a set for that one! (CP p. 488)

Morgan's acts of representation institute compromised autonomies
by placing each speaker in a point of view; and by varying the subject
position for speaking individuals he exercises an assumption that all represented utterances are political in the sense of claiming for their speakers particular positions in language. But by delivering represented
reading practices as recorded speech-performance on screen, he constructs the illusion of an illusion of an illusion. Not as fashionable collapse into endlessly recessive simulacra – Morgan is a linguistic agitator
and fictive simulacra are thematised in his video poems as elsewhere –
but perhaps to find scripted correlatives for the seam between space
and time that Fredric Jameson identified as the locus of video's form.[23]
A television-watcher feeling watched in poem 7 is convinced that 'the

slow opening of an eye' transformed a 'whole screen' of 'swirling dirty grey':

> until the grey clouds, the grey lids, gathered
> their hideous strength and grain by grain
> joined seamlessly together once again. (CP pp. 484–5)

Unpicking the seam between space and time as playback versus experiential instant, the speaker of a scratch video poem (6) who 'want[s] to be authentic', switches his attention 'from the set to the sky and back' to contrast a helicopter filmed between gables at sunset with a noiseless crow seen moving 'through the real red outside what we / call the real red':

> a scratch in air never to be solved scratch
> in air Steve said never solved as inside
> back went the helicopter to start again
> to start again I said those gables don't grow dark
> that's what I want to say they don't grow
> dark those gables on the set. (CP p. 484)

In parody of difference masquerading as sameness, the seam is advertised as commodified possibility in a brochure promoting portable televisions that will melt 'the boundaries between art and reality'. For a disappointed customer who took his set to Glencoe – 'there was a film about Glencoe' – a possible match between picture and place fails when the film disappears from his screen: so the portable receiver is placed next to a microwave oven, 'in the hope of precipitating an identity crisis / and if it results in mutual self-destruction / it will be worth it' (CP p. 495).

Poem 25 lays out Morgan's technique when six days of creation are set for a 'strange world jigsaw final' played out 'under the cameras', which proposes as competition subject an aerial photograph of 'as featureless a stretch as could be found' of the mid-Atlantic, 'hand-cut by a fiendish jigger to simulate, / but not to have, identical beaks and bays', and seen by the televiewing audience but not the competitor, who 'said he was a stateless person, called himself "Smith"'. By casting descriptive story and verbal image-making as speech-act, this account of a 'favourite programme' transforms an exercise in re-assembly into a redemptive challenge for a marginalised player who 'rose from his bed / ... on the third night' to complete the puzzle. 'But what I liked best', reports the speaker of a poem dramatising crossover between world and image:

was the last shot of the completed sea,
filling the screen; then the saw-lines disappeared,
till almost imperceptibly the surface moved
and it was again the real Atlantic, glad
to distraction to be released, raised
above itself in growing gusts, allowed
to roar as rain drove down and darkened,
allowed to blot, for a moment, the orderer's hand. (CP p. 498)

For a reader imagining a viewer watching an engrossed competitor whose 'mind, / if not his face, worked like a sea', verse and jig-saw take form together; and a shift from artifice to seeming naturalism to 'allow' the ordering hand to submerge in actuality pictures constitutes the kind of narrative transformation that 'affirms at once resemblance and differ-ence', and 'puts time into motion and suspends it, in a single movement'. Peter Brooks' comment on Todorov's description is relevant to proce-dures in Morgan's poem: 'The image of a double operation upon time has the value of returning us to the frequently eluded fact that narrative meanings are developed in time', not only in the world of reference but also in the narrative: 'if only because the meanings developed by narra-tive ... unfold through the time of reading'.[24] In Morgan's handling, typ-ically, the recognition (*anagnorisis*) classically prescribed for narrative intention is itself both topic and theme, filtering the Atlantic through a photograph, a jigsaw, a TV programme, a video box response, and the poem's reader; while 'blot' and the ordering hand disclose a writer at work. Illusions of the visible figure as interaction between technological naturalism and bemused subjectivity when a film of Giotto drawing his perfect freehand circle, once held to be a sign of artistic genius, moves one viewer from realist limit – 'I don't argue the case / that it really was the past' – to a conviction that film footage of the event really 'was Giotto's O'; a conviction the poem justifies (CP p. 499).

From the Video Box pushes serial soliloquy into strange places to pro-ject a variety of subject psychologies in acts of self-disclosure. The dis-placement of one communicating system by another is enjoyed by the first video speaker's response to a programme about imperial book-burn-ing in ancient China: 'the best the old classics / had ever done' for sol-diers and flunkeys who feed the fire: 'to warm a few hands / in a freezing night like that' (CP p. 481). Complaints about programmes that show 'without introduction, without discussion' 'the death of books, live, on screen' by a worried book-reader who watches 'the burning of the Library at Alexandria' encodes a rejection of the history he narrates; and

his distress extends only to the broadcasting authority. A bibliophile in
poem 3 closely familiar with the new British Library finds a film of it
going up in flames 'quite unusually riveting':

> Silent now the dead tongue in 11375.cc.13!
> Scandals of Cup.1000.c.7 all at rest!
> And 12452.w.3. quavering in his sprightly grave!
> Whoever was responsible for this show
> was a person of imagination, and bold to excess. (CP p. 482)

Each of these characters discloses Gutenberg's passage into electronic
transmission, though in the passion of their response they seem unaware
of it. Passage into uncertainty is topic when a scratch video poem about
the trials of Tantalus gets caught in a rewind loop that replays variable
sequence and so problematises both survival of the referent and semantic continuity in film or printed speech. At the moment in the programme's (and the poem's) transmission 'when the image of Ganymede
flashed through the spray':

> if he was allowed to touch it it was a shade
> if it was real he was not allowed to touch it
> if it was a shade he was allowed to touch it
> if he was not allowed to touch it it was real (CP p. 483)

Film text assimilates to print text when a scratch video poem uses
uncoordinated phrasal repetition to simulate the jerky crosscutting such
film often includes. The speaker/producer in poem 5 who goes into the
box not to talk about but to make a scratch video, blends Hogg's
Confessions of a Justified Sinner into a doubling of print and film that
brings visual representation into a relationship of speech:

> *this singular being read my thoughts in my looks*
> I have nothing more to show the camera
> *anticipating the very words that I was going to utter*
> to show the camera after I have let
> you see my friend who has been
> behind me all this time
> all this time and here he is
> beside me now here we are
> thank you thank you. (CP pp. 483–4)

Elsewhere in Morgan's baroque projections subliminal imaging fails to
transmit the Big Bang of cosmic origin during poem 16's 'messy story
about the Borgias': but a 'speeded mosaic of change' can redesign context at will for poem 17's mother confronting globally powerful systems:

>   – oh images, images,
> corners of the world seen
> out of the corner of an eye –
> subversive, subliminal –
> where have you taken my son
> into your terrible machine
> and why have you peeled off
> my grief like a decal
> and left me a nobody
> staring out to sea? (CP p. 492)

Lacan described Freud's domain as 'that of the truth of the subject', and we can read Lacan's conception of the decentred subject into Morgan's video box, where insertions of alienated subjectivity into the Symbolic arise in serial form.[25] In poem 18 the one unspoken word 'that should never be seen / except when you think you may have seen it / but are not sure', and for which 'neither noun nor verb / rules' is desire itself. Jameson came to consider video as 'likely candidate for cultural hegemony today', and headed his discussion of it 'Surrealism Without the Unconscious'. His comment about self-evident but often forgotten time-management in film sequence – that fictive scenes and conversations on screen are never coterminous with the time such moments take in real life – connects with Morgan's management of syntax and structure. *From the Video Box* explores a problem Jameson would identify concerning 'the construction of just such fictive or foreshortened temporalities (whether of film or reading), which are then substituted for a real time we are thereby enabled to forget':

> The question of fiction and the fictive would thereby find itself radically dissociated from questions of narrative and storytelling as such (although it would retain a key role and function in the practice of certain forms of narration): many of the confusions of the so-called representation debate (often assimilated to a debate about realism) are dispelled by just such an analytic distinction between fiction effects and their fictional temporalities, and narrative structures in general.[26]

Producing fiction effects as well as fictive temporalities in which to narrativise them is something Morgan has been doing for some time, and he plays inventive games with realist technique. By vocalising scripted difference his video poems prevaricate the technological assimilation of human subjectivity that Jameson sees as contingent on the compelling immediacy of film. A disgruntled viewer in poem 8 reports waiting for

his 'all-night movie' when his set starts to bleed and he touches it with
his hand: 'Look, I didn't wipe it off. See that, camera':

> I know we get our mail through the set, bills,
> bank balances, but blood is ridiculous.
> I want a clean dry screen from now on.
> Let them bleed elsewhere, whoever they are.

But linguistic subjectivity is both medium and message, and 'insofar as speech is pre-eminently social', as Jameson comments on another
occasion, 'the intersubjective objects which are works of literature
underscore the psychic function of narrative and fantasy in the attempts
of the subject to reintegrate his or her alienated image'.[27] Morgan's
video voices integrate self-image with strange contexts to encode a contemporary formulation of ideology as 'the representation of the subject's *Imaginary* relationship to his or her *Real* conditions of
existence'.[28] Poem 19's prospector on horseback in futuristic Patagonia
comes home to Glasgow because of a programme he saw on his wrist-
watch television. Recognising in footage from Mars a version of his
own activity, this speaker gives up his 'little tuneless clinking hoofbeaten
song / of mineralogy and materiality' to look for video celebrity: '
Did you ever have my type in your box?'. Looking for a more
emphatic displacement of the real by the imaginary, a sybarite in poem
20 wants to build wall-to-wall video in order 'to be there and feel
wall-ness':

> Try my wall,
> climb into my shell,
> sell your house, bring your family,
> sharpen your eyes and your wits until
> the dance is story and the story dance,
> and as you run forward you feel time run forward
> to fetch the age of gold.

Although 'language is the devil' for poem 22's speaker in Perthshire
whose faulty satellite dish brings words he doesn't understand, it remains
the medium of social universality and intersubjectivity, and its formal
inventions an archive of speech. The most memorable programme for
the closing poem's viewer is a 'Dance of the Letters' whose graphics,
'altogether / crisp and bright and strong and real', elaborate the deco-
ration around initial letters in medieval ecclesiastical manuscript as harsh
actuality images of the present, and undermine traditional closure by
spelling THE END descriptively.

The dance between referent and signifier is picked up in 'A City', one of seventy poems marking Morgan's seventieth year in *Hold Hands Among the Atoms* (1991), where the confusion of two cinema-goers watching a film about Glasgow shot partly in Moscow, partly in Chicago and partly reproduced by computer graphics, and where the sky is a listed property – 'change as it may' – leads one of them to conclude 'I'm not persuaded even of its existence':

> – What, *Glasgow?* – The city, not the film. – The city
> is the film. – Oh come on. – I tell you. (HH p. 25)

With the politics of representation again in play, *Hold Hands Among the Atoms* develops some of the issues raised in the video poems by opening up singular event to public inspection. In the eighth 'Whittrick' poem, the author of *The Living Brain* describes an artificial intelligence 'pro-grammed, elaborately / And with great faith in the logic of choice, to find / The end of every beginning, the probable / Haystack in the open field of the possible' (CP p. 114). Against the displacement of specific and variegated value by universal signs, Morgan's practised understand-ing that 'nothing going straight can pierce the jungle / of dimensions' now designs 'A Needle' to set a quest for the real as topic for the collec-tion by weaving metaphor as signifying context:

> invisible
> it cannot be but long unseen and longing
> to be seen: oh yes and to be used, to swoop through
> wounds it would knit, banners to be invested
> with futures of things known, frames to be figured
> to hopes as iron as Homer's woman fed on,
> against the odds of being only human. (HH p. 31)

Cross-figuring frames of reference are a series motif in *Hold Hands Among The Atoms*, where being human is tested in encounters with diverse forms of alterity, and where perceptions of and responses to his geopolitical present issue in some of the most directly referential poetry Morgan has produced. 'The Last Intifada' pays tribute to young Palestinians by projecting 'a million people' in a determining insurrec-tion that twists the dialectic between systems of power and people dying (HH p. 23). Hope has as hard a time of it when long-distance snipers in endlessly contemporary urban killing grounds target 'expendablest of the expendable' civilians who are 'too feeble to be seen by psyched-up fighters':

How great it must be not to be civilian
or anything but gun in hand, young, mobile,
slogan-fuelled better than machines are,
you cannot even hear the shattered housewife,
far less see her blood and bags and bread (HH p. 40)

A critique of political violence follows it across borders to develop
Marina Tsvetayeva's figure of human spines sailed over by brute power
in the text Morgan translated for *Sovpoems* into an 'annual, public,
ancient, and instructive' 'ritual of Trampling on the People' in Brazilian
shanty slums; whose surviving victims swear solidarity (HH, p. 15). Back
in the erstwhile USSR, the upsurge of iconoclasm that followed the tum-
bling of the Berlin Wall in 1989 provides 'A Statue' with occasion to measure the depth of change:

Then they were dancing
on fallen concrete epaulettes, a shoulder,
a block of rain-black cheek where the split face had
burst and spilt no blood or brain, no anything
apart from rusty rods that mocked each human
backbone with their undestroyed reminder
of iron laws and iron men. (HH p. 16)

Soviet deregulation brings a welcome revenge of the present when
'Difference' remembers the suppression of minority languages and promotion of the second-rate in order for 'the mass to move en bloc'. Of
the three writers named as silenced, Gennady Aigi's native Chuvash is
distinguished by its lack of mutual intelligibility with other Turkic languages; Iskander's Abkhazian is a language of the Caucasus which uses
both 'tongue-raising and lip-rounding in its impressive array of
palatalised, labialised, and labio-palatalised consonants'; and Rytkheu is
a Chukchee, 'a paleoasiatic people of extreme north-east Siberia' (OED).
The information becomes semantically functional when an 'empire /
expires in frozen edicts' and its politicians realise that 'there's no one /
bar the unassimilated – *bar-bar, bar-bar*' to help them: 'and why should
they, since you doomed them / to hold their tongue'. Punning on a
Scots word for barbarian the poem turns against former controllers
'songs that are not alien to the alien, / accreted stinging stories mock-
ing labials / where you are a *bar-bar* to them'; and celebrates 'endless
variousness':

How there can be such
difference we do not know but what we do know

> is that an absolute instinct loves it different,
> the world, the dialectic, the packed coaches
> whistling at daybreak through the patched countries. (HH p. 28)

Morgan's take on events of record includes an extended sentence responding to a 1989 report that a Communist Party weekly called *Hammer and Sickle* was to be renamed 'Friday'. Routine assumption of transforming sign into unchanging temporal sequence produces a warning that 'you can't do anything with Friday':

> it can live only in its bland abstraction
> from all the hard things that are great in hardness,
> the setbacks that still sting us crying us forwards,
> it has no face, and only an illusion
> of a smile, it beckons, but you must not buy it. (HH p. 36)

With 1917 as well as a post-communist revolution in play, an optimistic 'new' Russian speaking from the future remembers predecessors who also looked 'out where the universe was slanting / off and down, bright, full of forms, quite distant / but then very near and to be reached', and generates a ghostly pathos: 'It was vincible now, that illimitable' (HH p. 39).

The seventieth poem argues that 'often / there is a blank you must not fill with monsters. / It is all for what is to come after' (HH p. 81): but 'A Warning' focuses on 'the better life that / never seems to come' and sees in crumbling ideologies a new world order's ancient priest-craft resurrecting enchantment: 'opening of cathedrals, minuet of / vestments as they cross the ancient incense, ranks of dew-eyes dibbling trembling candles / in waxbound trays that never will grow freedom'. In tandem with these gothic stimulations, 'musty indefatigable reaction' revives, eager to believe that abolished thrones are again on offer: 'What, a republic a kingdom?' (HH p. 41). Morgan invests these poems with what he called 'very strong feelings':

> maybe because of a personal investment in the ideals that lay behind communism, I think that was there. I remember when various regimes began to collapse in 1988, 89, 90, watching extraordinary scenes on TV especially in capital cities of Eastern Europe; enormous crowds gathered together sometimes suggesting violence, sometimes peaceful demonstrations. It was just the extraordinary surprise this caused even to the pundits and sovietologists and to me too. I had been to various of these countries and thought I knew the history reasonably well and I too had thought that the regimes

then, by the middle 1980s were still pretty solidly established. I thought perhaps they were going to change bit by bit gradually, there had been little thaws here and there, but I was struck dumb just by what had happened. It was a mixture of feelings: I could understand why the people seemed to be so glad that they had shaken off the shackles of the Stalinist time; but at the same time I felt like warning them through the television set – do you really know what you've done, are you quite sure that it was the right thing to do, do you really know what problems lie ahead for you? I felt this very strongly just because I had hoped so much when I was young, I suppose.[29]

Changing with the times, and focusing Western affluence, the 'Dragon' that threatens a utopia discovered by 'sweating, angry, filthy, / adventurers dishevelled to our toecaps', has moved on from being hydra-headed into less definable dimensions: 'often not present, always sometimes present, / not to be calculated' as it undermines security:

> Papery arbours
> whisper softly. Gardeners with light wheelbarrows
> trundle themselves home to wife and children,
> not even glancing at what must be evening
> drawing dark wings high over the poplars. (HH p. 21)

Two epigraphs suggest ways into the book: the first from Laura Riding Jackson – 'There is something to be told about us / for the telling of which we all wait' – proposes story telling as revelation, and assumes a readership seeking self-definition. The second, given here in *Beowulf*'s Anglo-Saxon, translates in Morgan's version as 'the men cast off, / Eager voyagers, in their tight-timbered boat' (B p. 6). Grendel is the object of their quest and Beowulf's active intention complements and offsets Jackson's receptive audience. But both focus story and the first poem, 'A Chapter', tells a political fable about an urban community tidy in its dispositions but radically ill-at-ease with itself: 'baffled by the absence / of satisfactions they had strained their souls for'. In the public domain of 'a generation ... wasted by longings in the well-lit cities', any change constitutes external threat:

> Yet no one knew what laws must have been broken,
> or whether their malaise was good or evil.
> And that was when they heard the distant shouting. (HH p. 9)

Satirising domination by calculation in an economy that valorises only quantity, 'A Sale' proceeds on credit while anomic and reified shoppers exit 'into streets like slowly moving walkways / packed customer-tight, a marathon of inches / towards the bus lanes and the darkening suburbs', through which a dominant signifier endlessly circulates: 'it is the custom, customers; the custom' (HH p. 13). After its opening invitation to 'Imagine all the sea was turned to money', 'An Offer' identifies an environment controlled by currency values and sees its accumulators 'scrabbling with sacks through miles of paper'. Playing present perception off classic narrative the poem ends at the volcanic lake Virgil represented as hell's gateway:

> Imagine when this wealth has turned to coral,
> and banks of it rise up, as sharp as razors,
> and children with unwary feet are bleeding
> as they scamper on the ghosts of long-dead deutschmarks.
> What would you pay to have a new convulsion
> Send the reefs roaring to greed-grey Avernus? (HH p. 18)

'A Particular Country' measures desire reified in investment expectations against the life-world of rain forests: 'that / mass of change and chance and challenge where you / go out; sink in; draw deep at signs that daze you / as stock might, in the nights of your own country' (HH p. 54).

Reflecting on the collection's title and encoding the intersections it presupposes, both 'A Visit' and 'A Question' trace time-travelling encounters with otherness as integrations seemingly unavailable in the organised communities of social life, and both focus vanishing forms of print (HH pp. 51, 52). Troping an ultimate return of humankind to solar source as 'a bath of neutrinos', the speaker of 'Golden Apples' wonders 'would that not cleanse us?' and adds 'this is not science fiction'. 'Particle Poems' in 1977 showed Morgan's attraction to scientific grounding for spatialised metaphors of perception and being, and bathing in neutrinos is something we all do. Units of zero or negligible mass, their extremely low probability of interaction with matter means that neutrinos can travel many times across the interior of the earth with practically no chance of hitting anything. For which reason they constitute 'a unique tool in the study of weak forces in electromagnetic interactions' (OED). The pathways and properties of neutrinos serve as narrative paradigm for Morgan's different takes on our social and environmental structures and the way we move through them and they through us. 'A Skew' blows neutrinos of its own to filter the

known into the imaginable as a real world fable of creation (HH p. 45);
and 'Many intersections did somehow flow through one another' in 'A
Question' (HH p. 52).

Reference to Alfred Schnittke's experimental juxtapositions of radically disparate music from different epochs also suggest a relevance
beyond their immediate contrast with the steady flight of two swans in
'A Flypast': 'those muscles working, those webs, that eye, that purpose'
(HH p. 58). Schnittke's 'polystylism' intimates cognate procedures in
Morgan's kaleidoscopic muster; but some styles are preferred over
others. On the grounds that 'everything they did was an evasion / of fact
of mind, of (here he smiled) illusion', autotelic writing gets short shrift
from 'a little nutbrown hermit' who shrivels its paper in 'A Decadence'
(HH p. 12); and what 'self-reflexiveness' misses is topic for 'An
Argument' (HH p. 50). In contrast, the adventurer commanding a
'Vanguard' space patrol 'sent out to scotch or seal appalling rumours',
encourages jumpy troops by telling them 'whatever you have of imagination / you must use'. He is none the less nervous about 'celestial
mechanics / crumbling away' at the edge of the known world: 'No end
in time was near, or in space possible. / As for the dead, who am I to
appease them, / a scout, a ragged man, a storyteller' (HH p. 32).
Storytelling so extensively concerned with relationships of change and
systems of dominance cast sometimes locally, sometimes in off-world
space knows that a power of imagined futures set against their commodified trading in the material present faces awesome competition; as
from cosmic assayers 'well beyond the visible' calculating global returns
in 'The Last Scoria':

Controllers
press their final indifferent keys, the raking
begins, of empires, schools of thought, oppressions,
censors, treacheries, secret executions,
stonings, unknown soldiers, vivisections,
the starved, the slag, the sum of that, the scoria. (HH p. 63)

Trading actively in ideas of endless change and exchange, Morgan
subverts engrossing regimes of value by routing syntax and rhythm
through speaking voices in search of an operative dialectic between signifying systems and the world as it is and as it might become. He takes
his freedoms, has a grounded sense of what is real, and is optimistically
unimpressed by predictions of global homogeneity achievable through a
universal rationalisation of culture. In 'A Manifesto' (HH p. 77) it is
Futurists who hold hands among the atoms and across poems of intimate

address, political event, and speculative alterity seemingly subject to no rules of inclusion other than their presence on the page. Admission is anarchic but not without priorities. Certain contemporary practices don't operate in 'A Particular Country' of rain forests – 'Decreation, deconstruction died there' (HH p. 54) – and 'A Moratorium' on remembering while 'history's jugular drips' is refused in part by activating intimate memory and autobiographical event (HH p. 56). Meanwhile Morgan's self-regulating atoms assemble a range of deviant experience and heterodox perception, from the pathos of a rent-boy who speaks 'Il Traviato' (HH p. 27), to the black comedy of 'An Interview' with a vengeful Lazarus left to stink his life away: 'We know them / these holy men, death-bringers even when they're / bringing the dead to life. They crucify the spirit' (HH p. 38). For the carnivalised armed insurrection of an ethnically marginalised 'awesome advancing high-yaller charivari', 'there must be no harmony, no marching. / Each to his own' (HH p. 64); and a brothel-keeper teaches a transvestite hooker how to attract 'real men' (HH p. 65).

Suturing signifier to sometimes-arcane real world referent requires technical self-scrutiny, and *Hold Hands Among the Atoms* sifts its own procedures through a running fascination with the act of writing. A photograph of 'Aunt Myra (1901–1989)' registers slippage between memory, words and representation: 'Something is hard, not easy, though it's clearly / a man, a fan, a woman, a room, a picture' (HH p. 33). 'A Story' dramatises surreal and semi-autonomous narrative progress (HH p. 43), and 'A Defence' turns its celebration of thieving magpies into *jouissance* on 'this page': 'seeing / these things, first white, now white and black, to pay its / tribute to, and lay out, thus, its pleasure' (HH p. 46). 'A Water Horse' anglicises 'Kelpie' from *The Horseman's Word* (CP p. 211) as transforming thrust from formlessness to a slow canter across the universe (HH p. 61), and possible real world leverage for crafted utterance is thematised when 'Sunday in East Mars' launches the 'strenuous pleasure' of discovery against conceptual closure. A speaker in deep space transmitting singularity as preferred collective code is out to disconcert the receiver of his message:

> We want you not to know, and not to manage.
> We think you manage far too much. We'd never
> send you a scenario, a storyboard, a legend,
> but we do and in our time endlessly will
> give you signals that show greater power's
> in stories than in story.

Rather than programmed image-management acclimatising viewers and consumers to encoded values, 'Sunday in East Mars' asks instead: 'What is adjustment? / Giving up. What is a whole? A sum of / parts done wrong'.[30] Relevant to the series as well as the message at hand, this voice claims: 'Delight is / use and use delight, and when you write you / move the shape of things that millimetre / it needs to breathe', so that it 'grows, re-forms but never forms, advances / in its own dimensions'. Describing 'scarlet nasturtiums / twin[ing] with vigorous will between the boulders', he reaches the end of his message with 'I love to watch them when I'm not transmitting. / We'd send you one, but then you have it, don't you?' (HH p. 67). 'You have it' idiomatically bridges the ambiguity it triggers between 'you understand the difference between world and word,' and 'you have received the transmission that confirms their inseparability'.

Morgan returns to a collapsed Soviet Union when 'Red Flag Down', opening poem in *Sweeping Out The Dark* (1994), asks 'Who is going to praise those crowing / over the lowering?' and bears disabused witness to post-communism's first New Year: 'slipping through the bars of the moon / to thud and wail on our filthy snow'. A substitution of commonwealth (*sodruzhestvo*) for empire is the linguistic deception on which political elites depend when the impact of unregulated markets on deregulating economies makes for 'a steamy, seamy time' everywhere: 'skew-whiff for *mesteremberek* [craftsmen], / brilliant for peddlers in shop doorways, / deadly for grannies with ice-cracked bones'.[31] A later poem describes imagination as 'the nose-cone of the race'; and in *Sweeping Out The Dark* the first of a six-sonnet sequence called 'Trajectory' writes revolutionary burn-out as a nose-cone's re-entry to 'grit and rust and dark and love and gall'. Taking a longer perspective on 'the ball of earth alone unhung / on any golden chain', 'The Blue Ring' existentialises Henry Vaughan's vision of eternity in favour of a real world 'aspiration to explore / vulnerablest things devoid of fear' (SD p. 2). Seen from a distance that resolves into immediacy, 'The Revolution' in sonnet 3 moves in a world of luxurious consumption and permissive control, and is attentive to machine intelligence as perpetuating instrument for real world and representational systems, when the power to programme becomes actually existing power's programme: 'a made world'; 'an artifice'. The poem's seemingly omnipotent 'they' exercise instant global transmission of context-changing practice, and they appropriate the political dispensation of Ghandi's term for resistance: 'Satyagraha? You have only to ask'. Against which our speaker maintains that in the right light 'you could actually see right through' the process:

> Millions were still content to grunt and bask
> in designer spas, pink jacaranda rooms
> run up a moment before, out of nothing. (SD p. 3)

This poem's revolution is a 'green' one with teeth: 'our / drills went in and gouged the viscous looms / they'd programmed. It's the earth, green. Smell! Look!' (SD p. 3). Real world contexts in the last three sonnets of 'Trajectory' reformulate the dialectic as a 'Thesis' that fabulates western decline and fall, an 'Antithesis' of buccaneering energy where 'the fit, the bad, the bold were mercenaries / with starry bedroll and a wad of banknotes'; and a 'Synthesis' that incorporates feelings from both for a damaged survivor who sees rougher times coming but finds in the shadow of Vesuvius a figure of persistence who gives the collection its title: 'No promises! Hell can be ahead. / In backstreet Naples, under her living cliff, / A woman vigorously sweeps out the dark' (SD p. 4).

If written language is a shadow-world then translation is an exercise in its effects, to which Morgan brings the spice of variety. The activity has been instrumental for him, from sound poetry to the 'revelation of nature as relentless metamorphosis' he found in the Hungarian poet Sándor Weöres (CT pp. 61, 59–101). 'One should explore everything', Weores claimed: 'including those things which will never be accepted, not even in the distant future. We can never know, at the start of an experiment, where it will lead … not even after we have completed it'.[32] One can see why Morgan was drawn; and when the editors of *European Poetry in Scotland*, to which Morgan was a major contributor, quote George Steiner they suggest a relevance for the fact that translations make up a third of *Sweeping Out The Dark*: 'Poetry translation plays a unique role inside the translator's own speech. It drives inward. Anyone translating a poem, or attempting to, is brought face to face, as by no other exercise, with the genius, bone-structure and limitations of his own native tongue'.[33] In the year *Rites of Passage* was published, Morgan agreed that 'like a good original poem' a successful translation 'has the effect of slightly altering the language it is written in, and I do not mean within the immediate context of the poem alone, but as regards the available potential of that language' (NNGM p. 234). Work he included in *Sweeping Out The Dark* shows him taking stock; part of an effort to accommodate global transformation and to measure existential time. He does Claudian's 'On the Old Man of Verona: A Deconstruction' into Scots to satirise a stubbornly self-centred order

stifling the aspirations of young people (SD p. 95), and uses a Scots version of Michelangelo's 'In me la morte' to personalise dying. The
wretched conditions of Leopardi's life make available a practised pessimism for a Scot mourning his loneliness; and for the comfortless figure
speaking Leopardi's 'Tae his sel' (included in an English version in *Rites
of Passage*), life is 'a wide wersh wanrufe' [dispiriting unrest], and the
world 'the last wanhope' [despair] (SD p. 101). Morgan's Pushkin generates resonance from the dying year by asking: 'Were you ever taken /
By some unrobust girl wasting away:

> Strange, but it's like that. She is stricken,
> Death-bent, poor creature, unrepining prey
> Of unseen jaws whose grip will never slacken;
> She smiles still, with red lips that fade to grey;
> Her face has twilight in its blood, not dawn;
> Alive today, tomorrow she is gone. (SD p. 103)

When the year turns, Pushkin's 'rhymes race forward to the rendezvous';
and Morgan includes both a use of Scots to catch the sound-poem
Velimir Khlebnikov built around the Russian *smekh* [laughter] (SD
p. 109), and the human nightmare that interrupts and overpowers
Khlebnikov's shouts and hootings in 'Ha-oo!' (SD p. 110). He also
includes translations from Gennady Aigi, whose sometimes-religious
feelings are person-centred and of this world. Aigi's 'A Note: Apophatic'
weighs biblically derived Orthodoxy against physical state terror as actually existing systems of subjection:

> but the night of this world should have been
> enormous terrifying like the Lord-not-Revealed
> such a thing could be endured
> but murder-people
> have seeped into the darkness of this white night:
> terrifyingly-simple
> terrifying Moscow night (SD p. 150).

Morgan remembers the 'immediate and powerful impact' of his first
discovery (in the late 1950s and in Italian translation) of Attila József's
'deep urban pathos and concern' (NNGM p. 115).[34] The inclusion of
25 József poems in *Sweeping Out The Dark* helps to ground a wide-
ranging project by reconstituting structures of feeling during a time of
their seeming obliteration. József (1905–37) – whose father deserted
the family and left a mother to survive by taking in washing, and who

managed to gain admission to Szeged University only to be expelled for
his subversive poetry, two volumes of which were published by the time
he was nineteen – ran foul of government and was charged with blas-
phemy. An anti-war poem Morgan calls 'Blighty Numbers' generates
radical effect out of ideological transformation: 'Stammering Christ's
are / Calcifying into one, till the bacchanalia / Of death-rattles mounts
up into a / Terror-sermon on the mount' (SD p. 137). Until he threw
himself under a train in 1937 József preserved a radical poetics in the
face of serious mental stress and instability partly by valorising interior
space: 'How good it would be to buy a ticket and travel to Oneself, it
is / there all right, alive, inside us' (SD p. 117). He centres intimate
pictures of working-class life around his washerwoman mother, and
extends the quality of feeling in that relationship to others labouring in
harsh conditions. 'March 1937' sets an international context for local
urgency in a struggle for social value:

> The papers say that mercenaries
> are ravaging the face of Spain.
> A brainless general in China
> chases peasants from hill to plain.
> The cloth we use to wipe our boots
> comes laundered back in blood again.
> All round, big words bemuse and smooth
> the voiceless miseries in men. (SD p. 138)

Drawn by a 'dry heart's leap of recognition … to a landscape that is
bone of my bone', József hones singular perceptions where freight sheds,
workshops and clanking trains are backdrop for 'A Night in the Suburbs'
to become the 'Night of the poor' and identify the poem's industrial
energy:

> Be my coal,
> and the smoke at my heart's core,
> cast me in your ore,
> make me a seamless forge,
> and make a hammer that labours and rings,
> and make my blade strike till it sings.

Meanwhile, the poem dryly prays: 'May the lice leave our bodies whole'
(SD p. 147). It is not difficult to see why his writing attracted official
hostility: 'Dead Landscape' accuses large landowners of engrossing natural resources to the exclusion of others, and 'The Woodcutter' wants to

lay his axe to the whole set-up (SD pp. 134–5, 136). For much of his earlier life József took work wherever he could find it: a speaker in 'Unemployed' – 'Eighteen months now / the bird can't rise from the ground' – looks back at a series of labouring jobs and continuing hunger. In a social order where 'everything's old', the old personify resistance: 'Revolution / coughs as it crouches on sharp-edged stones / ready for pelting, and with hands all bones / holds a bright penny: my best creation' (SD p. 131). Refusal of organised religion as a discipline of fear informs a response that 'has faith / but is silent before creed or oath'. A poem called 'They'd Love Me' develops alienation on a 'thankless earth' as basis for reconstructive commitment:

> If I was transformed
> to a god, in place of the god they know,
> men would love me in truth, with all their soul. (SD p. 132)

Jószef knew about writing in bourgeois society: 'All this is a game, you know. I'm writing here / in pencil. Gentry's money paid the paper'; and figures an experienced anger: 'These letters have no machine-gun rat-tat-tat / yet. Like poverty they gouge, like lice they bite' (SD p. 120).[35] From the voice of a twenty-year-old through to epitaph and a final 'set[ting] out for the gods above, / in opposition' (SD p. 149), Morgan links the way things were in 1930s Hungary with the way things are in a translating present: 'Going behind the heavy tread of the real, / look deep into yourself, see / where you were born' (SD p. 141). 'It is probably true,' Morgan commented, 'that the translator must come to a very peculiar awareness of the way in which the quest for the most native will turn out to draw him into the most universal. He pauses in an astounding landscape, almost afraid to move. When he moves, he is no longer himself. And that is it' (NNGM p. 235).

Notes

1 Tom Leonard, *Radical Renfrew*, Edinburgh, 1990, p. xxi.
2 Morgan, *Hold Hands Among the Atoms*, p. 32. Hereafter HH.
3 Interview in Nicholson, *Poem, Purpose and Place* p. 76.
4 Cairns Craig, *Out of History: Narrative Paradigms in Scottish and British Culture*, Edinburgh, 1996, p. 201.
5 Edwin Morgan, *Sonnets From Scotland*, Glasgow, 1984, p. 11. Hereafter referenced as *Collected Poems* (CP, p. 438).
6 Edwin Morgan, *Gilgamesh*, second version, 1997, unpublished typescript; John Frow, 'What Was Postmodernism?', in *Time and Commodity Culture: Essays in Cultural Theory and Postmodernity*, Oxford, 1997, p. 27.

7 MacDiarmid, *Complete Poems*, vol. I, p. 573. See also the explanatory note on the facing page.
8 Lynch, *Scotland: A New History*, pp. 13–14.
9 Tacitus, *The Agricola and The Germania*, trans. H. Mattingly, Harmondsworth, 1970, pp. 80–1.
10 Craig, *Out of History*, p. 201.
11 Douglas Dunn, 'Morgan's Sonnets', in Crawford and Whyte (eds), *About Edwin Morgan*, pp. 79, 83.
12 Craig, *Out of History*, pp. 201–2.
13 Dunn, 'Morgan's Sonnets', p. 83.
14 Raymond Williams, *On Television: Selected Writings*, ed. Alan O'Connor, London, 1989, p. 9.
15 Interview in Nicholson, *Poem, Purpose, and Place*, pp. 73–4.
16 Julia Kristeva, *Desire in Language: A Semiotic Approach to Literature and Art*, ed. L. S. Roudiez, trans. T. Gora, A. Jardine and L. Roudiez, London, 1984, p. 74.
17 See stanza 52 of Shelley's 'Adonais'.
18 Debord, *The Society of the Spectacle*, pp. 136–7.
19 Gilles Deleuze, *The Logic of Sense*, ed. C. V. Boundas, trans. Mark Lester, New York, 1990, pp. 261–2, cited in Claire Colebrook, *Ethics and Representation: From Kant to Poststructuralism*, Edinburgh, 1999, p. 202.
20 Jean Baudrillard, *For a Critique of the Political Economy of the Sign*, trans. C. Levin, St Louis, 1981, p. 172.
21 Walter Ong, *Orality & Literacy: The Technologizing of the Word*, London, 1995, p. 177.
22 Hans Magnus Enzensberger, 'Constituents of a Theory of the Media', in *The Consciousness Industry*, New York, 1974, p. 97; Williams, *On Television*, p. 5.
23 Fredric Jameson, *Postmodernism, or, The Cultural Logic of Late Capitalism*, London, 1991, p. 76.
24 Tzvetan Todorov cited by Peter Brooks, in *Reading for the Plot: Design and Intention in Narrative* [1994], Massachusetts, 1998 pp. 91–2.
25 Cited by Peter Dews, *The Limits of Disenchantment: Essays on Contemporary European Philosophy*, London, 1995, p. 260.
26 Jameson, *Postmodernism*, p. 74.
27 Fredric Jameson, 'Imaginary and Symbolic in Lacan: Marxism, Psychoanalytic Criticism and the Problem of the Subject', *Yale French Studies*, 55–6, 1977, p. 352.
28 Louis Althusser, 'Ideology and Ideological State Apparatuses', in *Lenin and Philosophy and Other Essays*, trans. Ben Brewster, London, 1971, p. 152.
29 Interview (17 August 1998).
30 Compare Adorno's refusal of Hegel's insistence that the whole is the true: for Adorno 'the whole is the untrue' partly because 'the thesis of totality is itself untruth, being the principle of domination inflated to the absolute'. (*Hegel: Three Studies*, p. 87.)
31 Edwin Morgan, *Sweeping Out The Dark*, Manchester, 1994, p. 1. Hereafter SD.
32 Cited by William Jay Smith, 'Foreword', in Sándor Weöres, *Eternal Moment: Selected Poems*, ed. M. Vajda, trans. Edwin Morgan, William Jay Smith et al., Budapest and London, 1988, p. 9.

33 George Steiner, Introduction, *Penguin Book of Modern Translation*, 1966, cited in Peter France and Duncan Glen (eds), *European Poetry in Scotland: An Anthology of Translations*, Edinburgh, 1989, pp. xv–xvi.

34 Morgan, *Collected Translations*, p. xxi.

35 See 'Attila József: Curriculum Vitae (1937)', and 'Chronology', included in *Winter Night: Selected Poems of Attila József*, trans. John Bátki, Budapest, 1997, pp. xiii–xix.

7 Not fade away

You can't smoke Magritte's pipe. You can't eat Burns's haggis, even though it's 'warm-reekin, rich'. (Edwin Morgan)[1]

Images of endless repetition, yet never quite the same, haunt my mission, which I can't know. (Edwin Morgan)[2]

Renewal is figured differently when the talkative sperm on 'A Voyage' that initiates all others stretches orgasmic instant into exploratory narrative for radio listeners to enjoy an unusual love-in.[3] As this spermatozoon politikon launches into language and on to a large but momentary intra-uterine stage, small space generates expansive metaphor where interior and exterior change places. In the first but endlessly compulsive odyssey of every adventurer eager for experience – 'hungry prow high-pointed towards the Other' – figures talking successful copulation is the grounding conceit for a narrative journey from linguistic conception to epithal-amium. Travelling from soliloquy to dialogic union with a self-identifying and sensuous feminine egg, Morgan's communicative sperm shapes perception as he goes: 'The caves are full of – what are they full of? – us', or: 'When I say "like", / What do I mean? Could two sperms fall in love? / I am given to speculate, but there's no time'. In an already made and constantly remaking context, a description of muscle and tissue encodes cognition interacting with chance:

> How strange to think
> This mechanism, this place with all its splendours
> Interlocking, planned, crafted, long perfected,
> Should be a cradle of adventitiousness
> At our level,

and subsequently: 'Contingency keeps order on its toes' (VR p. 16). Since we are moving in language, that order is partly signified in the rhyming couplets of an initially self-contained but also self-determining feminine entity moving to the triplet of union, when action animates being. 'In the beginning was the sound', writes fellow-Glaswegian Tom

Leonard, and because at Morgan's first frontier with alterity it is the female egg who 'had the wit / to say "I am"', coolly displacing a Judaeo-Christian patriarchal paradigm, the beginning was her sound-world.[4] As the birthplace of intersubjectivity and necessary grounding of relation-ship, speech is the first repository of memory and origin of history. Egg and sperm enter the Symbolic with appropriate convulsions when an orgasmic Big Bang – 'The explosion was volcanic, / The release, the scat-tering, the four, five waves / Were like the climax of some giant act / We were and were not part of' – locates beginnings in language. In this medium, microorganisms develop sense and sensibility (and a social mutuality): 'By tinglings, breathings, scents and apprehensions / – Impossible but there it is – of goals, / Ends, embraces, giving and taking of treasures' (VR p. 17). In a brief history of time the material millions of ejaculation move through their instant as an exacting and exhausting challenge in our speaker's remembering present; which is the single site of reference – 'that's the point. It's my story' (but one that will fuse with another as it mutates and reproduces) – for time passing, present, and prospective future. The egg has her own narrative awareness: 'I am not here to frighten you', she says, 'Well yes I am! But that's the way / To pull the hero into play' (VR p. 17). Naming a world that moves them as they move through it, for sperm and egg organic chemistry and fictive stratagem combine to trace the arrival of subjectivity and story. Nefertiti, Bonnie Prince Charlie, Sigourney Weaver (knocked out of the race by an alien cell), the Argonauts; all are a-flowing, part of 'an army / Of explor-ers, aspirers, tunnellers, Galahads', which 'A Voyage' moves through everyday linguistic practices of the speaking subject – 'At that joke I snapped out of it'. Dramatising the inevitability of discursive being and reconstructing medium as message, Morgan delivers an oral context for shared self-making.

As recorded voice entering ears over electronically transmitted sound waves, the poem finds airspace for scripted speech-worlds. And since to yield their meanings all acts of writing have to be related some-how to the world of sound, 'the natural habitat of language', we are use-fully reminded that 'reading' a text means converting it to sound, aloud or in the imagination, because:

> thought is nested in speech, not in texts, all of which have their
> meanings through reference of the visible symbol to the world of
> sound. What the reader is seeing on this page are not real words
> but coded symbols whereby a properly informed human being
> can evoke in his or her consciousness real words, in actual or

imagined sound. It is impossible for [writing] to be more than marks on a surface unless it is used by a conscious human being as a cue to sounded words, real or imagined, directly or indirectly.[5]

But speech in turn nests in texts which thereby historicise its use, and poetry is an archive of the process. When the voyaging sperm penetrates the hitherto unexperienced shape of the egg, he recognises primal repetition as continuity: 'I have to re-enact the very deed / that gave me life'. Activating prior script as both speech and recorded action he wonders whether 'ghosts from some earlier encounter' might include the shade of Belshazzar, slain after Daniel interpreted the letter of his judgement (Daniel V, 1–31); then opts for survival by physical intervention metaphorically conceived. 'The head,' he says, 'like a snake's wedge, / Must weave from side to side, the tail must thrash / With rhythm, the whole body must trace the five points of a star' (VR p. 14).

Points which the whole body must trace include the development of a literate society. How that society sustains itself is theme for 'The Five-Pointed Star' of varying responses to Robert Burns; in the first of which Catherine of Russia's sexual needs are spoken in soliloquy but absent from the letter of invitation she sends to Scotland: 'All this I did not write, but he can read / Between the lines, for his need is my need' (VR p. 38). Catherine expresses reservations about Burns's republicanism: 'James Macfarlan', an urban Glaswegian poet from the industrial generation that followed Burns, sees him 'strutting / Through the salons in his best breeches, rutting / In a cloud of claret, buttonholing / Lord This, sweet-talking Doctor That', to the disregard of those who 'thrive / Or fail to thrive by foundry fires, or try / To find the words … to show the new age its dark face'. Burns owed his position as Excise Officer in Dumfries to the Earl of Glencairn, and recanted his earlier politics to keep his job. Macfarlan may also have been aware that after 1793 Burns penned patriotic anti-French verse:

> 'Liberty's a glorious feast,' you said.
> Is that right? Wouldn't the poor rather have bread?
> Burns man, I'm hard on you, I'm sorry for it.
> Your flame dazzled, folk gave you glory for it.
> I think such glory is dangerous, that's all.
> Poetry must pierce the filthy wall
> With cries that die on country ways. The glow
> Of bonhomie will not let the future grow. (VR p. 39)

Wordsworth thought Burns 'a man of extraordinary genius': 'Whose light I hailed when first it shone, / And showed my youth / How verse may build a princely throne / On humble truth'. Had the two known each other they would have been 'true friends though diversely inclined'; the latter demonstrably true. But Wordsworth thought the well-intentioned damage done to Burns's reputation by his first editor would have been avoided if James Currie had been blessed with 'one of the noblest characteristics of Englishmen, that jealousy of familiar approach, which, while it contributes to the maintenance of private dignity, is one of the most efficacious guardians of rational public freedom'.[6] To redress cultural and political perceptions north and south of the border, Morgan devises a familiar approach for a later Scot who rationalised an English lexicon and thereby opened access to its instrumentality. 'Sir James Murray', a tailor's son from Hawick who became editor of *The New English* which in turn became *The Oxford English Dictionary*, echoes Burns ('O lovely words and lovely man') with 'I pick a daimen icker from the thrave / And chew it thoughtfully'; and then – 'I must be brave and fight for this' – exercises an exuberant alterity as he maps an imperial vocabulary:

> My English colleagues frown
> But words come skelpin rank and file, and down
> They go, the kittle skimmers, they're well caught
> And I won't give them up.

Aware of his readers' sensitivities – 'Some, though not I, will jib at houghmagandy: / We'll maybe not get that past Mrs Grundy' – this Scotsman abroad knows what he is about: 'We steam along, we crawl, we pause, we hurtle, / And stir this English porridge with a spurtle' (VR p. 40). While Murray was indexing a metropolitan lexis for the English-speaking world, 'Franz Kafka' in Austria was an official in the accident prevention department of the state-sponsored Worker's Accident Insurance Institution; from where he reviews Burns's case as well as his own. 'Kafka' makes intertextual sport of bad faith as it explores writing complicit with governing power: 'How can [Burns] brood / Over the shillings in his ledger – the king's / Shilling! – when heads are rolling and rings / Are cut from the half-dead on battlefields?'. Complicity then echoes in present circumstance:

> Nearer home nothing yields
> To pity. My last client lost his arm
> On the shop floor. Everyone knows the harm

Was 'accidental', management was clean.
No one's going to subpoena a machine. (VR p. 41)

The fifth point of this star offers testimony about machine-readable
transmission – 'It's all on CD-ROM. Look under Song':

Digitized Burns is mixed from every portrait,
Strides like life across the fields, goes straight
To his chair, frowns, hums, fidgets, sings.
Remember his 'rich, deep' voice? It rings
Through the room, his eye smoulders the wallpaper. (VR p. 43)

Deictic and encompassing, multi-media representation of Burns here
inscribes loss in plenitude: 'Its strange perfection disinherits thought',
and against over-determined digital simulation, print text is preferred for
the internalising license exercised by participation: 'The real songs linger
at a fugitive table, / Amazing, changing, bold, supreme, able / To get
the hardest eye to glisten, heart / To throb, vessels of a profuse art'. The
voice of 'An Anonymous Singer of the 21st Century', feels like Morgan's,
seventy-seven years old when *Virtual and Other Realities* was published,
raising a glass to Burns and to lyric surviving compound simulacra:

I sing to please myself now, or for friends.
Great songs may have uncovenanted ends.
The stream of love, hope, memory, incitation
's too naked for this packaged generation.
But hear me if you will, and then you'll take
A joyful draught with me for that man's sake. (VR p. 44)

The sequence that follows 'The Five-Pointed Star' gives the collection
its title, and explores for a generation packaged or otherwise some of the
uncovenanted ends contingent on electronic networking and a world
wide web that seems limitlessly extensible.

Generally understood as the use of computer modelling and simulation
to enable a person to interact with an artificial, three-dimensional visual
or other sensory environment, in Morgan's handling 'virtual reality' has
been metaphoric resource and textual practice for some time. As part of
a series initiated by Peter McCarey and first published in *Verse* as 'Rehabs
and Reconstructions' (vol. 4, no. 2, June 1987), the imaginary space of
'Variations on Omar Khayyám' (CP pp. 503–7) introduces ancient text
to multi-media futurity when a vividly rendered yet minimally sketched
desert camel train's dawn awakening transpires as film, 'almost like life,

/ in close-up or in long-shot, wound off a reel / in the dark archive bay',
watched by an unruly crew in an intergalactic flotilla itself under surveillance from a cosmically distant monitor:

> and that panel flickered, not crowded round
> by angels, not in heaven, but hung one moment
> in annihilation's waste, the console glowed
> unplayed by fingers, the code changed
> every instant, a cold wind hurried down the steps
> and ruffled the fresh dark well of life (CP p. 504)

Seizing the day acquires contemporary urgency when 'rolling dead
young men' are 'left for film crews'. 'Variations' animates a linguistically
simulated environment to move its reader through changing viewpoints
and perspectives: rhythms and phrases it uses as sensors to guide contact
with both textual precedent and its own unfolding are taken from a nineteenth-century translation into English that became popular enough to
be known as 'Fitzgerald's Rubaiyat'. A characteristic time- and scene-
shift returns Morgan's poem from deep space to ageless desert, where
Khayyám and his lover couple under the stars and speak decidedly
modern idiom. But 'shaft me' also reaches from penis-signifier back to
Anglo-Saxon roots in creation, origin; involved in making or constituting nature or species (OED). Because its medium is linguistic,
'Variations' constructs a mirror of its own production. 'Virtual and Other
Realities' refracts these techniques through an interactive sequencing
that makes interface a technological condition of scripted existence as it
now is for many people across a spectrum of message transmission and
reception. To a degree that troubles some real-world analysts, social integration of these simulations and deliveries is advanced by special effects
in films that familiarise audiences with and acclimatise them to machine
assimilations of human subjectivity. Screen cyborgs, cybernauts, and self-
programming (and therefore autonomous) computers are now staple
representational fare, where forms of simulation routinely shape and
transmit dimensions of the actual.

When different forms of text are signifying nodes in the networks
of a developed economy; film, print and electronic techniques intersect
with weapons development, as cyborg behaviour and associated narratives repeatedly display. E-mail developed out of an American military
requirement for a dispersed communications system that might survive
nuclear attack; and according to *Encyclopaedia Britannica*, virtual reality came of age in the 1980s, when the US military and the National
Aeronautics and Space Administration began creating new systems for

computer-generated imagery. 'In 1989 the U.S. Department of Defence launched Simnet (simulator network), [an experimental link-up between] microcomputer-based workstations that enabled military personnel to practice combat operations on interactive, real-time training systems; Simnet was used to prepare U.S. troops for the Persian Gulf War in 1991'.[7] Virtual was always already a moulding of other realities, and its original linkage with an ethical valorisation of engagement with the public good is part of an historical transition to which Morgan's sequence is sensitive. Although in optical science 'virtual' applies to the effect of reflection or refraction on rays of light, its earliest surviving appearance denoted individually willed, context-changing capacity exercised by virtuous citizens acting sometimes singly sometimes collectively. The word took a turn to the invisible world during seventeenth-century conflict about how bread and wine signified, and subsequently became an almost entirely notional category when microphysicists used it to theorise energy loss and gain in molecular processes too instantaneous to measure. With these contexts in play, 'Virtual and Other Realities' defamiliarises the sense made widespread by networked computer-use, of something 'not physically existing as such but made by software to appear to do so from the point of view of the user'. To service this point of view the term is especially applied to 'memory that appears to be internal although most of it is external, transfer between the two being made automatically as required' (OED).

Morgan's poem 'In Night City' refers to William Gibson's *Neuromancer*, a science-fiction adventure judiciously published in 1984 that helped to integrate cyberspace into novel-writing territory where there is no community, only relations of dominance. Human figures, some invested with flesh and blood, some partly so and others holographic projections from memory banks mediating feral power, move through an urban jungle where flora and fauna are computer-designed and cloned replacements for originals lost in a distant and now hardly remembered past.[8] Gibson's cyberpunk protagonist Henry Case, managing to give as good as he gets before his final assumption into the Net that locates and specifies much of the novel's action, is paradigm postmodernist hero, transformed into the simulations that articulate his being. Neural technology occupies his body and invades his mind, and the environment through which he moves alters sometimes decisively his behavioural possibilities. In his world as ours electronic space is where context-changing transactions are routinely communicated, and jacking in to its virtually existent global network as 'real' an activity as any other, including for access to the black and grey markets where

Case survives. Gibson's prose takes Case flatlining into a predatory cyberspace where human and machine intelligence become inseparable and where rival corporations resolve market penetration. His narrative delivers a spatialised world of audio and visual projection, sometimes holographic and undetectably simulated so that Case and the reader have difficulty discriminating one virtual reality from another. Meanwhile, under a 'hologram sky glittered with fanciful constellations suggesting playing cards, the faces of dice, a top hat, a martini glass', artificially reproduced subjectivity is refined to the point where Neuromancer himself, avatar of a successor generation of android intelligence, can say in robotic staccato that ironises as it existentialises his performance: 'Unlike my brother. I create my own personality. Personality is my medium.[9]

In 'Poetry and Virtual Realities', a lecture given at a 1998 Edinburgh Science Festival, Morgan quoted Phil Tippett, who runs an animation studio in Berkeley, California:

> We now have the ability and the technology to make things look photorealistic using the computer. But this revolution is going to surpass the industrial revolution, and there's going to be a lot of blood on the floor ... the computer demands that you be very procedural and use specific language.... It's not the same thing at all as having a relationship with materials. My concern is that ... one can tend to lose touch and sight of the real physical world.[10]

Tippett's concern about alienation from the material world is shared by others:

> The repetitive structure of what [Baudrillard] calls the simulacrum (that is, the reproduction of 'copies' which have no original) characterises the commodity production of consumer capitalism and marks our object world with an unreality and a free-floating absence of 'the referent' (e.g., the place hitherto taken by nature, by raw materials and primary production, or by the 'originals' of artisanal production or handicraft) utterly unlike anything experienced in any earlier social formation.[11]

But the late twentieth-century emergence of electronically mediated cognitive moulding will also, it has been suggested, free learning from coercion: 'the essence of the coming integrated, universal, multi-media, digital network is discovery – the empowerment of human minds to learn spontaneously, both independently and co-operatively, Morgan has his suspicions:

There's a kind of dialectic going on as to whether we should
rejoice that simulation can now be so expert we don't always
recognise it: on the other hand where does this leave us, what
kind of world are we living in if we don't know what we see and
feel and so on? I think that over the sequence as a whole it's
probably left as an ongoing argument in my mind, because I
haven't decided myself. I find very fascinating the idea that if you
had the helmet and the gloves and they were more sophisticated
than they are at the moment and you were giving yourself and
were being given experiences which were possibly even more convincing than real life; it's both a kind of triumph of things that
were unimaginable some time ago yet on the other hand it has
an element of fear about it because you maybe think that you are
no longer in control of what you are doing. It's the element of
control and power that lies behind it that is the worrying thing.
['Virtual and Other Realities'] does come back to people living
in cardboard boxes so maybe that is the interim final statement
about it. I think there is still an uncertainty in my own mind
about the whole thing. I find it very fascinating but I have worries about it as I think probably many people do have. It won't
stop, and we have to get to grips with it somehow.[12]

Catching the Japanese/American axis of *Neuromancer*, a demotic,
knowing Glaswegian personality whose medium is 'In Night City' also
has his doubts:

> Ur aw thae radgie nuts in Cybernippon
> guys and dolls yer hauns kin get a grip on,
> an if they're no, whit screens ur they a blip on?

Idiomatic reference here to the 1955 Hollywood film version of Damon
Runyon's 1931 story 'Guys and Dolls' suggests that intertextuality is
endemic to both speech and story and the perceptions they encode.
Rhyme-adjusted reference to Marcel Duchamp's 'La Mariée mise à nu
par ses célibataires, même' (The Bride Stripped Bare by her Bachelors,
Even) suggests something similar and different by creating other contexts for one of the great enigmas in twentieth-century image projection
that began in 1912 as a pencil sketch on tracing paper, developed into a
compound of literary and graphic forms including a 'Musical Erratum'
and comprised elements that had been independent artworks.
Duchamp's so-called 'Large Glass' was begun in America in 1915 and by
1923 had reached the 'definitively unfinished' state in which it was exhib-
ited; a visual construct constituted by a cluster of associated productions

each having its own validity and each contributing to a work that has
been described as one of the most mysterious of all time.[13] Contingency
kept order on its toes when the 'Large Glass' was smashed on its way
from exhibition in 1926: ten years later Duchamp put the shattered
pieces together. 'It's a lot better with the breaks', he told Pierre Cabanne,
'a hundred times better. It's the destiny of things'.[14]

Provoked into a double take at Gibson's printed representations of
visual representations of imaged presence, Morgan's doubting Scot
wants to know more:

> Is it blid, is it juice, is it a chairge, ur they randy?
> Is their denner pretend-sampura wi trash-shandy?
> Whit d'ye mean ye're no sure. That's handy! (VR p. 76)

The prosthesis he utters delivers a Scottish astonishment at real time
Glasgow ('toon') contexts: 'See thon? See power? Whit a stoon!' This
will be a strategy across the sequence; bringing into language alternative space for subjectivity as knowable site of comprehending power
and motivating agency. And since epic occupation of deep space is now
a continuing function of technology, and colonisation of discursive
space a daily composition of local and global telecommunications,
'Virtual and Other Realities' moulds expansive scale to an everyday
world where faxing is a widely normalised evolution in the speed and
variety of text transmission. A grounded speaker feeding paper into the
machine notes the shift from Gutenberg he is already internalising –
'The signals go, the page remains' – and talks about the weather and
his garden. Despite the charms of elusive signifiers, in the sentient world
of 'March' a fidelity to the body in the phenomenal world measures
the real in triplet time:

> The fax
> is in the land of numbers, covers its tracks,
> its impulses like rations brought in packs
>
> across a thousand miles can only say
> the dialling hand is up and on its way,
> braced by one raffish, restless, rude spring day. (VR p. 47)

The difference from physical impact that is the aporia all signifying systems must accommodate is de-and reconstructed here and across the
sequence: but as a technical instrument where 'the virtual and the real /
are married', language in 'The Race' directs energetic simulations into
'our longing for the plenum of the weal' (VR p. 67).

'The land of rhyme is active' in 'The Ferry' because nothing is static in cognitive experience, and claims of user-friendly mutuality between virtual and other realities – 'it searching you, you it' – are vigorously displaced: 'buffet, buck, breach / dimensions like meniscuses, give speech, / cry out, scrunch your keel right up the beach' (VR p. 48). 'The Ferry' measures slow chugging through water against windsurfers skimming over it into the vanishing distance, and projects real world time in invented image:

> The sailboard like an angel-fish head on
> has virtually vanished, only to don
> a shimmer that long after it has gone
>
> you could stand watching, waiting for the time
> when it must turn and be itself, and chime
> with what you know is real on waves of rhyme. (VR p. 48)

If surfing the internet is subliminal metaphor here, Jack Kerouac provides the opening line of the next poem for an initially destabilising category shift from terra firma to 'Mare Firmum': 'Walking on water wasn't built in a day'. In a poem where 'Only the naked foot must make its name', a tried and tested print projection of Jesus buoyant and Peter sinking (Matthew XIV, 25–33) becomes shared imagining in a virtual transcendence that relates more readily to a Logos understood in its original combination of 'reason' and 'word'. In order 'to tell us we must sometimes walk there too', 'Mare Firmum' strips windsurfers of their equipment and reintroduces a 'sailboard like an angel' to send an adventurer 'across the choppy tops, a saint alone, / till faint and fading he is the sea's own'. A watcher invited to people this 'Mare Firmum' does so by generating visual effect:

> At last it seems nothing will do. You sit
> on the machair, the dawn mist lifts a bit
> as you stare at imagined figures threading it. (VR p. 49)

A fundamental simulation in the series, the illusion that mediates many of its effects, is a linguistic animation of speaking voices; and a high-tech cycle advertising the shift from orality through literacy and print to electronic media is necessarily tuned into printed words as visual coding of the elusive world of sound. For a user hoping to arrest time, the throwaway pen with which he writes on paper – 'I'm holding fast to everlasting snows' – invites the elegy that marks its passing. 'The Pen' brings speech and script together in recognition that while means of delivery change, visible signs of writing do not dispense with orality. But because speech dies in the breath of its transmission, for its utterer orality is transient; 'gone into the world of sound' as the voice of 'Into Silence' puts it: 'There is no cutting-room floor, no ground. / I speak, and I am nowhere to be found'. As it spatialises the capacity of language to 'lap then zap the circuit', 'Into Silence' listens for peace and quiet:

> I think it would be good to hear that place.
> The finished tape would not re-trace but trace
> its noble scroll in one untampered space. (VR p. 50)

Astronomer Bernard Lovell tampered with space often enough to know that 'no one knows our universe is unique'. 'Flip' is the term that William Gibson uses when his protagonist switches into cyberspace, and the poem called 'Universes' uses a sixteenth-century Scots variant to fold back the cosmos, reinvest memory and speech as coeval, and wonder at possible realms past, present and coming by focusing on peopled narrative: 'some are scarcely born, and some so old / no time exists for their story to be told'. In preference to drifters who 'glean / nothing but what interminably might have been', the poem opens a space-time continuum that 'is of ancient stock', where 'Night and day the universes dock'. Its last triplet's launching pad for language mobilises John's gospel beginning as creation myth in active service of a connecting present:

> And day and night the gantries slip from sight,
> the horn is heard that puts our doubts to flight,
> the word moves out in casings clean and tight. (VR p. 69)

Challenge to ruling orthodoxy provokes governing reaction: word-worlds created and perceived by eye and ear of passionate subjects brought Christopher Marlowe to untimely end, as violent if not occult as the death of his famed protagonist. According to *The English Faust Book*, when the Doctor's students went to look for their teacher on the night his contract expired 'they found no Faustus':

> but all the hall lay besprinkled with blood, his brains cleaving to the wall: for the devil had beaten him from one wall against another, in one corner lay his eyes, in another his teeth, a pitiful and fearful sight to behold. Then began the students to bewail and weep for him, and sought for his body in many places: lastly they came into the yard where they found his body lying on the horse dung, most monstrously torn and fearful to behold, for his head and all his joints were dashed in pieces.[15]

Rehearsing this death scene as elegy to a free-thinking ethics: 'the very paradise / of seeing and saying left there for rats and mice', 'Marlowe' co-ordinates scripted speech by addressing questing character through secular dramatist: 'O Faust, Johannes, broken, spirited out / into your terror, I'll write you and I'll shout / your godless power until it comes about' (VR p. 89).

On one occasion when Gibson's Case is wearing a virtual reality helmet, it 'filled with a confused babble, roaring static, harmonics howling down the years'.[16] Morgan's 'Under The Helmet' slows things down when its speaker plays simulated circumstance off against imagined possibility; watching 'a camel saunter through the eye / of a needle and become a cable', then with immediate transition seeing 'two broad-winged pigs taxi and fly'. Constituting an imaginary domain where things happen, 'Under the Helmet' differentiates and connects enabling technology and the interactive space of *Beowulf*, including invented nightmare:

> Someone will pick it up to range again
> through all worlds imagination's men
> loom up with like old Grendel in his fen. (VR p. 56)

Living nightmares invented for survivors in 'The Fourth World' – 'Stumps are weeping, sodden rags are stinging' – are disclosed in emphatic detail when imagination's man scouting a fifth dimension from the core of Third World misery looms up with an old woman singing from a starkness that defies challenge: 'In order to make sure that the untold // stories are told'. Challenge is effected when feminine iconography moves from 'Daybreak bloodies a foundered caryatid / that shoulders only dust', to 'one so old' who 'stands up and flaps a shawl into the cold', and dramatises a relationship between image and reality that puts the copula in the sequence's title to work. And if the 'other' realities move towards an expansion of lifeworld possibilities ('The Fourth World' produces ringing defiance), those possibilities can be disconcerting in expansive ways. Contingency keeps order differently on its toes when '"A bunch of asparagus in a teapot" / comes at us' from domestic context, 'not quite part of the plot / but life all the same', and therefore valorised. 'In the Kitchen', a voice that takes 'order with a pinch of salt' is sensitive to 'the sturdy meaningful straight-bat // incongruity of that crock of tendertops' because: 'I love the *sdvig* [disruption] that tells the pomp to halt' (VR p. 52).

In the interactive dreams, projections and expectations that constitute 'Virtual and Other Realities', Leprechauns who 'extort a fitting fee'

are real-time players for a stoned Irishman in 'A Dream Recalled', unwilling to accept that 'the stiff windless ranks of sedge' are 'only themselves,
as he must learn to be'. His unhappy attempt at hallucination leaves him
still longing for the green light in the west. Half way through 'More
Questions Than Answers', its speaker agrees that 'So far this poem does
not have a focus' and compares sharing its activity to passing around a
cannabis joint. Readers left with more questions than answers by this are
assured that they 'are not likely to find nothing of note' (VR p. 59).
Whatever its problems, image-transmission managed by and interacting
with the human subject is sequence-theme, and Ezra Pound was a skilled
practitioner who lived through the 'thin film of images' (Canto 4) of
cinema's early impact. Rather than Pound's perception of the 'Poet' as
'simply the great true recorder', the writer represented here with triplet
rhythm as probe takes the line into anger and describes an expanded range:

> Words, bitter as tears, are overflowing.
> Words better than tears are doggedly hoeing
> fields that seem past harvesting or sowing.

> What poor creature then? 'He limps, he prowls,
> winces when something deep inside him howls.
> His line reminds, entices, soars, grieves, howls'. (VR p. 63)

'1818' reconstructs the attempted suicide and double death of
Matthew Clydesdale, a miner hanged for murder whose body was taken
to Glasgow's anatomy hall for an experiment:

> the avantgarde chemist, the galvanic battery. Air
> enters his lungs, his tongue wags, eyes flutter,
> limbs convulse, he stands, amazed, aware –

> his death is not in order!

So Matthew's jugular is lanced (VR p. 54). Morgan reminds us that the
event was supposed to have taken place a few months after the publication of Mary Shelley's *Frankenstein* and wonders whether the experimental scientist had read the book, and was trying to make life imitate
art.[17] Genres, canons and categorical imperatives, scripted or screened,
are miscible in this ordered disordering, whether in a 'Dialogue' between
remembering sensibility and punk present – 'What gunk / has jammed
your mind-set' – for brashness to win through by 'releasing and seeding
feelings we never knew' (VR p. 73); or spinning context for Marco Polo's
'not tall tale' about hauntings 'In the Stony Desert' of North West
China, where 'footfalls leave no footprints for his eyes':

The djinn laugh softly, don't materialise.

He sweats, swears, shouts, gallops half-possessed
until he sees the lighted tents at rest
as if only order and peace were manifest. (VR p. 79)

'A Mongol Saying' generates image through 'the great lord // Jenghiz, the unforgotten', and mingles 'real mirages' with effective subjection:

In his stirrups he rises,
his helmet points, his eye pierces, he advises.
Westward the unimaginable prizes

mingle with real mirages, whinnies, snorts,
dust-clouds of embassies from shaking courts,
letters of submission from rich forts. (VR p. 80)

In its interplay of virtual imaging and simulating script, the series provides for seemingly random access both to a real-time present and to a hyper-real environment where 'Rhetoric, like colour, melts off the edge'; and as with all semantic transmission slippage is endemic. When the speaker of 'Really Red' who walks out 'to find the really real, / from early morning into cochineal' reflects that 'that first mistake still seems to have appeal', it is a question whether the mistake (and the appeal) relate to represented movement or its immediate glide into metaphor. Either way, the category-master materialising here dissolves time and space in desire:

I entered cochineal at half past five.
The red was really lividly alive.
I halted with my mind in overdrive.

Mile upon mile, dimension on dimension,
a crimson chaos panted for invention,
for love, for the impossible intention. (VR p. 77)

'Apprehended, silent presences' in 'For Love' – 'We move towards them, feel that they enfold us, / plead with them to really want to hold us. / They disengage; they had to; so they told us' – urge a seizing of the day:

Armies of time, once summoned, are soon massed.
We run to meet them, disappearing fast
into a future that soon too is past. (VR p. 78)

Post-apocalyptic but still 'Brisk Thoughts towards Town' (VR p. 57) makes a plea for live music – 'A fife // throbs to be shrill, but cannot, in its case / by the door' – on behalf of people enjoying 'the run of things as grateful to be rife / as ever mouse and cursor were'; and a run of things that can be grateful and rife animates the reified order Marx saw as market society inevitability. In terms that become relevant to the poem called 'Marginalisation' – 'You can almost see our starving atoms' – Georg Lukács described this developing order in subjectivities mainly transacting through the purchasable goods of an apparently responsive market, goods which acquire a 'phantom objectivity' to service 'an autonomy that seems so strictly rational and all-embracing as to conceal every trace of its fundamental nature: the relation between people'. The freedom to purchase and possess, Lukács suggested, accumulates as a 'second nature'.[18] 'Who has not felt this', Morgan's poem asks, 'as Gramsci once'. Antonio Gramsci's 'We have increasingly become phantoms' is the opening line for 'Marginalisation' to set both textualised reason and printed apocalypse against shrinkage. 'We flit from Areopagus to Patmos':

> We pass through bastions, dungeons, pyramids.
> Nothing stirs in the stone. Our heavy lids
> drowse on the grilles and tills and screens and bids
>
> of an unclassic time. (VR p. 93)

Signifiers passing across space and through materiality suggest a returning relevance for neutrinos; and perhaps for Baudrillard's perception of currency value as itself the ultimate transmission system: 'A pure artefact, it enjoys a truly astral mobility … the orbit in which it rises and sets like some artificial sun'. Globalising access to its highly selective freedoms developed perceptions of the replicating image as itself the prevalent form of value-generation; but now less a process of exchange than an omnipresent saturation of selfhoods pursuing constantly reproduced simulacra of desire. Images of the real so expertly packaged for immediate consumption encode political and ideological dimensions in a mode of representation that is itself a culture product and 'by a long shot not historical reality itself'.[19] This liminal movement generates material structures: corporate capital and awesome power are both 'now in orbit above our heads on courses which not only escape our control, but, by the same token, escape from reality itself'.[20] Except that in Morgan's poem they don't so much escape from reality as endlessly replicate emptied selfhood in a surveillance society of managed consumption:

> Phantoms pushing nothing across counters,
> phantoms in malls, a maze of non-encounters,
> phantoms clocked by cameras and bouncers –

a blur, a shadow, something grey, half seen,
things to think back to, never really been,
an unclicked turnstile – the undead, the unclean! (VR p. 93)

'Images of endless repetition' produce the earthly 'Nightmare' of a paranoid speaker for whom 'everything's desperate': 'language, money, documents all gone' (VR p. 81). 'Transclusion' locates a paranoiac in cyberspace – 'a wild man far out in the Net' – and counsels him to transform his nightmare of universal debt into an everlasting rain check on despair. 'The Mass', perhaps in response to the despair about earthly futures Chernobyl blew across half the world, pluralises its title from a description of matter to include large-scale human assembly and addresses a nuclear obliteration that would makes a social exclusion zone of the planet, absolute for the peoples that disappear, promising cryogenic future to the self-selected few. The poem wonders about the survival of exploitative hierarchies: 'Kill all the species and yet keep the class?' (VR p. 96); a question partly answered when 'The Saluki' sets against an abstracting discourse of science – 'all phenomenal objects are bundles of qualia' – its energetic Arabian hound 'unbundling qualia everywhere' (VR p. 92). Disclosure involves self-disclosure and Morgan puts candour on the line when reference to a sixteenth-century Belgian anatomist suggests if obliquely that Matthew Clydesdale haunts a speaker's acceptance that a life of writing is subject to the nemesis of the signifier. 'To the Librarians, H.W. and H.H.' reads the notion that 'New shelves' of books represent 'new selves' as a delusory consolation that operates only until 'the hard white of existence':

> halted me in my tracks with its insistence
> on asking me if I felt no resistance
>
> to peeling layer on layer like a flaying,
> did I not hear the winds, the distance baying,
> where was my life, what was Vesalius saying? (VR p. 71)

'Death', says Walter Benjamin, 'is the sanction of everything that the storyteller can tell', the only end that can determine meaning.[21] In 'To the Librarians' a bid for truthful witness resolves life and writing into a life of writing to keep the figure of death at bay: 'What you have been and done's not set aside. / Your files are you, and file through one divide'. A mother's remembered words push fear into fable 'At the Last', and 'The Dead' connects autobiography with sequence-theme – 'How can living shapes be so invaded?' – by locating personal memory in public space. Perfectly balanced, 'The Glass' figures a moving objectification of emotion. 'Someone'

elegises a loved one in the virtual reality of intense memory traced by
'nothing but a poem to gather and keep' (VR p. 88); and a soldier who
seized the day whenever he could but doesn't like paying for the favour
takes us into some 'Real Times' of gay society that form part of an imagined community also projected 'In a Bar'; and where 'Not that Scene' res-
cues pleasure from unpromising context.

As the sequence measures large and particular sympathies, from
physical sex to a gestating universe, it also ironises its own procedures by
following Fyodor Tyutchev's 'A thought articulated is a lie' with a seeming demonstration: 'The threadworm challenged lobsters prancing by'.
Tyutchev was a diplomat as well as poet, and 'Indefinables' plays articu-
lation into a suspicion of the way that 'plated jointed thoughts get their
victory':

> Articulated, hence articulate?
> Thoughts in grammar picking out the state?
> Thoughts in metre sent at highest rate? (VR p. 85)

Thought articulating with systems of material power is disconcerted
when broken speech finds a measure of meaning that leaves threadworm
safe and lobsters potted. Believing that 'Minds rest no more than seas,
though they may try', 'Indefinables' sets surrealist cartoon against controlling discourse, and includes the sky in its bid for freedom. Making
alternative space for signifying subjectivity, 'On the Level' subverts and
restores its title by imitating the disconnected syntax and signifiers of
L=A=N=G=U=A=G=E poetry, whose protocols are found inadequate
because they 'find a pressure point, run out of sight' (VR p. 86). In the
invented syllables of 'Zaum', on the other hand, 'the human tongue /
has shot into the mind': 'When virtual poetry joins the caravan, / not
what it cannot, please, but what it can // is your criterion for its board
and keep'. In praise of Khlebnikov's sounds, ordered syntax makes space
for non-syntactic rhythm, achieved measure delivers difference, rhyme
assimilates quoted syllables that remain free-floating signifiers for each
reader's use: 'And no it's not encrypted, for its plan / is to keep virtual'
(VR p. 87).

Wittgenstein's proposition that the limit of our words is the limit
of our world recognises language as instrumental guidance system for
sentient thought. That words limited to fields of reference sanctioned
by governing practice thereby sanction governing practice is a proposition ironised in 'Realism' as 'a mind too green / to kick-start action
from the dream machine'. The poem turns from realism as a type of
imagining divorced from action – 'velleities of crime' – to a seeing and

saying that redefines its title by transfiguring the object world; not into a fantastic narrative but as a metamorphosis in perception and in things perceived:

> how to say the cup is waiting there
> but does not know it is, shining to share
> a shining, bare as waiting lips are bare. (VR p. 74)

If realism 'counts the cracks in crags', 'Imagination' 'springs from the flagstones with a crack of fire', and pushes at known boundaries. Which is very much what Giordano Bruno's did until 'earthly powers' in the Vatican burned him alive with his tongue in a gag for suggesting 'Configurations still unfigurable', and for tapping into 'powers to come, still impermissible'. Necessarily (and dangerously) committed to uncensored investigation and reciprocal debate whatever the implications for biblical writ, Bruno imagined plural universes, as the epigraph he provides for *Virtual and Other Realities* makes clear; and 'Multiple worlds need multiple incarnation'. In return for his speculations about atomic matter and being, 'Giordano Bruno' conscripts neutrinos in support of the possible over the known:

> Ah but transcending it
>
> are specks we see, and specks we cannot see
> but must imagine, in that immensity.
> It is reason sets imagination free. (VR p. 91)

Shelley reasoned imagination into forms of freedom partly by dramatising his Fairy Queen as figure of expanding energy against England's social order. Relevant to a continuing interest of Morgan's, 'Queen Mab' witnesses the alienated subjectivity interpellated by a governing system which, 'like a desolating pestilence, / Pollutes whate'er it touches':

> and obedience,
> Bane of all genius, virtue, freedom, truth,
> Makes slaves of men, and, of the human frame,
> A mechanized automaton.[22]

Shelley re-cast 'Queen Mab' (1813) as 'The Daemon of the World' (1816) whose protagonist is encouraging movement from darkness into light when she speaks the epigraph for *Virtual and Other Realities*:

> For birth but wakes the universal mind
> Whose mighty streams might else in silence flow

Thro' the vast world, to individual sense
Of outward shows, whose unexperienced shape
New modes of passion to its frame may lend;
Life is its state of action, and the store
Of all events is aggregated there
That variegate the eternal universe.[23]

Like its mother text, 'The Daemon of the World' opened to human
observation both a complicit clerisy and professional engineers as agents
of spiritual and physical slaughter:

Shadows, and skeletons, and fiendly shapes,
Thronging round human graves, and o'er the dead
Sculpturing records for each memory
In verse, such as malignant gods pronounce,
Blasting the hopes of men, when heaven and hell
Confounded burst in ruin o'er the world:
And they did build vast trophies, instruments
Of murder, human bones, barbaric gold,
Skins torn from living men, and towers of skulls
With sightless holes gazing on blinder heaven.[24]

Both 'Queen Mab' and 'The Daemon of the World' shifted 'Nature'
from an assembly of Newtonian laws founding the world's intelligibility
to an energising power then visionary in early nineteenth-century prelude to historical fulfilment as republican, free-thinking and democratic
subjectivity; the revolutionary big ideas of the day which drew serious
reaction. Morgan shifts the agency of dissent into a *Demon* sequence of
twenty poems written in twelve months from January 1998, whose
space-and time-ranging reporters might also owe something to
Gilgamesh: 'a brave glitter, but a darkness inside', who is 'a demon of
activity by day and by night'; and perhaps more to Enkido with whom
Gilgamesh bonds, and who 'arrive[s] to change the order of things' with
'the force of the wilderness' in his veins'.[25] 'There are demons and
demons' says one of them refusing an invitation to torment the human
lifeworld; and the first speaker to tell his tale in *Demon* is a shape changer
whose 'job is to rattle the bars', who looks into the 'peeling miasma' of
an urban 'underworld' and makes 'perfectly visible' an underclass still
making music. Seeing Orpheus as a street busker working 'Pluto's glim-
mery piazza', and seizing a moment of ruling susceptibility induced by
the busker's song and detected in a 'shining wetness at the corner of
Pluto's eye', 'A Demon' turns street entertainment into resistance and

keeps one jump ahead of his pursuers: 'The visors are after me. Too late, grey ones! / I've done my bit. Orpheus is learning along':

> I scramble like a monkey
> From stake to stake and spar to spar and rattle
> My rod, a ratchet for the rungs, a grating
> Of something from gratings that has nutmegged,
> Pungenced, punched, punctuated the singing
> And made the singer devilish angry,
> Devilish fearful, and at last devilish strong.[26]

Affective music in rebellious voice activates a pre-Christian signification of demon as form of conscious agency somewhere intermediate between imagined gods and imagining people; and as such a human capacity for good and ill. 'A Demon' opens a series that re-positions a power to imagine alterity in speakers and characters ambiguously positioned in relation to an unambiguously human lifeworld.

In *Demon*'s *realpolitik*, the angry figure who puts iron into Orpheus's song is on the run from 'the vizors'; 'The Demon Winged' looking to close down a missile attack has 'militant seraphs' to cope with. Occult encounters with policing agencies in the service of determined power include perverted energy in brutal action when 'The Demon at the Frozen Marsh' reflects human agency at a nadir of organised society. Noting a certain thickness in the air above the death-camp at Auschwitz: 'something fogged and hoary about / But it won't settle', this demon enjoys the flash of sunlight on his body, and the shadow it casts of his lifted hand, 'spilling indescribable metal / over the shallow crust of ice on the pond' he looks down at. He also refuses any softening of the camp's reality: 'Nothing had better be beautiful while I am here', and his hardened ego roams the earth at will: 'I am off to where after Oświęcim. Watch' (D p. 6). A sympathetic and chatty 'Submarine Demon', whose 'hands, / Feet, sift sand, silt, squelch mud, clench / Tucks and puckers of the skin of the world', is 'drawn to a scene' on a seabed not measureless to man, but not easily fathomed either. Where the sun is not needed neither is Genesis, and in a hitherto undiscovered realm of freedom this maker and namer has much to keep him occupied:

> I'll stay awhile. No angels here, thank god,
> With their hymns and whips. I shall talk
> To the sea-beasts, give them names, teach them
> There are stars they'd be no better for seeing,
> And houses, new or ruined to pass by.
> I'll learn the good of what they only are. (D p. 8)

'The Demon in Argyle Street' intervenes to point hallucinating denizens of Glasgow's wino underworld towards disruptive agency; and 'The Demon Winged', keen to exercise its 'great reserves of soaring', is conscious of the need 'to fight the guardians of the time / On foot, where it hurts' (D p. 10). In localised space 'The Demon at the Brig O'Dread' is out to disturb 'another satisfying day of managing' – 'I saw we had had enough of that' – with effective reminders of mortality; and a demon's hymn grounds its marriage of heaven and hell in a clear sense of priorities:

> You'll never hear a harpstring
> If we can smuggle it
>
> Away from the high heavens
> And tease it out to bind
> Every grasping evangelist
> Right out of his mind. (D p. 12)

Making alternative music, 'A Little Catechism From the Demon' encodes an existential project: 'Study my life and set out now' (D. p. 28); and another of these spirit-visitors remembers a 'demon fancier' from the human world, 'With a bag of fruit and a flambeau,' who 'flashes a thigh and drops an apple'. Underwhelmed by the proposition, this demon instead shakes 'her hand, his hand (who knows?)' and incites response:

> Is it braille? Can you follow? I don't mean
> The text, I mean me! Do you even know
> What a demon is? Could you *be* one? Well? (D p. 9)

The demon who 'Goes To Kill Death' visits Middle East battle-grounds where all sides boast godly sanction: 'shelled villages were smoking shells / Or hells, though shellers crowed to heaven'. Unsuccessful there, he tries Third World hospitals where 'stubbly doctors dropped asleep / By empty cupboard doors that swung and creaked'; then watches 'muffled refugees' in mountain passes 'slipping with bundles from country to no country. / Old women were silent, with bleeding feet' (D p. 29). These contemporary reports include a Balkan war-fighting zone where all combatants routinely claim divine mission and where 500 years ago a youthful Albanian, Gjergj Kastrioti, converted to Islam while hostage to the Turkish Sultan who renamed him after Alexander the Great. Skanderbeg crossed over to rejoin his countrymen when the Turks were defeated at the Serbian city of Niš (in 1443), and repeated his success against Islamic forces often enough for the Vatican to name

him Captain General of the Holy See. In Morgan's re-location, unstable
currents are staple for a demon plotting carnage with 'restless diodes in
his mind'. But this is his day off, and God's momentary withdrawal from
war-fighting leaves a restless speaker to coin his wonder: 'Once in how
many thousand years is it, / This heavenless hellless place, this peace, this
pause?':

> He does not know; he does not think; he dreams.
> The sunken wrecks don't rise, and Skanderbeg
> Is motionless on his horse. There is nothing,
> Not even weather, nothing at all. (D p. 17)

The dream truce is brief; history will surface again, and despite its
demon's peaceful-seeming rest, the poem suggests, 'you will not take
that one home with you'.

'The Demon in the Whiteout' who looks for 'what I'd been told I
must not try to find / (best reason for a demon's trudge!)', replays creation myth through Mary Shelley's experimental figure here discovered
in Arctic wastes looking for ways to end it all; a mission our demon – 'I
knew his story' – seeks to postpone by recommending Promethean alienation as stimulant to outcast energy:

> 'We need a knot in the wood of good.
> Heaven crumbles just a little – and that's great –
> When the alien god staked out on the rock
> Discovers he can snap his chains, and does.

Confident that figures of invention 'would live to trouble both gods and
men', and aware that 'It may be a human thought to want to die, / But
it is more human not to', this demon heads for warmth 'whistling my
hearty, unsafe amen' (D p. 16). Compelled to internalise suffering, the
speaker of 'The Demon And The World' remembers Aeneas carrying his
father from burning Troy and draws a line between fable and lived experience: 'The poetry of departures / Jolts, grinds, judders, whines,
pounds, climbs – / And then you have, alone, to get on with your life'
(VR p. 18). In daemonic configuration that aloneness is a social phe-
nomenon, whereas Antony of Egypt, traditionally the founding father of
Christian monasticism, spent years getting on with his life in desert solitude where he was plagued by devilish visions. 'The Demon Judges a
Father' by including detail from Hieronymous Bosch's 'The Temptation
of St Anthony'; temptations here described as nothing otherworldly, but
'The cess and soss and process of his selfhood'. 'I know you won't speak

to me', this demon says to Antony: 'you think I am virtual', and voices
his real-world accusation:

> you solitary non-server
> Of the people, your persecutors are shadows
> Because you persecute yourself. Shadow
> Of a man, you have lost the coat of many colours.
> Oh how you hate the brightnesses of the world! (D. p 23)

Those brightnesses constitute 'A Demon's Distraction' as an orgy of
human movement where 'delights increase and multiply', before the
scene is wiped and 'horror recomposes' (D p. 25): but 'The Demon
Admires The Stars' because no one made them – '*lux* without *fiat*' – and
he points his purpose by connecting Morgan's concrete sequence with
Pictish inscription: 'if it was permitted / I would breathe a horseman's
word to bring / The runes of Aberlemno back to life' (D p. 27). The art
of story finds space for movement when 'The Demon Considers Day and
Night' by reinventing the world he scans 'under many million stars /
That shiftily declare absolutely nothing, / Not even everything', in an
internalising tale whose activating impulse reaches for the reader: 'to pull
you / Into my imagined land – I call it land – / To study the power to
do and to undo' (D p. 21). The constellation is still an invitation.

Morgan's 1949 'Conclusion' for 'The Triumph of Life' recognised
that:

> Sleepless are the barbarisms of Goya's malediction,
> Stephen is stoned although his name grows dim,
> And demons need so superseding fiction (CP p. 547)

In that early poem Rousseau's ghost invites Morgan's speaker to 'make
this sharp ascent, / Which may resolve or feed your heavy doubt' (CP p.
542). Half a century later, with nothing to keep him going but recorded
activity, prior representation, and the articulate conviction that what does
not change is the will to change, 'The Demon At The Walls Of Time'
will climb 'until I see stars / beyond what is only rampart rampart rampart', and will continue making mischief where he can. 'I don't come
unstuck', this figure insists, 'I don't give up. / I'll read the writing on
the wall. You'll see' (D pp. 30–1). 'The Demon on Algol' – 'demonic
caravanserai / If ever there was one, livid place, brilliant! – / It winked
into space, was called the evil eye – / I liked that' – plays on the Arabic
derivation of its name, and tropes the fact that Algol is an eclipsing
binary; one of two stars moving so closely in orbit that the light of one
eclipses the other, hence the poem's wink. Given the fabled association

of this second brightest star in the Perseus constellation with Medusa and the Gorgons, 'demonic caravanserai' is accurate; and any angel touching down there a self-convicted fool – 'dead thick'. Ludic subversion of orthodox hierarchies includes a cartoon reduction of ruling icons when a chorus of demons out-shouts a heavenly interloper:

> The angel jumped so sharp it shed its rags,
> Ran across the lava wailing something
> In its poor piping dialect. What a coarse roar
> We demons then sent after its toty buttocks
> Twinkling pinkly through a rain of cinders! (D p. 22)

Reviewing *Poems of Thirty Years* in 1983, Kenneth White quoted Georges Bataille, 'one of those radical poet-thinkers that are rare anywhere and in some places practically extinct': 'Poetry that is not engaged in an experience going beyond poetry will never be real movement, but only the residue of agitation'.[27] Morgan's development of an essentially political poetics of subjectivity through a carnival of scripted speech and interactive story seems endlessly renewable and plausibly humane; its only unthinkable thought being the absence of alternatives. Often-prodigious bridgings of the public and the personal, the fantastic and the real are included in meaning-making practices that multiply context for social and personal experience often at odds with both syntactic limit and tyrannies of style. 'I don't think there's anything you can't say,' Morgan commented in 1991, 'that wouldn't make sense if only you could devise a context for it. That sort of thing is in my work a lot, I'm sure'. The driven and driving figure climbing the walls of time who closes his *Demon* sequence agrees: 'Is challenge the word or is it not?':

> feeling and following
> The life-lines of unreadable inscriptions
> Cut by who by how I don't know, go
> Is all I know. (D p. 30)

Notes

1 Edwin Morgan, 'Poetry and Virtual Realities', lecture delivered at the 1998 Edinburgh Science Festival.
2 Morgan, *Virtual and Other Realities*, p. 81. Hereafter VR.
3 'A Voyage' was commissioned by the BBC and broadcast on Radio 4, 12 June, 1996.
4 Tom Leonard, on the front cover of *Intimate Voices: Selected Work 1965–1983*, Newcastle, 1984.

5   Ong, *Orality & Literacy*, p. 75.
6   William Wordsworth, *The Prose Works*, vol. 3, pp. 122, 344; *The Poetical Works*, vol. 3, p. 66.
7   'virtual reality', *Britannica Online* (www.britannica.com).
8   William Gibson, *Neuromancer* [1984], London, 1995.
9   Gibson, *Neuromancer*, pp. 180, 305.
10 Typescript supplied by Morgan.
11 Fredric Jameson, *Signatures of the Visible*, London, 1992, p. 17.
12 Interview with Morgan, 17 August 1998.
13 Richard Hamilton, *The Bride Stripped Bare By Her Bachelors Even Again: A Reconstruction*, Newcastle upon Tyne, 1966, n.p.
14 Pierre Cabanne, *Dialogues with Marcel Duchamp*, trans. Ron Padgett, New York, 1971, p. 75.
15 J. H. Jones (ed.), *The English Faust Book*, Cambridge, 1994, p. 180.
16 Gibson, *Neuromancer*, p. 238.
17 Morgan, 'Poetry and Virtual Realities', p. 14.
18 Georg Lukács, *History and Class Consciousness: Studies in Marxist Dialectics*, London, 1971, pp. 85–6.
19 Jameson, *Signatures of the Visible*, p. 22.
20 Jean Baudrillard, *The Transparency of Evil: Essays on Extreme Phenomena*, trans. J. Benedict, London, 1993, pp. 27–8, 33.
21 Walter Benjamin, 'The Storyteller', in *Illuminations*, p. 94.
22 Percy Bysshe Shelley, 'Queen Mab', in *The Complete Works*, vol. 1, p. 88.
23 Percy Bysshe Shelley, 'The Daemon of the World', in *The Complete Works*, vol. 1, p. 224.
24 *Ibid.*, p. 216.
25 Edwin Morgan, 'The Demon at the Frozen Marsh', and 'Submarine Demon', *London Review of Books*, 20: 12, 18 June 1998, p. 12.
26 Edwin Morgan, *Demon*, Glasgow, 1999, p. 5. Hereafter D.
27 White, 'Morgan's Range', p. 34.

Edwin Morgan: 'Pieces of Me'

Glasgow

In the tram with my mother –
I was five or six –
drunk man leaned across
offered me a sixpence.
'Ur ye a good boay?
Sure ye're a good boay.'
I was not so sure.
My mother hissed
'Take it, take it,
always take
what a drunk man gives you!'
I remember how nicely
he clasped my hand round the coin.

Rutherglen

For a while the walk
home from school
seemed without end.
My evil spirit,
my well-named bully
Harry Maule
followed, waylaid me,
punched me, punched me,
never said why.
I tried different routes
but that has its limits.
He was fond of winter,
threw stones in snowballs.
Not that I cried.
But he never said why.

North Berwick

Being about twelve
on the beach at North Berwick
I saw an enormous
sudden freak
wave pound
a swimmer down
and crashing cast him
limp on the sand.
Amateur hands
ran to pump him.
Blue; too late.
My first dead body.

Blantyre

Sydney Graham
sitting up in bed
pyjama jacket
open to the waist
tearing into a steak
clutched in both hands:
the poet at home.
I watched fascinated
as gobbets of gristle
spattered the sheets.
'Christ,' cried Nessie,
'we *have* got a plate!'

Rutherglen

With my call-up papers
I stood at the tram stop
talking to Jean.
'Don't know when I'll see you,
everything's uncertain.'
'I don't know' she said
very sharp 'if I like
to be included in everything.'
'Well – ' I said,
turned on my heel
and quickly walked off.

Cairo

After we medics
were regaled on the troopship
with admonitory close-up
grisly colour slides
of advanced chancres
we trooped to the Cairo
brothels but only
Jackie stayed long enough
to come back with a dose
and was flung treatment
but no sympathy.

El Ballah

On the open lorry
jolting into the desert,
pressed against the sweating
back of my favourite
blond-haired swaddy
I came.

Sidon

When we had set up camp
we watched the beautiful
skeleton of a fishing-boat
being built on the shore.
Arabs would occasionally
appear, hammer a bit,
sing, disappear.
Month after month
its see-through planks
framed their ravishing
patches of sea blue.
In waves of heat
the boat would shimmer
ghostlike, Phoenician.
We left after a year
for a new war zone,
said goodbye to a craft
still baking and shining
in perfect unfinishedness,
a ruin in reverse!

Rutherglen

Having split, with patience,
my first pound note
I kept the two halves
in case of disbelief.
They gave me a glow.
But I was now wound up
tingling for conquest
and as I stared at them
I seized another note
washed my hands
examined my nails
took chair to table
In best midday light
made one note two

removed metal strip
made two one again.
A happy hour!
So I kept the strip
recirculated the note
thought of whoever
would hold it to the light.
O the consequences!
O the delight!

Kiev

Kilted in Kiev
picking postcards
at a street kiosk
I failed to notice
my four colleagues
had stealthily vanished
hiding in a doorway.
Business concluded
I turned about
to find no one
gazed around
sketched a few
frank bewilderments –
O the conspicuous!
A crowd gathered
From nowhere like filings
to a magnet, muttering,
whispering, pointing,
man in a skirt –
in another moment
hands-on experience
loomed - panic! –
Four grins materialised
clapped me on the back -
O quite the best
joke of the tour!

Glasgow

A man like a shade
fastened onto me
along Gordon Street.
'Gie's a pound.
 Hink Ah don't know ye?
 Ye' ll no shake me aff.
C' moan c'moan c'moan.
- Right. That's be'er.
You know the score.
Try Buchanan Street Station,
toilet's busy therr.'
Janus, blackmailer
 of the friendly city.

Amsterdam

Brimming jenevers,
an evening of that,
and then some wildness
in that nice hotel.
They had to change the sheets
but they didn't throw us out.

Glasgow

When I told Morven
that John had died
she gave me the greatest
of hugs that showed me
I should not be totally
without comfort, not
totally, although
it seemed that way.

Rovaniemi

'Hold tight!' he cried, and did I!
The skidoo whooshed forward
over our frozen lake
and we whooped with it
double furry biker
cloned centaur
clinging and swishing
magic circles
Lappish flakes
to kiss our faces.

Istanbul

Climbing a hill
to look down on the city
I saw it gradually
rise into view
slowed my step
savouring the gradualness
as if the ground was sacred,
and perhaps it was.
When more than minarets
appeared, and the whole
crowding of domes,
gleam of waterways
crowded with ferries,
the bridges and the light,
far-off horns and cries
crowded the very
emptiest spaces
of the heart
I tried to stifle
sobbing but could not,
could not stop tears.

Bibliography

Adorno, Theodor, *Prisms*, trans. S. Weber and S. Weber, London, 1967.

—— *Negative Dialectics* [1966], trans. E. B. Ashton, New York, 1973.

—— *Notes to Literature*, [1965–66], trans. S. W. Nicholsen, Columbia, 1991.

—— *Hegel: Three Studies* [1963], trans. S. W. Nicholsen, Massachusetts, 1993.

Althusser, Louis, 'Ideology and Ideological State Apparatuses', in *Lenin and Philosophy and Other Essays*, trans. Ben Brewster, London, 1971.

Altieri, Charles, 'What is Living and What is Dead in American Postmodernism: Establishing the Contemporaneity of Some American Poetry', *Critical Enquiry*, 22:4, 1996.

Arendt, Hannah, 'Philosophy and Politics', *Social Research*, 57:1, 1990.

Bakhtin, M. M., *The Dialogic Imagination: Four Essays*, ed. M. Holquist, trans. C. Emerson and M. Holquist, Austin, 1981.

—— *Art and Answerability: Early Philosophical Essays*, eds M. Holquist and V. Liapunov, trans. V. Liapunov and K. Brostrom, Austin, 1990.

—— *Towards a Philosophy of the Act*, eds V. Liapunov and M. Holquist, trans. V. Liapunov, Austin, 1993.

Baudrillard, Jean, *For a Critique of the Political Economy of the Sign*, trans. C. Levin, St Louis, 1981.

—— *Symbolic Exchange and Death*, trans. I. H. Grant, London, 1993.

—— *The Transparency of Evil: Essays on Extreme Phenomena*, trans. J. Benedict, London, 1993.

Benjamin, Andrew (ed.), *The Problems of Modernity: Adorno and Benjamin*, London, 1989.

Benjamin, Walter, *Illuminations*, ed. Hannah Arendt, trans. Harry Zohn, New York, 1969.

—— *Reflections*, ed. P. Demetz, trans. E. Jephcott, New York, 1986.

—— *The Origin of German Tragic Drama* [1963], trans. John Osborne, London, 1998.

Benveniste, Emil, *Problems in General Linguistics*, trans. M. E. Meek, Miami, 1971.

Berman, Marshall, *All That is Solid Melts Into Air: The Experience of Modernity*, London, 1983.

Bernstein, J. M., *Recovering Ethical Life: Jurgen Habermas and the Future of Critical Theory*, London, 1995.

Bhaskar, Roy, *Dialectic: The Pulse of Freedom*, London, 1993.

Black, David, 'From Glasgow to Saturn', *Lines Review*, 49, 1974.

—— 'Scottish Poetry in the Sixties', *Akros*, 10:28, 1975.

Blackburn, John, 'Edwin Morgan', in *Hardy to Heaney: Twentieth Century Poets: Introductions and Explanations*, Edinburgh, 1986.

Blake, William, *The Complete Poetry and Prose*, ed. D. V. Erdman, New York, 1988.

Bold, Alan, *Modern Scottish Literature*, London, 1983.

—— (ed.), *The Letters of Hugh MacDiarmid*, London, 1984.

—— *MacDiarmid: A Critical Biography*, London, 1988.

Boyne, Roy, 'Postmodernism, the Sublime and Ethics', in J. Good and I. Velody (eds), *The Politics of Postmodernity*, Cambridge, 1998.

Brooks, Peter, *Reading for the Plot: Design and Intention in Narrative* [1984], Massachusetts, 1998.

Brown, Edward J., 'Mayakovsky's Futurist Period', in George Gibian and H. W. Tjalsma (eds), *Russian Modernism: Culture and the Avant-Garde, 1900–1930*, Ithaca, 1976.

Burnyeat, M. F., 'Art and Mimesis in Plato's "Republic"', *London Review of Books*, 20:10, 21 May 1998.

Cabanne, Pierre, *Dialogues with Marcel Duchamp*, trans. Ron Padgett, New York, 1971.

Calder, Angus, 'Morganmania', *Chapman*, 64, 1991.

Certeau, Michel de, *Heterologies: Discourse on the Other*, trans. Brian Massumi, Manchester, 1986.

Chukovsky, Korney, 'Akhmatova and Mayakovsky', in E. J. Brown (ed.), *Major Soviet Writers: Essays in Criticism*, Oxford, 1973.

Colebrook, Claire, *New Literary Histories: New Historicism and Contemporary Criticism*, Manchester, 1997.

—— *Ethics and Representation: From Kant to Poststructuralism*, Edinburgh, 1999.

Cooke, Dorian, J. F. Hendry, Norman MacCaig, Robert Melville, Nicholas Moore, Philip O'Connor, Dylan Thomas and Henry Treece (eds), *the new apocalypse: an anthology of criticism, poems and stories*, London, 1939.

Craig, Cairns, *Out of History: Narrative Paradigms in Scottish and British Culture*, Edinburgh, 1996.

Crawford, Robert, 'Recent Scottish Poetry and the Scottish Tradition', *Krino*, 3, 1987.

—— '"To Change / The Unchangeable" – The Whole Morgan', in Robert Crawford and Hamish Whyte (eds), *About Edwin Morgan*, Edinburgh, 1990.

—— 'Morgan's Critical Position', *Chapman*, 64, 1991.

—— *Identifying Poets: Self and Territory in Twentieth-Century Poetry*, Edinburgh, 1993.

Critchley, Simon, *The Ethics of Deconstruction: Derrida and Levinas*, London, 1992.

—— *Ethics – Politics – Subjectivity: Essays on Derrida, Levinas and Contemporary French Thought*, London, 1999.

Damer, Sean, *Glasgow: Going for a Song*, London, 1990.

Davie, Donald, *Thomas Hardy and English Poetry*, London, 1973.

—— *The Poet in the Imaginary Museum*, ed. Barry Alpert, Manchester, 1977.

Debord, Guy, *The Society of the Spectacle* [1967], trans. D. Nicholson-Smith, New York, 1994.

Deleuze, Gilles, *The Logic of Sense*, ed. C. V. Boundas, trans. Mark Lester, New York, 1990.

Dews, Peter, *Logics of Disintegration: Post-structuralist Thought and the Claims of Critical Theory*, London, 1987.

—— *The Limits of Disenchantment: Essays on Contemporary European Philosophy*, London, 1995.

Donnachie, Ian and Christopher Whatley (eds), *The Manufacture of Scottish History*, Edinburgh, 1992.

Donoghue, Denis, 'Ten Poets', *London Review of Books*, 7:19, 7 November 1985.

Dunn, Douglas, 'Morgan's Sonnets', in Robert Crawford and Hamish Whyte (eds), *About Edwin Morgan*, Edinburgh, 1990.

Eagleton, Terry, *The Ideology of the Aesthetic*, London, 1990.

Easthope, Antony and John O. Thompson, *Contemporary Poetry Meets Modern Theory*, Hemel Hempstead, 1991.

Edgecombe, R. S., 'The Poetry of Edwin Morgan', *Dalhousie Review*, 62, 1983.

Eliot, T. S., 'Tradition and the Individual Talent', in *The Sacred Wood: Essays on Poetry and Criticism* [1920], London, 1960.

—— *The Complete Poems and Plays*, London, 1969.

Enzensberger, Hans Magnus, *The Consciousness Industry*, New York, 1974.

Erlich, Victor, *Modernism and Revolution: Russian Literature in Transition*, Massachusetts, 1994.

Fazzini, Marco, 'Edwin Morgan: Two Interviews', *Studies in Scottish Literature*, 29, 1996.

—— 'Playing Translation with Morgan and MacCaig', *Forum for Modern Language Studies*, 33:1, 1997.

—— 'From Glasgow to Outer Space: Edwin Morgan's (Un)Realities', in *Crossings: Essays on Contemporary Scottish Poetry and Hybridity*, Venezia Lido, 2000.

Fergusson, Bernard, *Hubble Bubble*, London, 1978.

Fergusson, James (ed.), *The Green Garden: A New Collection of Scottish Poetry*, Edinburgh, 1946.

Foster, John, 'Red Clyde, Red Scotland', in Ian Donnachie and Christopher Whatley (eds), *The Manufacture of Scottish History*, Edinburgh, 1992.

Foster, John and Charles Woolfson, *The Politics of the UCS Work-in*, London, 1986.

France, Peter and Duncan Glen (eds), *European Poetry in Scotland: An Anthology of Translations*, Edinburgh, 1989.

Fraser, G. S., 'Apocalypse in Poetry', in J. F. Hendry and Henry Treece (eds), *the white horseman: prose and verse of the new apocalypse*, London, 1941.

Freeman, Carl, 'Beyond the Dialect of the Tribe: James Joyce, Hugh MacDiarmid, and World Language', in Nancy Gish (ed.), *Hugh MacDiarmid: Man and Poet*, Edinburgh, 1992.

Frow, John, 'What Was Postmodernism?', in *Time and Commodity Culture: Essays in Cultural Theory and Postmodernity*, Oxford, 1997.

Frykeman, Erik, 'Loneliness in Edwin Morgan's Poetry', in *In Other Words: Transcultural Studies in Philology, Translation and Lexicology Presented to H. H. Meier*, Providence RI, 1989.

Fulton, Robin, *Contemporary Scottish Poetry: Individuals and Contexts*, Loanhead, 1994.

Fussell, Paul, *The Great War and Modern Memory* [1975], Oxford, 2000.

Gardner, Helen, *The Art of T. S. Eliot*, London, 1949.

Garioch, Robert, *Complete Poetical Works*, Edinburgh, 1983.

Gascoyne, David, *A Short Survey of Surrealism* [1935], London, 1970.

Gibson, Andrew, *Towards a Postmodern Theory of Narrative*, Edinburgh, 1996.

Gibson, William, *Neuromancer* [1984], London, 1995.

Glen, Duncan, *Hugh MacDiarmid (Christopher Murray Grieve) and the Scottish Renaissance*, Edinburgh, 1964.

Graham, W. H., 'Notes on a Poetry of Release', *Poetry Scotland*, Glasgow, 1946.

Gramsci, Antonio, *Selections from the Prison Notebooks*, eds Quinton Hoare and Geoffrey Nowell Smith, London, 1986.

Grant, Damien, 'Walls of Glass: the Poetry of W. S. Graham', in Peter Jones and Michael Schmidt (eds), *British Poetry Since 1970: A Critical Survey*, Manchester, 1980.

Gregson, Ian, 'Edwin Morgan's Metamorphoses', *English*, 39:1, 1990.

—— *Contemporary Poetry and Postmodernism: Dialogue and Estrangement*, London, 1996.

Hamburger, Michael, 'Translation as Affinity', in *Testimonies: Selected Shorter Prose 1950–1987*, Manchester, 1989.

Hamilton, Richard, *The Bride Stripped Bare By Her Bachelors Even Again: A Reconstruction*, Newcastle upon Tyne, 1966.

Hamilton, Robin, 'The Poetry of Edwin Morgan: Translator of Reality', *Akros*, 15:43, 1980.

—— *Science and Psychodrama: The Poetry of Edwin Morgan and David Black*, Frome, 1982.

Hassan, Ihab, *The Postmodern Turn: Essays in Postmodern Theory and Culture*, Ohio, 1987.

Hawthorn, Geoffrey and Camilla Lund, 'Private and Public in "Late-Modern" Democracy', in J. Good and I. Velody (eds), *The Politics of Postmodernity*, Cambridge, 1998.

Heaney, Seamus, *Beowulf: A New Translation*, London, 1999.

Hendry, J[ames]. F[indlay]. 'Myth and Social Integration', in *the white horseman: prose and verse of the new apocalypse*, London, 1941.

—— 'The Apocalyptic Element in Modern Poetry', *Poetry Scotland*, Glasgow, 1945.

—— and Henry Treece (eds), *the white horseman: prose and verse of the new apocalypse*, London, 1941.

Herbert, W. N., 'Morgan's Words', in Robert Crawford and Hamish Whyte (eds), *About Edwin Morgan*, Edinburgh, 1990.

Herron, Frank, *Labour Market in Crisis: Redundancy at Upper Clyde Shipbuilders*, London, 1975.

Holmes, Richard, *Shelley: The Pursuit* [1974], London, 1994.

Houston, Amy, 'New Lang Syne: *Sonnets from Scotland* and Restructured Time', *Scottish Literary Journal*, 22:1, 1995.

Hyde, G. M., 'Mayakovsky in English Translation', *Translation and Literature*, 1, 1992.

Ingpen, Roger and Walter E. Peck (eds), *The Complete Works of Percy Bysshe Shelley*, New York, 1965.

Jack, R. D. S., *Scottish Literature's Debt to Italy*, Edinburgh, 1986.

Jakobson, Roman, *Selected Writings*, The Hague, 1962–82.

—— 'On a Generation that Squandered its Poets', in E. J. Brown (ed.), *Major Soviet Writers: Essays in Criticism*, Oxford, 1973.

Jameson, Fredric, 'Imaginary and Symbolic in Lacan: Marxism, Psychoanalytic Criticism and the Problem of the Subject', *Yale French Studies*, 55–6, 1977.

—— 'Beyond the Cave: Demystifying the Ideology of Modernism', *The Ideologies of Theory: Essays 1971–86*, vol. 1, *Situations of Theory*, London, 1988; vol. 2, *The Syntax of History*, London, 1989.

—— *The Political Unconscious: Narrative as a Socially Symbolic Act*, London, 1989.

—— *Postmodernism, or, The Cultural Logic of Late Capitalism*, London, 1991.

—— *Signatures of the Visible*, London, 1992.

Jangfeldt, Bengt, *Majakovskij and Futurism, 1917–1921*, Stockholm, 1976.

—— and Nils Åke Nilsson (eds), *Vladimir Majakovsji: Memoirs and Essays*, Stockholm, 1975.

Jones, Daniel, *English Pronouncing Dictionary* [1917], London, 1964.

Jones, J. H. (ed.), *The English Faust Book*, Cambridge, 1994.

Jones, Peter and Michael Schmidt (eds), *British Poetry Since 1970: A Critical Survey*, Manchester, 1980.

Joyce, James, 'Ireland, Island of Saints and Sages', in Ellsworth Mason and Richard Ellman (eds), *The Critical Writings of James Joyce*, London, 1959.

József, Attila, *Winter Night: Selected Poems*, trans. John Bátki, Budapest, 1997.

Krease, John, 'Some Comments on "The Computer's First Code Poem"', *Poetry Nation*, 2, 1974.

Kristeva, Julia, *La Révolution du langage poétique: l'avant-garde à la fin du XIXe siècle: Lautréamont et Mallarmé*, Paris, 1974.

—— *Desire in Language: A Semiotic Approach to Literature and Art*, ed. L. S. Roudiez, trans. T. Gora, A. Jardine and L. Roudiez, London, 1984.

—— 'The Ethics of Linguistics', in *Desire in Language: A Semiotic Approach to Literature and Art*, ed. L. S. Roudiez, trans. T. Gora, A. Jardine and L. Roudiez, Oxford, 1984.

—— 'Word, Dialogue, and Novel', in *Desire in Language: A Semiotic Approach to Literature and Art*, ed. L. S. Roudiez, trans. T. Gora, A. Jardine and L. Roudiez, Oxford, 1984.

—— 'The System and the Speaking Subject', in Toril Moi (ed.), *The Kristeva Reader*, Oxford, 1986.

Lacan, Jacques, *Écrits: A Selection*, trans. A. Sheridan, London, 1977.

Langbaum, Robert, *The Poetry of Experience: The Dramatic Monologue in Modern Literary Tradition*, Chicago, 1985.

Lawrence, D. H., *Apocalypse, and the Writings on Revelation*, ed. Mara Kalnins, Cambridge, 1980.

Leonard, Tom, 'Poster for POETSOUND '84', Third Eye Centre, Glasgow, 1984.

—— *Intimate Voices: Selected Work 1965–1983*, Newcastle upon Tyne, 1984.

—— *Radical Renfrew*, Edinburgh, 1990.

Lewis, Helena, *Dada Turns Red: The Politics of Surrealism*, Edinburgh, 1990.

Lindsay, Maurice, 'Editorial', *Poetry Scotland*, Glasgow, 1943.

—— (ed.), *Modern Scottish Poetry: An Anthology of the Scottish Renaissance, 1920–1945*, London, 1946.

—— *History of Scottish Literature*, London, 1992.

Lukács, Georg, *History and Class Consciousness: Studies in Marxist Dialectics*, London, 1971.

Lynch, Michael, *Scotland: A New History*, London, 1992.

Lyotard, Jean-François, *The Postmodern Condition: A Report on Knowledge*, Manchester, 1979.

MacCaig, Norman (ed.), *Honour'd Shade: An Anthology of New Scottish Poetry to Mark the Bi-centenary of the Birth of Robert Burns*, Edinburgh, 1959.

McCarey, Peter, 'Edwin Morgan the Translator', in Robert Crawford and Hamish Whyte (eds), *About Edwin Morgan*, Edinburgh, 1990.

McCarra, Kevin, 'Morgan's "Cinquevalli"', *Scottish Literary Journal*, 12:2, 1985.

—— 'Edwin Morgan: Lives and Work', in Robert Crawford and Hamish Whyte (eds), *About Edwin Morgan*, Edinburgh, 1990.

MacDiarmid, Hugh, 'A Theory of Scots Letters', *The Scottish Chapbook*, 1, 1922.

—— *Lucky Poet. A Self-Study in Literature and Political Ideas*, London, 1943.

—— 'Six Scottish Poets of To-Day and To-Morrow', *Poetry Scotland*, Glasgow, 1943.

—— (ed.), *The Golden Treasury of Scottish Poetry* [1940], London, 1946.

—— *The Company I've Kept: Essays in Autobiography*, London, 1966.

—— *Complete Poems*, eds M. Grieve and W. R. Aitken, Manchester, 1993.

McGill, Jack, *Crisis on the Clyde: The Story of the Upper Clyde Shipbuilders*, London, 1973.

Mackenzie, Alexander, *The Prophecies of the Brahan Seer* [1877], Essex, 1977.

Marsack, Robyn, 'Edwin Morgan and Contemporary Poetry', in Robert Crawford and Hamish Whyte (eds), *About Edwin Morgan*, Edinburgh, 1990.

Marshall, Herbert (ed.), *Mayakovsky and his Poetry*, London, 1942.

—— *Mayakovsky*, London, 1965.

Marx, Karl, *Capital*, vol. 1, Harmondsworth, 1976.

Mayakovsky, Vladmir, *The Bedbug and Selected Poetry*, ed. P. Blake, trans. M. Hayward & G. Reavey, London, 1961.
—— *How Are Verses Made*, trans. G. M. Hyde, London, 1970.
—— 'Speech at the Dispute "Futurism Today"', in *Selected Works in Three Volumes*, ed. Alexander Ushakov, trans. Dorian Rottenberg, Moscow, 1985.
—— 'The Workers and Peasants Don't Understand You', in *Selected Works in Three Volumes*, ed. Alexander Ushakov, trans, Dorian Rottenberg, Moscow, 1985.
Melville, Robert, 'Apocalypse in Painting', in J. F. Hendry and Henry Treece (eds), *the white horseman: prose and verse of the new apocalypse*, London, 1941.
Milton, Nan, *John Maclean*, Bristol, 1973.
Montefiore, Jan, *Feminism and Poetry*, London, 1987.
Morgan, Edwin, 'When the Blind Dream'; 'Twilight'; and 'Maya: Dream-Reality/Reality-Dream', *Glasgow University Magazine*, 2 February 1938.
—— 'Women and Poetry', *Cambridge Journal*, 3:2, 1950.
—— 'Dunbar and the Language of Poetry', *Essays in Criticism*, 2:2, 1952.
—— *The Vision of Cathkin Braes and other Poems*, Glasgow, 1952.
—— *Beowulf: A Verse Translation into Modern English*, Berkeley, 1952.
—— 'Modern Makars Scots and English', *Saltire Review*, 1:2, 1954.
—— 'Jujitsu for the Educated: Reflections on Hugh MacDiarmid's poem "In Memoriam James Joyce"', *The Twentieth Century*, 160:955, 1956.
—— 'MacDiarmid Embattled', *Lines Review*, 15, 1959.
—— *Poems from Eugenio Montale*, Reading, 1959.
—— 'Who will Publish Scottish Poetry?', *New Saltire*, 2, 1961.
—— 'Poet and Public', *The Scotsman*, 12 March 1962.
—— 'The Beatnik in the Kailyard', *New Saltire*, 3, 1962.
—— 'The Beat Vigilantes', *New Saltire*, 5, 1962.
—— *Starryveld*, Switzerland, 1965.
—— 'Diabolical Experiment', *Times Literary Supplement*, 7 December 1967.
—— 'Concrete Poetry', in Bernard Bergonzi (ed.), *Innovations: Essays on Art and Ideas*, London, 1968.
—— *The Second Life*, Edinburgh, 1968.
—— *Wi The Haill Voice: 25 Poems by Vladimir Mayakovsky*, Oxford, 1972.
—— *Instamatic Poems*, London, 1972.
—— *From Glasgow to Saturn*, Cheadle, 1973.
—— *Essays*, Cheadle Hulme, 1974.
—— *Fifty Renascence Love-Poems*, Reading, 1975.
—— *Hugh MacDiarmid*, London, 1976.
—— *Rites of Passage: Translations*, Manchester, 1976.
—— *The New Divan*, Manchester, 1977.
—— 'Provenance and Problematics of "Sublime and Alarming Images" in Poetry', *Proceeding of the British Academy*, LXIII, 1978.
—— *Star Gate: Science Fiction Poems*, Glasgow, 1979.
—— *Scottish Satirical Verse: An Anthology*, Manchester, 1980.
—— 'James Joyce and Hugh MacDiarmid', in W. J. McCormack and Alistair Stead (eds), *James Joyce and Modern Literature*, London, 1982.

—— 'Some Classical Ephemera', *Times Literary Supplement*, 5 February 1982.

—— *Poems of Thirty Years*, Manchester, 1982.

—— *The Apple-Tree: A Medieval Dutch Play*, Glasgow, 1982.

—— *Master Peter Pathelin*, Glasgow, 1983.

—— *Sonnets from Scotland*, Glasgow, 1984.

—— *Selected Poems*, Manchester, 1985.

—— *From the Video Box*, Glasgow, 1986.

—— *Newspoems*, London, 1987.

—— *Themes on a Variation*, Manchester, 1988.

—— *Collected Poems*, Manchester, 1990.

—— *Crossing the Border: Essays on Scottish Literature*, Manchester, 1990.

—— 'Books I have Read (1927–1940)', in Robert Crawford and Hamish Whyte (eds), *About Edwin Morgan*, Edinburgh, 1990.

—— *Hold Hands Among the Atoms*, Edinburgh, 1991.

—— *Edmond Rostand's Cyrano de Bergerac*, Manchester, 1992.

—— *Sweeping Out The Dark*, Manchester, 1994.

—— 'Long Poems – But How Long?', W. D. Thomas Memorial Lecture, University of Wales Swansea, 1995.

—— *Collected Translations*, Manchester, 1996.

—— *Gilgamesh* (second version, 1997), unpublished typescript.

—— *Virtual and Other Realities*, Manchester, 1997.

—— 'Planet Wave', *P. N. Review*, 24:3, January–February, 1998.

—— 'A Mirrear Dance Mycht Na Man See', *Times Literary Supplement*, 20 March 1998.

—— *Christopher Marlowe's Doctor Faustus: In a New Version*, Edinburgh, 1999.

—— *Demon*, Glasgow, 1999.

—— *Phaedre: A Tragedy*, Manchester, 2000.

—— *New Selected Poems*, Manchester, 2000.

—— *A.D. A Trilogy of Plays on the Life of Jesus*, Manchester, 2000.

—— 'Attila József', *The Dark Horse*, 11, 2001.

—— 'Pelagius', *The London Review of Books*, 23:19, 2001.

Morris, Pam (ed.), *The Bakhtin Reader*, London, 1994.

Muir, Edwin, *Scott and Scotland: The Predicament of the Scottish Writer*, London, 1936.

Mulhern, Francis (ed.), *Contemporary Marxist Literary Criticism*, London, 1992.

Nicholson, Colin, *Poem, Purpose and Place: Shaping Identity in Contemporary Scottish Verse*, Edinburgh, 1992.

Olson, Charles, 'Projective Verse' [1950], in D. M. Allen and W. Tallman (eds), *The Poetics of the New American Poetry*, New York, 1973.

Ong, Walter, *Orality and Literacy: The Technologizing of the Word*, London, 1995.

Opie, Iona and Opie, Peter (eds), *The Oxford Dictionary of Nursery Rhymes*, Oxford, 1992.

Osborne, Peter, *The Politics of Time: Modernity and Avant-Garde*, London, 1995.

Plato, *The Republic*, trans. Paul Shorey, London 1937.

Pound, Ezra, *Personae: Collected Shorter Poems of Ezra Pound*, London, 1952.

Proffer, E. and Proffer, C. R. (eds), *The Ardis Anthology of Russian Futurism*, Michigan, 1980.

Raban, Jonathan, *The Society of the Poem*, London, 1971.

Read, Herbert, *Art Now* [1933], London, 1948.

—— *Poetry and Anarchism*, London, 1938.

Rich, Adrienne, 'When We Dead Awaken: Writing as Re-Vision', in B. C. Gelpi and A. Gelpi (eds), *Adrienne Rich's Poetry*, New York, 1975.

Rosemont, Franklin, *André Breton and the First Principles of Surrealism*, London, 1978.

Rushdie, Salman, *In Good Faith*, London, 1990.

Schmidt, Michael, 'Edwin Morgan', in *An Introduction to Fifty Modern British Poets*, London, 1979.

—— and Peter Jones (eds), *British Poetry Since 1970: A Critical Survey*, Manchester, 1980.

Scott, Walter, *The Heart of Midlothian*, ed. Clare Lamont, Oxford, 1982.

Shell, Marc, *The Economy of Literature*, Baltimore, 1993.

Shelley, Percy Bysshe, *The Complete Works*, eds. Roger Ingpen and Walter E. Peck, London, 1965.

Shklovsky, Victor, 'Art as Technique', in *Russian Formalist Criticism: Four Essays*, trans. L. T. Lemon and M. J. Reis, Lincoln, 1965.

—— *Mayakovsky and his Circle*, ed. and trans. Lily Feiler, New York, 1972.

Sinfield, Alan (ed.), *Society and Literature 1945–1970*, London, 1983.

—— *Literature, Politics and Culture in Postwar Britain* [1989], London, 1997.

Smith, Iain Crichton, 'Vintage Morgan', *Cencrastus*, 32, 1989.

—— 'The Public and Private Morgan', in Robert Crawford and Hamish Whyte (eds), *About Edwin Morgan*, Edinburgh, 1990.

Snow, Michael and Margaret Snow (eds), *The Nightfisherman: Selected Letters of W. S. Graham*, Manchester, 1999.

Steiner, George (ed.), *Penguin Book of Modern Translation*, Harmondsworth, 1966.

Tacitus, *The Agricola and The Germania*, trans. H. Mattingly, Harmondsworth, 1970.

Thomas, Dylan, *Collected Poems: 1934–53*, eds W. Davies and R. Maud, London, 1993.

Thomson, Geddes, *The Poetry of Edwin Morgan* [Scotnotes 2], Aberdeen, 1986.

Treece, Henry, *How I See Apocalypse*, London, 1946.

Trotsky, Leon, 'The Suicide of Vladimir Mayakovsky' [1930], in P. N. Siegel (ed.), *On Literature and Art*, New York, 1970.

Virilio, Paul, *The Lost Dimension*, New York, 1991.

Walter, W. Grey, *The Living Brain* [1953], Harmondsworth, 1961.

Watson, Roderick, '"Water Music" and the Stream of Consciousness', *Scottish Literary Journal*, 5:2, 1978.

—— 'Edwin Morgan's "Glasgow Green"', *Akros*, 17:52, 1983.

—— *The Literature of Scotland*, London, 1984.

—— 'Internationalising Scottish Poetry', in Cairns Craig (ed.), *The History of Scottish Literature: vol. 4, The Twentieth Century*, Aberdeen, 1987.

—— '"An Island in the City...", Edwin Morgan's Urban Poetry', *Chapman*, 64, 1991.

—— 'Edwin Morgan: Messages and Transformations', in G. Day and B. Docherty (eds), *British Poetry from the 1950s to the 1990s: Politics and Art*, London, 1997.

Weöres, Sándor, *Eternal Moment: Selected Poems*, ed. M. Vajda, trans. Edwin Morgan, William Jay Smith *et al.*, Budapest and London, 1988.

Wheeler, Wendy (ed.), *The Political Subject: Essays on the Self from Art, Politics and Science*, London, 2000.

White, Kenneth, 'Morgan's Range', *Cencrastus*, 12, 1983.

Whyte, Christopher, 'Now You See It, Now You Don't: Revelation and Concealment in the Love Poetry of Edwin Morgan', *Glasgow Review*, 2, 1993.

Whyte, Hamish, 'MacDiarmid and the Beatniks', *Scottish Literary Journal*, 13:2, 1986.

—— (ed.), *Edwin Morgan: Nothing Not Giving Messages: Reflections on his Work and Life*, Edinburgh, 1990.

—— 'Edwin Morgan: A Checklist', in Robert Crawford and Hamish Whyte (eds), *About Edwin Morgan*, Edinburgh, 1990.

Williams, Raymond, *Marxism and Literature*, Oxford, 1977.

—— *On Television: Selected Writings*, ed. Alan O'Connor, London, 1989.

Wittgenstein, Ludwig, *Tractatus Logico-Philosophicus* [1921], trans. D. F. Pears and B. F. McGuinness, London, 1974.

Wood, Barry, 'Scots, Poets and the City', in Cairns Craig (ed.), *The History of Scottish Literature*, Aberdeen, vol. 4, 1987.

Wordsworth, William, *The Poetical Works*, ed. E. de Selincourt, 5 vols, Oxford, 1940–49.

—— *The Prelude: or Growth of a Poet's Mind*, ed. E. de Selincourt, rev. ed. Helen Darbishire, Oxford, 1959.

—— *The Prose Works*, eds W. J. B. Owen and J. W. Smyser, Oxford, 1974.

Wright, Tom and Hugh Rae, 'Burns and the Poets of Today', *Scottish Field*, 109:709, January 1962.

Young, Alan, 'Three "Neo-Moderns": Ian Hamilton Finlay, Edwin Morgan, Christopher Middleton', in Peter Jones and Michael Schmidt (eds), *British Poetry Since 1970: A Critical Survey*, Manchester, 1980.

Young, Douglas, *'Plastic Scots' and the Scottish Literary Tradition*, Glasgow, 1946.

Žižek, Slavoj, *The Sublime Object of Ideology*, London, 1989.

Index

Note: 'n.' after a page reference indicates the number of a note on that page.

Adorno, Theodor 31, 91, 167n.30
Aigi, Gennady 156, 164
anarchism 26, 35, 66, 98, 161
Anglo-Saxon 15, 20, 31, 35, 43–6, 158, 174
Apocalypse, New 10, 23, 24, 25, 26, 27, 53
Arendt, Hannah 4
Arnold, Matthew 134
Attila, József 3, 11, 83, 164–6
Auden, W. H. 46

Babbage, Charles 133
Bacall, Lauren 33
Bakhtin, Mikhail 1, 11, 64, 133, 134
Bataille, Georges 193
Baudelaire, Charles Pierre 64, 83
Baudrillard, Jean 120–1, 148, 176, 184
BBC 16, 19, 38
Beat poets 25, 40, 41, 47, 88
Beethoven, Ludvig 37
Benjamin, Walter 77, 91, 185
Benveniste, Emil 112
Berman, Marshall 83
Bhaskar, Roy 123
Bible, the 24, 31, 32, 138, 164
Biko, Steve 134
Bishop, John Peale 88
Blake, William 27, 119
    'America' 27
    'Proverbs of Hell' 27
    'Visions of the Daughters of Albion' 119
Bogart, Humphrey 33
Bold, Alan 5
Bory, Jean-François 97
Bosch, Hieronymous 53, 54, 191
Brahan Seer, the 55
Brecht, Bertolt 86, 94, 139
Breton, André 66, 106, 107
Brontë, Emily 54
Brooks, Peter 151
Bruce, George 42

Bruno, Giordano 187
Bukowski, Charles 88
Burns, Robert 33, 94, 142, 143, 169, 171–3
Burnyeat, M. F. 124
Burroughs, William 41
Byron, George Gordon 133, 134
    'Sonnet on Chillon' 134

Calgacus 141
Campbell, Roy 37
Capital 98
    see also Marx, Karl
Chiesley, Rachel (Lady Grange) 142
Clydesdale, Matthew 182, 185
Cocteau, Jean 53, 54
Cold War 11, 32, 41, 83–4, 108
Columba, St 138, 139
Communist Manifesto 76, 94, 98, 99, 133
concrete poetry 4, 42–3, 90–8 *passim*, 108
Crane, Hart 7, 36
Crawford, Robert 78
Creeley, Robert 52–3, 88
Currie, James 172

Dadaism 66, 92, 97, 98
Dante Alighieri 28, 94, 115
Davidson, John 41
Davie, Donald 65
da Vinci, Leonardo 36
Debord, Guy 98, 99, 147
    Situationiste Internationale 98
    The Society of the Spectacle 98
De Quincey, Thomas 41, 142
devolution 16, 137, 146
Dishonour'd Shade: Seven Non-Abbotsford Poets 39
Divan poetry 115–16
Donne, John 33
Donoghue, Denis 3
Doughty, Charles 41
Douthwaite, Pat 128
Dózsa, György 121

Duchamp, Marcel 177–8
Dunbar, William 32, 34, 46
Dunn, Douglas 145

Eliot, T. S. 7, 41, 45, 47, 50, 64, 65, 71,
    83, 87, 88
  Murder in the Cathedral 45
  Sweeney Agonistes 45
Encyclopaedia Britannica 174
English Faust Book, The 180
Enzensberger, Hans Magnus 148
European Poetry in Scotland 163

Fergusson, Bernard 19
Fergusson, James 16, 17, 18, 19
  *The Green Garden: A New Collection
    of Scottish Poetry* 17, 18
Finlay, Ian Hamilton 39, 42, 95
Fraser, G. S. 24
Freud, Sigmund 25, 60, 125, 153
Fry, Christopher 47
Fulton, Robin 6, 7
futurism 10, 14, 40, 60, 63, 64, 66, 67,
    87, 90, 97, 113, 117, 160
  Mayakovsky and 14, 60, 63, 66, 67, 87
  Russian 65, 66, 90

Gaelic 17, 18, 22, 43, 50, 51
Gaelic League 17
Gardner, Helen 45
Garioch, Robert 41, 42
Gascoyne, David 106, 107
gay poetry 2, 11, 15, 35–7, 88, 89, 90,
    104–6, 128–9, 132, 185–6
Geddes, Jenny 33, 34
Ghandi, Mahatma 162
Gibson, Andrew 116
Gibson, William 175–6, 180, 181
  Neuromancer 175, 177
Gilgamesh 138, 188
Ginsberg, Allen 41, 88
  'Howl' 88
Giotto (Di Bondone) 151
Glasgow 3, 4, 8, 10, 14, 16, 20, 21, 25,
    73, 74, 75, 76, 88, 89, 99, 139,
    142, 146, 154, 155
Glasgow Herald 16
Glasgow University 7, 14, 15, 36
Gomringer, Eugen 90
Graham, William Sydney 23, 25, 26, 31,
    43
Gramsci, Antonio 14, 19, 184

Graves, Robert 128
Grey, Zane 94
Guevara, Ernesto (Che) 109
Gulf War 6
Gutenberg, Johannes Gensfleisch 141,
    152, 178

Hardy, Thomas 97
Heaney, Seamus 44
Heisenberg, Werner Karl 122
Henderson, Hamish 23
  Elegies for the Dead in Cyrenaica 23
Hendry, J. F. 23, 24, 25, 26, 27, 59
  The Orchestral Mountain 25
  *the white horseman: prose and verse of
    the new apocalypse* 24
Herbert, W. N. 50
history 6, 8, 15, 21, 28, 59, 69, 74, 82,
    88, 90, 104, 113, 119, 129,
    139–41, 151, 170, 191
Hogg, James 152
  Confessions of a Justified Sinner 152
Honour'd Shade 39
Hopkins, Gerard Manley 142
Hutton, James 142
  A Theory of the Earth 142

Iser, Wolfgang 115, 116
Iskander, Fazil 156
Izvestia 67

Jackson, Laura Riding 158
Jacobson, Roman 59, 64, 71, 72, 90
Jameson, Fredric 7, 69, 74, 104, 149,
    153, 154
Jamieson, John 48
  *Etymological Dictionary of the Scottish
    Tongue* 48
Jones, Daniel 20
  English Pronouncing Dictionary 20
Joyce, James 37, 47–52 *passim*,
  Finnegans Wake 47, 49, 51
  Ulysses 48

Kafka, Franz 40, 172
Kastrioti, Gjergj 190
Khayyám, Omar 173, 174
Keats, John 108
Kentigern, St 139
Kerouac, Jack 41, 179
Khlebnikov, Velimir 59, 63, 64, 85, 90,
    164, 186

King Lear 79
   see also Shakespeare, William
Klee, Paul 41
Knox, John 21, 33, 34, 141
Kristeva, Julia 59, 60, 64, 68, 71, 72,
   147
   La Révolution du langage poétique
   59
Kropotkin, Peter 27
Kubrick, Stanley 127

Lacan, Jacques 125, 153
Lallans 17, 19, 21, 22, 38, 39, 52
   see also Scots
Langland, William 32
Larkin, Philip 65, 88
Lauder, Harry 35
Lawrence, D. H. 24, 25
Lear, Edward 144
Lenin, Krupskaya 67
Lenin, Vladimir Ilyich 62, 66, 69, 73
Leonard, Tom 3, 137, 169–70,
Leopardi, Giacomo 164
Lévi-Strauss, Claude 96
Lewis, Cecil Day 46
L'Humanité 66
Liberace 134
Liebknecht, Karl 73
Lindsay, Maurice 17, 18, 19, 21, 25, 26,
   42
   Modern Scottish Poetry: An Anthology
   of the Scottish Renaissance 17
Lines Review 66
Lorca, Federico García 7
Lovell, Bernard 180
Lukács, Georg 184
Lynch, Michael 74
Lyotard, Jean-François 8
Lyte, Henry 34

MacCaig, Norman 26, 39
McCarey, Peter 173
McCrae, John 118
MacDiarmid, Hugh 6, 10, 14, 16, 17–26
   passim, 37, 38, 39, 40, 42, 43,
   47–52 *passim*, 54, 60, 61, 73, 76,
   78, 88, 120, 139
   an Anglo-Scot 22
   'The Battle Continues' 37, 38
   Collected Poems 38
   'Cornish Heroic Song' 48
   and feminism 54

'Glasgow 1960' 76
Golden Treasury of Scottish Poetry 17,
   18, 23, 54
'In Memoriam James Joyce' 47, 49
'The Kind of Poetry I Want' 48, 61
Lucky Poet 50, 61
'On a Raised Beach' 120
Penny Wheep 37
'Perfect' 139
Sangshaw 37
The Scottish Chapbook 48
'Water Music' 48
Macfarlan, James 171
McGinn, Matt 143
McGonagall, William 33
Mackintosh, Charles Rennie 78
Maclean, John 73, 74
MacLean, Sorley 22, 23
MacNiece, Louis 43
Magellan, Ferdinand 10
Magritte, René 169
Malevich, Kazimir 90
Mallarmé, Stéphane 90
Marlowe, Christopher 2, 3, 180–1
   Doctor Faustus 2
Martynov, Leonid 86
Marx, Karl 133, 184
   see also Capital; *Communist*
   Manifesto
Mayakovsky, Vladimir 7, 10, 14, 22, 23,
   27, 36, 45, 59–72 *passim*, 82,
   84, 85
   'How Are Verses Made?' 74
   May One Become a Satirist? 69
Measure for Measure 148
   see also Shakespeare, William
Melville, Herman 36
   Moby Dick 133
Melville, Robert 53
Michelangelo 36, 164
Milton, John 115, 126, 134, 141
modernism 6, 7, 8, 11, 41, 49, 60, 61,
   64–5, 68, 69, 74, 83, 87, 90
   Anglo-American 7, 69, 74, 87
   Eliot and 65
   ideology of 7
   MacDiarmid and 41, 49
   Mayakovsky and 65
   Morgan reconstructs 6, 7, 11, 41, 47,
   60, 61, 68, 69, 87
   Pound and 65
   Russo-European 87, 90

Monroe, Marilyn 4, 55, 89
Montale, Eugenio 11, 82, 83
Movement poetry 61
Muir, Edwin 21, 25
Murray, James 172
My Lai massacre 100
myth 24, 25, 51, 73, 93, 119, 127, 128,
    139
    classical 128–33 *passim*
    documentary 99

Neruda, Pablo 87, 88
    Universal Song 87
New Criticism 7
New Saltire 39, 41
Nureyev, Rudolf 101

Olson, Charles 52, 115
    Maximus 115
    'Projective Verse' 52
Ong, Walter 148
Oppenheimer, J. Robert 42
orality 1, 8, 16, 19, 21, 41, 42, 44–52
    passim, 59, 68, 71, 88, 95, 101,
    116, 143–4, 146–7, 148,
    169–71, 179, 180, 188
    drama and 1, 2
    Scots and 16, 19, 21
Oxford English Dictionary, The 172

Paolozzi, Eduardo 101
Paris, Matthew 141
    Historia Anglorum 141
Park, Mungo 35
Pasternak, Boris 85, 87, 88
Petrarch, Francesco Petrarca 75, 137
Piaf, Edith 4, 89
Pilate, Pontius 140
Pirandello, Luigi 47
'Plastic Scots' 16, 19, 21, 31, 94
    see also Lallans; Scots
Platen-Hallemunde, August Graf von
    104–5
    see also gay poetry
Plato 4, 11, 123–6 *passim*, 148
    The Republic 125
PN Review 2
Poe, Edgar Allan 119, 142
Poetry Scotland 25, 26
Politics 1, 4, 8, 14, 15, 16, 17, 20–7
    passim, 32, 34, 38, 42–3, 60–8
    passim, 73–5, 84, 104, 107, 123,

125, 137, 140–5 *passim*, 156,
    158, 161, 162, 184, 189
    see also futurism; modernism;
    surrealism
Polo, Marco 182
Poor, Old, Tired, Horse 39
Pope, Alexander 134
postmodernism 7, 114, 116–17, 120,
    122, 175
Pound, Ezra 7, 41, 46, 65, 87, 115, 182
    Cantos 115
    'The Seafarer' 46
Pushkin, Alexander Sergevic 164

Quasimodo, Salvatore 82

Raban, Jonathan 92
Racine, Jean 2, 3
    Phaedre 3
Read, Herbert 26, 27, 97
    Poetry and Anarchism 26
    Surrealism 27
    see also anarchism
realism 11, 89, 117, 120, 122, 124, 128,
    130, 145, 179, 184, 186–7
    documentary 11
'Red Clyde' 73, 74
Referendum 11, 16, 137, 138, 146
    see also devolution
Reid, James (Jimmy) 77, 78
renascence, Scottish 17, 19, 22, 42, 52
revolution 73, 97, 107, 157
    modernist 61
    Russian 60, 62, 63, 66, 67, 72, 84, 86
Rich, Adrienne 130
Rimbaud, Arthur 64, 97–8
Ross, Anthony 42
Rostand, Edmond 2
    Cyrano de Bergerac 2
Rushdie, Salman 116
Rytkheu, Yuri 156

Sartre, Jean-Paul 47
satire 69, 91, 97, 110, 159, 163
Saunders, R. Crombie 19
Saussure, Ferdinand de 64
Schnittke, Alfred 160
science fiction 4, 8, 10, 11, 27–8, 53,
    63, 92, 104, 109–15 *passim*,
    118–23 *passim*, 126–8, 132, 137,
    139, 144–6, 154, 159–61,
    173–7, 180–1, 187, 192

see also virtual reality
Scots 2, 3, 15, 16–23 passim, 26, 39, 42,
        43, 48–50, 51–2, 59, 61, 64, 65,
        68, 69, 72, 73, 76, 82, 93, 163,
        164
    see also 'Plastic Scots'
Scotsman, The 39
Scott, John 89
Scott, Walter 9, 31, 143
    Lay of the Last Minstrel 31
Scottish Field 39
Scottish International 42
Scottish Poetry 42
Seferis, George 143
Semeonoff, Konstantin 47
Shakespeare, William 33, 134, 148, 149
Sharpeville massacre 91, 102n.16
Shelley, Mary 182, 191
    Frankenstein 182
Shelley, Percy Bysshe 26, 27, 28, 133,
        147, 187–8
    'The Daemon of the World' 187, 188
    'The Mask of Anarchy' 27
    'Ozymandias' 133
    'Prometheus Unbound' 27
    'Queen Mab' 27, 187, 188
    'The Triumph of Life' 27, 192
Shklovsky, Victor 31
Smith, Iain Crichton 4, 5, 6
Smith, Sydney Goodsir 22, 39
Smith, Tommy 2
Socrates 124
Spender, Stephen 46
Stevens, Wallace 41, 87, 134
story 7, 9, 95, 110, 113, 122, 127, 139,
        144, 150, 153, 154, 158, 160,
        161, 170, 182, 185
    and poetry 9
    and speech 170–1 177, 188, 193
    sublime, the 8, 127
surrealism 10, 11, 23, 24–5, 27, 66, 50,
        87, 97, 98, 106–8, 111, 153
    Manifesto of Surrealism 106
    Platform of Prague 108
    The Second Manifesto of Surrealism 107

Tacitus, Publius 140–1
    Agricola 140
Tempest, The 149
    see also Shakespeare, William

Thomas, Dylan 23, 31, 41, 43
    18 Poems 23
    Deaths and Entrances 31
    Twenty-Five Poems 23
Thomson, 'B. V.' 83
Tippett, Phil 176
Todorov, Tzvetan 151
translation 1–7 passim, 22, 23, 35, 46,
        68, 69, 74, 82, 83, 84, 163, 164,
        166
Treece, Henry 26
Trotsky, Leon 60, 73
Tsvetayeva, Marina 86, 156
Tyutchev, Fyodor 186
Tzara, Tristan 107

Ulanova, Galina 55
Upper Clyde Shipbuilders 74, 77

Verlaine, Paul 23
Vesalius, Andreas 185
Virilio, Paul 116
virtual reality 111, 174–5, 181

Wallace, William 145
Walter, W. Grey 53,
    The Living Brain 53, 155
Weöres, Sándor 163
White, Kenneth 3, 47, 193
Whitman, Walt 41, 61
    'Song of Myself' 61
Whyte, Hamish 10, 40
Williams, Raymond 148
Williams, William Carlos 41, 88
    Paterson 41
Wittgenstein, Ludvig 96, 117, 186
    Tractatus 96
Wordsworth, William 34, 56 n.16, 87,
        98, 121, 123, 133, 172
    'The Prelude' 123
    'Tintern Abbey' 123
Wright, Tom 39

Yeats, William Butler 41, 87
Yevtushenko, Yevegeny Aleksandrovich
        86, 88
Young, Douglas 17, 19, 21
    'Plastic Scots' and the Scottish Literary
        Tradition 21
Young, Thomas 141